# Restoring Classic & Collectible Cameras

by Thomas Tomosy

Amherst Media, Inc. ■ Buffalo, New York

Published by:
Amherst Media, Inc.
P.O. Box 586
Buffalo, NY 14226
Fax: 716-874-4508

Publisher: Craig Alesse
Senior Editor/Project Manager: Richard Lynch
Associate Editor: Frances J. Hagen

ISBN: 0-936262-59-1
Library of Congress Catalog Card Number: 97-77827

Printed in the United States of America
10 9 8 7 6 5 4 3



**Read before attempting any maintenance or repair of cameras or accessories:**
Follow safe work procedures at all times when doing any work on cameras or accessories. You are responsible for reading, understanding and following the safety procedures and instructions that apply to the tools you use. Wear eye protection at all times during maintenance or repair procedures. Keep your workplace and any maintenance or repair related materials completely out of the reach of children. Some of the substances referred to in this book are flammable and emit harmful vapors. Follow every precaution when working with these substances. Do not inhale vapors. Read carefully, understand and practice any and all warnings and/or cautionary statements on the containers and with the literature of solvents, glues, oils, lighter fluid or any other chemical substances before using them. The area in which you use or store these substances must be properly and adequately ventilated at all times. Do not use heat or flame until the vapors of any solvents, oils, glues, lighter fluid or any other chemical substances are no longer present.

Read this book completely before attempting any work on cameras or accessories, and then reread the particular section pertaining to the equipment you intend to work on before beginning procedures. Practice all maintenance or repair techniques on old, discarded, "junk" cameras or accessories to become skilled with the procedures before attempting any work on valuable equipment.

# Table of Contents

# Introduction

Collecting cameras is an exciting hobby in itself, but maintaining and restoring the samples in your collection adds another, important dimension to the hobby. By routinely improving on your finds, not only will you acquire more intimate knowledge of your prized collection, but can actually increase its aesthetic and monetary value.

When you restore an old object for your own enjoyment, you're free to set rules and standards as you please. However, if you're thinking of selling at a future time, or even if you just like to show off your collection to like-minded friends, then you must observe the rules of "sympathetic restoration." Chapter One offers some guidelines.

Rare antiques tend to reside in museums or in permanent collections; they are not accessible to you or to me, except for observation purposes. This is a practical book. This book features models that are readily obtainable for reasonable sums; however, the principles of restoration apply equally to rare or common models. The information presented here will enable you to restore a true rarity — if you happen to find one — even if it's not specifically featured in this book.

Once you understand the principles and have successfully restored a wooden camera, you can restore the next one just as easily even though it may be a different make, format, or vintage. The same doesn't necessarily apply to mechanical restorations. Even though similarities abound in design and construction, you can never take the similarities for granted. Early lens shutters, for instance, may be quite unique in design and distinctly different from later examples.

The material in the book is arranged roughly in the order of difficulty, with models in each chapter serving as illustrations for specific projects as well as providing examples on general restoration methods.

From simple cleaning and touching up, through complete strip-down, refinish, and build-up, to detailed mechanical disassembly and repair, you will find instructions on practically all aspects of classic camera restoration and maintenance you are likely to encounter.

While it may not always be essential, a certain amount of camera mechanics knowledge as well as some experience in disassembling, diagnosing, and repairing cameras often comes in handy when working on a restoration project. For your convenience, the most important precautions and general repair methods are abstracted from my previous books, ***Camera Maintenance and Repair, Volume One*** and ***Volume Two*** and are found in the section entitled, "Abstracts" at the end of the book.

Since some of the classic and collectible cameras are extremely valuable, be careful when working on expensive equipment. It's easy to cause damage but difficult to put it right — especially since parts for older models are often unavailable. Practice on "junk cameras" first, and approach the more valuable models only when you have the necessary experience and confidence.

It is also important to remember that restoring a camera is often more than just an evening project. Indeed, some complex projects may take weeks, perhaps months. When restoring cameras, you must be patient, methodical, and meticulous; otherwise, you might not be satisfied with the results.

Above all, practice good and safe working habits. Have fun and appreciate the rewards of restoring classic and collectible cameras and equipment.

## How to Use this Book

I suggest that you read the whole book from cover to cover before embarking on a restoration project. The methods described in each chapter are unique and may be useful for your project even though your particular model may be different. The Table of Contents and Index will aid you in finding a specific model or method.

In case you come across a basic method you're not familiar with, turn to the Abstract section at the end of the book where the method is outlined. If more extensive help is needed, the Abstract section will also provide details on where to find more information on each method.

If you are learning camera restoration from scratch, I suggest obtaining several of the specific models featured in this book. Restoring those models with instructions in hand would be a relatively easy way to proceed. As each model in the book is used to illustrate some principle or method of restoration, buy as many of them as you can. Most of the models featured are reasonably priced.

## Safety

Restoring cameras is probably one of the safest occupations there is; nevertheless, a few precautions must be observed. You will be using solvents, glues, and oils. These materials may be flammable and emit harmful vapors. Read the warnings on all containers and abide by them. Whenever you're using heat (soldering iron, hair drier), and especially any open flame (propane torch, cigarette lighter), be aware of the fire hazard. If you must smoke a cigarette, take a break, and smoke away from your work area.

If you have children around, make sure they can't get at industrial substances, electricity, or cutting tools.

## Before We Begin

You may wonder why some people prefer to collect old items in their filthy, unrestored condition. The answer is that some so-called antiques have no intrinsic value or beauty of their own, in which case the filth on them is necessary to signify their age.

This may impart some meager value to an otherwise worthless piece. Cameras, however, having brand name, model name, serial number, and various other identifying features don't need to be filthy and worn to prove their age or value. A camera is both beautiful and functional in its own right. The filth and other signs of wear which accumulate over the years detract from the camera's value.

### Sympathetic Restoration

One must be aware of the kind of restoration he or she undertakes if keeping or increasing the value of the item is important. The term used in the antique furniture field is "sympathetic restoration." The term means bringing the piece as close to its original condition as possible, not only in appearance, but in the methods and materials used to restore the object.

Sympathetic restoration is the best practice for restoring cameras. Parts and fittings on a camera must be removed and restored one by one. There is no magic wand that makes the camera appear sparkling and better-than-original. Without disassembly, only minor retouching or partial cleaning is possible. This should be of no concern, as disassembly is usually quite easy with older cameras.

Sprayable restoring agents should be avoided, as most leave a film which is detectable at close scrutiny. They often change the sheen or the hue of the finish. You don't want the result to look overdone.

When a part must be replaced and a sample is not available, you must fashion the part in such a way that its shape and material matches the original. If all the fittings are brass, use brass replacements. Screws must have the same kind of slots as all the other screws in the camera. Phillips, Robertson, or any other modern slots must be avoided in older cameras. Even the plating must match. If the existing parts are nickel plated, then chrome-plated screws or parts will stand out. See "Screws" in Chapter Five.

## The Authorized Service

We may postulate that Leicas and Leica collectors belong in a special class. Not only will a Leica collector demand external originality, but he may ask for certificates to prove the origin of the piece and ask for service records from the Leica factory. This certainly happens concerning top of the line models traded among the top echelon of collectors and investors. When trading ordinary Leica models at a swap meet, however, discussions on certificates will not likely come up.

Leica is not alone. According to McKeown's, Deardorff studio cameras must be restored by the authorized service center to meet with collectors' and users' approval. However, it's really the quality of the work that counts and not who has performed it. If these considerations worry you, just stay away from troublesome brands such as Leica and Deardorff. Certainly the rules for investment quality collectibles are stricter. There are many examples of valuable collectibles that are changing hands in non-working condition simply because no one has the nerve to disassemble the camera or trust the authorized professional to take tools to cosmetically perfect cameras. (Investment quality denotes mint examples of the most valuable models of classic cameras.) At any rate, examples in that category are not supposed to need restoration or maintenance.

## Level and Extent

The extent of restoration you endeavor to undertake is up to you. Often external cleaning and some minor retouching will do wonders for the appearance of the item. If external parts are missing, they can be replaced easily. The only problem is finding the original part (see Chapters Five and Six).

If you decide to get fully involved, you will undertake a complete strip-down, overhauling the mechanism, refinishing the body exterior, making and replacing bellows or other missing or damaged parts, and a complete reassembly.

Another fairly involved method of restoration is finding two examples of the same model both damaged or incomplete. The parts salvaged from one are used to restore the other, making, in effect, one out of two. Sometimes extensive disassembly of both cameras will be required. Later on we will have numerous examples of both minor and major restorations you can chose from to suit your level of skill.

Chapter One

# Preliminaries

## Removing Adhesive Tape

People often stick adhesive tape or labels onto the body of the camera as a price tag, an ID tag, or an attempted repair. Any tape or label must be peeled off as soon as you take possession of the camera. Adhesive tape can damage the finish whether it's leather, wood, or a painted surface.

Some adhesive tapes or labels actually peel off without leaving any residue or mark whatsoever, but most do not. Some adhesive surfaces will harden completely, given enough time. The backing may peel off, but the hardened adhesive might have to be scraped off. Some types of adhesive residue will dissolve in lighter fluid, and most types will dissolve in Acetone™.

Try lighter fluid first as it will not damage the finish. If you must use Acetone™, make sure the camera finish is not dissolved also. Most baked enamel is impervious to Acetone™. Leather, unless coated, will not be bothered by Acetone™ either. A lacquered surface might dissolve however. If nothing else works, use wood or plastic to scrape off the residue. On leatherette or leather, you can carefully try a blunt knife if solvents don't work.

Porous surfaces such as leather or wood might soak up the adhesive substance, and after it is thoroughly cleaned, the surface will remain discolored. Nothing can be done about this short of replacing the whole piece, if that's possible.

You should never stick any adhesive tape or label onto your camera. If labeling is necessary, a price tag on a string provides the best solution. If you must tape some parts together as a temporary measure, use cloth insulating tape or black athletic tape. Never use vinyl or cello or duct tape; they are the worst offenders of contamination. Besides, they don't work very well. Vinyl tape unwinds all by itself and leaves a sticky mess. Duct tape slips under tension, and cello hardens over time and loses its adhesiveness.

## Restoring the Camera Case

The case of a valuable camera is valuable itself. Even if not priced separately, a nice, original case adds value to the package. Common problems found with cases are usually the carrying strap or handle, the stitches, the hinges, and any foam paddings (photo 1.1).

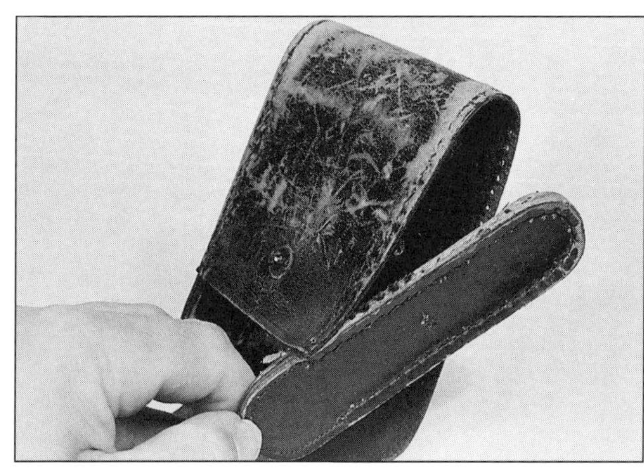

***1.1:*** *This case needs restitching.*

The usual choice of fasteners is thread or rivets. Glue may be used for some inner repairs or in conjunction with thread. It is important to remember never to use adhesive tape, staples, or wire for any repair on a case.

Before doing the stitches, see if the inside of the case is sound. If some of the linings or paddings have come undone, reglue them with contact cement. Make sure the cement is not smeared over on the outside and doesn't plug the original needle holes.

Some cases may have a foam padding inside them which has deteriorated to dust or a sticky semi-liquid. If you find such substances in a case, you must scrape them out thoroughly; otherwise, the case will contaminate the camera. Replace the foam with a new one or just glue down the loose lining after the mess is cleaned out.

You might have seen cases stitched together with a completely different thread and stitch pattern from the original. You should never do this. On a good portion of the case, study the pattern of the stitches. You will have to use the original holes and follow the original sewing pattern.

Using a strong set of tweezers, pick out the broken thread fragments from the leather. Obtain a thread that closely resembles the original both in color and gage. Using a blunt-point needle with a sufficiently large eye to take the thread, pull the thread through the existing holes.

Usually a double-stitch pattern is used. That is, you either use two needles that mirror each other, or you insert the alternate loops going one way, then come back and fill in the missing loops. This process is not difficult if you pay attention to the original pattern.

Trim off any frayed edges with a sharp pair of scissors. Brush shoe polish into the leather to remove the dust and dirt. If it's fairly smooth, use a soft rag to rub the shoe polish deep into the leather. Let it dry for 15 minutes then buff it up with a soft brush if there is deep grain, or with a soft rag on smooth grain.

If the glossy top coat is chipping, scrape off the loose scales. Generously rub shoe polish into the leather. Apply another coat after the first coat has soaked in. Buff it with a soft shoe brush.

## Restoring Straps and Handles

If a long strap is broken, cut off the frayed ends, and rivet them together with tube rivets. At least two rivets will be required. If the strap is broken right at the root, drill off or break out the rivets from the case, drill or punch new holes into the strap, and rivet it on again following the original arrangement. Tube rivets, tools, and other accessories for leather work are available from your local leather supplier.

Quite often in 35mm cases, the bottom hinge of the front lid breaks. This problem calls for reinforcement. Cut a one-inch strip from a piece of leather that closely resembles the original. Glue the patch strip on before stitching. Since in this case, there are no original holes, use a sewing machine, or use an awl to pre-punch the holes for the needle. For this job, use finer thread with the color matching that of the leather.

Handles on folding cameras are often impressed with a brand name or logo. Therefore, try to salvage the original whenever you can. See the Kodak handles on the photo below.

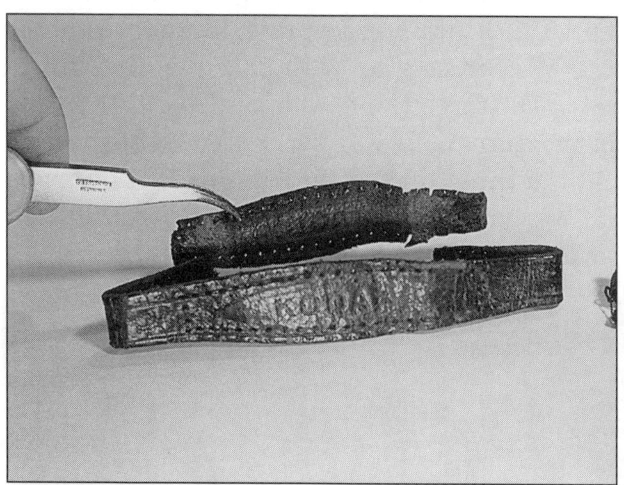

***1.2:** Hopeless-looking Kodak handles.*

The one on the left can be repaired, the other is beyond help. Sometimes redoing the stitches with stronger thread is enough. If the leather is broken, you may glue an extra reinforcing layer inside the original, and stitch through this sandwich. You can impress decorative lines into a new leather handle by the methods described in Chapter Five, Folding Brownie Model A.

A household sewing machine is adequate for sewing most camera cases, flat side, but corner stitches you encounter must be done by hand.

## Making Leather Lens Caps

A leather cap on a large view-camera lens bespeaks of elegance, originality, and completeness. Alas, the cap is often missing.

To make a leather lens cap, start with a cardboard skeleton, then cover it with leather. While it might be possible to find a jar lid that is the right size, it's easier and almost as fast to make the blank from cardboard. The thickness of the cardboard stock is 0.4mm. You may also use cover stock (0.3mm) from your stationery supplier.

As caps come in different sizes, you must come up with your own measurements. The measurements I use here are for a cap to fit the Vitax Portrait Lens fitted to the Wollensak shutter (discussed in Chapter Four). Cut off several strips of cardboard from a shoe box, 15mm wide by 340mm long. Wind two layers of the strips around the mouth of the lens and secure them with adhesive tape. This is just a spacer ring, it's not part of the cap. Mix white glue with an equal amount of water. Dip three 12mm wide cardboard strips into this mixture. Wind wax paper over the spacer ring and the three soaked cardboard strips on top of the wax paper. Tie them down with ordinary sewing thread and let the assembly dry overnight (photo 1.3). This will be the rim of the cap.

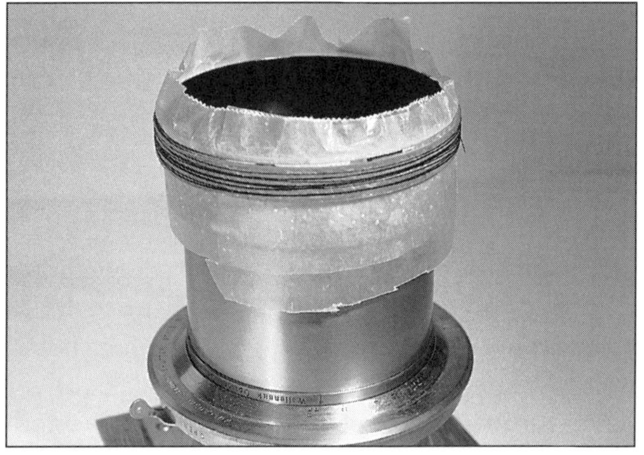

***1.3:** Wind sewing thread over the strips.*

Carefully pry the ring off the next day. Cut out a disk from a stiff cardboard at least .6mm to 1mm thick, depending on size.

Make the disk the same size as the outside diameter of the rim ring. In my case, it's 110mm. Glue this disk onto the rim ring using white glue at full strength (photo 1.4). Weigh it down and let it dry. After the glue has dried, clean up the blank with #150 sandpaper, and round off the sharp edges.

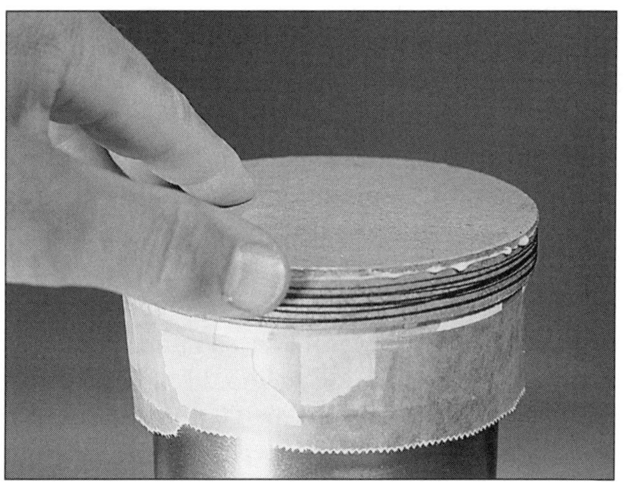

***1.4:** Glue on the top disk.*

Glue a layer of black or colored felt onto the inside disk, but leave the rim bare for now. Replace the spacer ring and the blank over the lens. Find a suitable-colored sheepskin or goatskin to cover the blank (see Chapter Two for staining skin). Cut a circle the size of the outside diameter of the cap (110mm), plus the height of the rim (14mm), plus at least 20mm all around for something to grip while stretching the skin. This yields a circle with a diameter of 175mm.

Soak the skin in lukewarm water for a few minutes. Squeeze the water out between sheets of blotting paper or paper towels. Smear white glue onto the blank. Stretch the skin over the top, and snap a fairly strong elastic band just under the rim of the cap to hold the skin in place (photo 1.5).

Smooth the top portion of the skin toward the rim to stretch it and to work out the air bubbles. At the same time pull the overhanging skirt down to work out the wrinkles (photo 1.6).

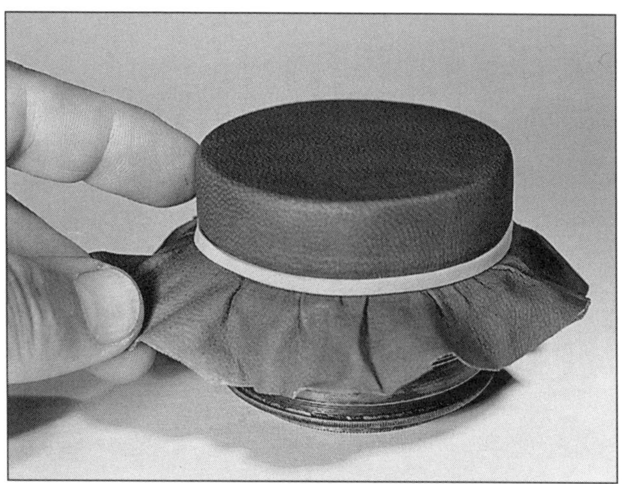

*1.5: Snap an elastic band over the skin.*

Go around the cap several times until the skin on the top as well as around the rim is completely wrinkle-free and all the air bubbles are worked out. Let the assembly dry for at least 24 hours.

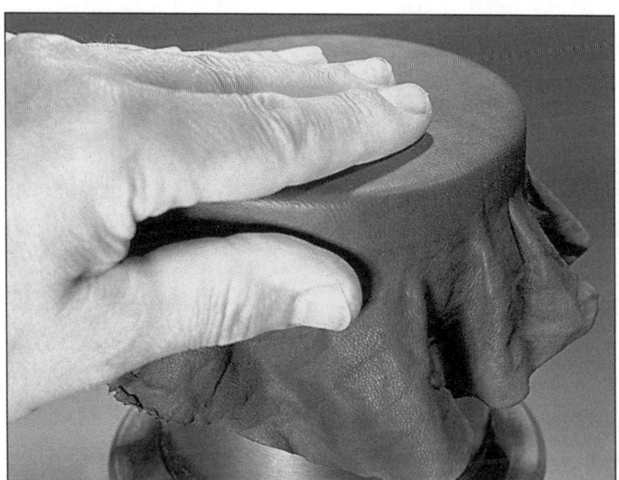

*1.6: Work out the wrinkles.*

Pry the cap off the lens carefully. In this example, the skirt must be trimmed to a length of 13mm. Smear contact cement onto the inside of the rim.

Fold the overhang inside around the rim, and pat it down over the glue. Fit the finished cap onto the lens to give it support while drying.

In order to impress a circle into the top of the cap, support the inside while pressing a suitable round object into the outside of the top (photo 1.7). Photo 1.8 shows two finished caps.

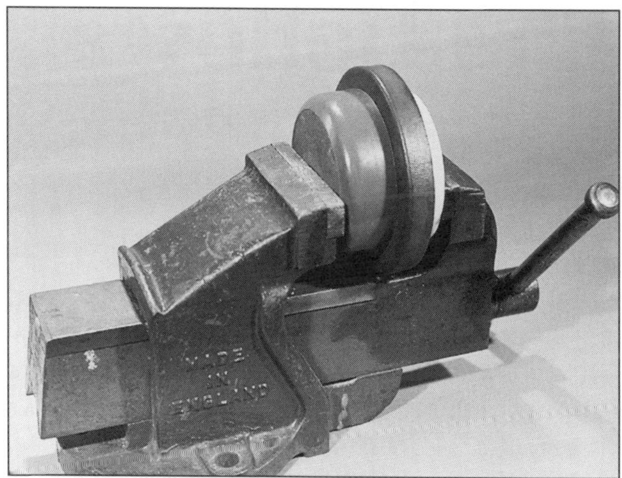

*1.7: Impressing a circle.*

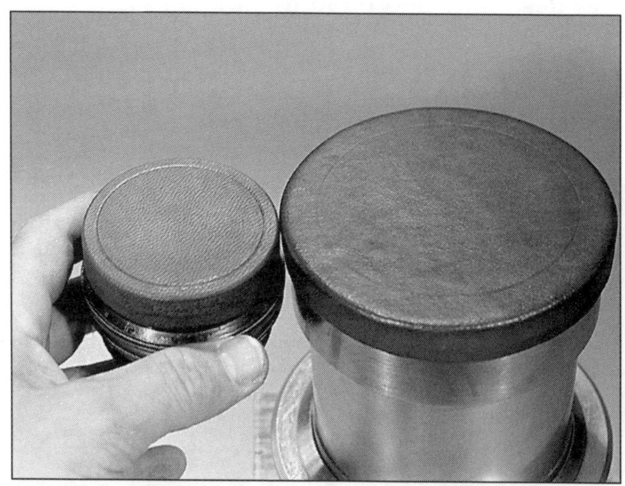

*1.8: The finished caps.*

# Chapter Two

# The Bellows

Bellows are an important part of many older, as well as modern, large-format cameras. Alas, bellows are often the first thing to go. If you're restoring cameras, repairing and building bellows are essential skills you must learn.

Even if bellows looks quite hopeless, examine them to see if they could be repaired. Repairing some bellows might require a lot of work, but so does designing and building new ones.

## Caring For Your Bellows

Before folding up a view camera, make sure that the lens standard is centered properly. If the camera is closed and stored for a long time with the lens standard off center, permanent distortion to the bellows will be inevitable (photo 2.1).

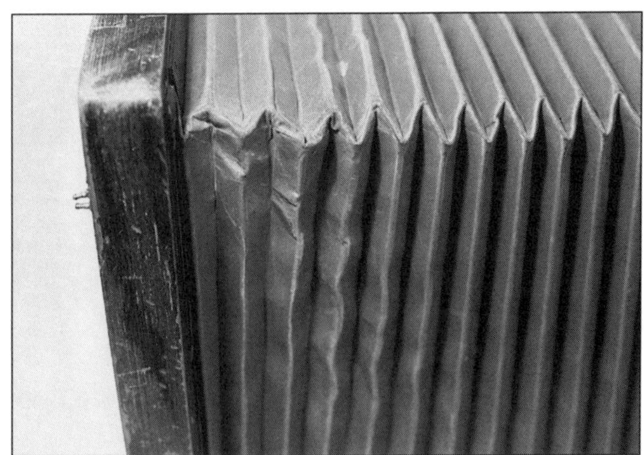

***2.1:** Distorted bellows.*

You will often find bellows that have been stored for a long time with some of the folds inverted. Once the inversion becomes permanent, the bellows will refuse to fold up properly. In this case, first ascertain that the layers are not separating (see below).

If the bellows, aside from the inversion, is sound, fold the camera up slowly while arranging the folds into their proper position. Use both hands for helping the bellows from the inside as well as from the outside. Storing the camera with the bellows properly folded usually restores the shape of the bellows.

Sticky bellows materials result in the folds getting glued together. You must always check this because if some of the folds don't open, the rest of the bellows will be overstrained when extended, and wear much faster.

This happens more readily to colored bellows, such as those found in the Kodak Boy Scout models. If they're stuck together, you must carefully pull the folds apart by reaching inside with a finger through the film gate. The folds can usually be pried apart without causing any damage. Once separated, they don't usually stick together again.

## Restoring Bellows

The possible restoration methods are: 1. filling in pin holes and corner frays; 2. replacing the outer skin; and 3. regluing the original layers.

### Method 1

Some bellows are still in reasonable shape except that the corners are frayed and leaking light through pinholes. Aside from the light leaks, the frayed corners must be repaired for aesthetic reasons. Open the back of the camera, and hold the bellows up to a strong light. Looking through from the inside you should see the pinholes.

Taping the corners is not a proper restoration method, but it does work if all you're interested in is taking pictures. Use good quality cloth tape (not solid vinyl or duct tape). Remove the bellows, pull it straight, and tape the corners lengthwise with a single length of tape (photo 2.2). Support the bellows from the inside and press the tape on hard. Fold up the bellows again.

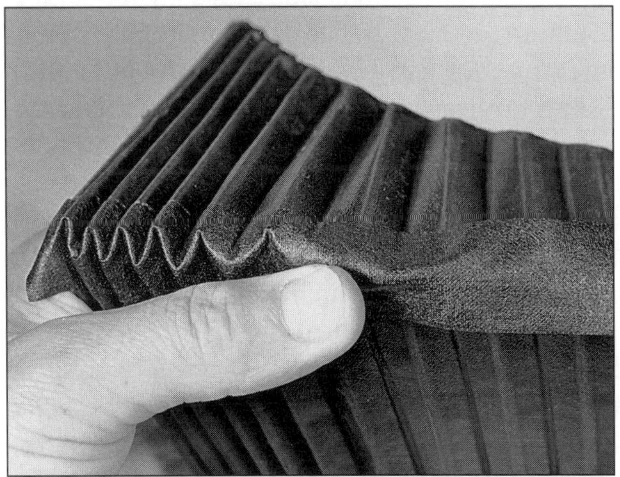

*2.2: Repairing corner fray with tape.*

It's more difficult, but possible to apply the tape with the bellows in place. Extend the bellows as far as it will stretch. Apply the tape lengthwise as before while supporting the inside with your fingers. Conform the tape to the folds as you're applying it.

If you care about cosmetic appearances, repair the corner frays by filling them in individually. Plasti Dip™, vinyl repair compound or paper glue mixed with paint are possible candidates for filling in corner holes. You must often experiment to find out which method works best with the bellows at hand.

Plasti Dip™ comes in different colors, including black, and looks like thick paint, but it doesn't run or smooth over the way most paints do. To apply it, take a small spatula such as a screwdriver blade. Work the plastic into the hole or fray and smooth it down perfectly before it dries. You have to work fast. This substance becomes unworkable in about 20 seconds.

If you didn't get complete coverage you can add more plastic after about 20 minutes. Work with the thickest portion of the plastic, such as that found at the bottom of the can or the underside of the lid. Don't stir or shake the can; you want the thick of it.

Vinyl repair compound usually comes in a repair kit (photo 2.3). There are several different colors in the kit that may be mixed to match the color of the bellows. This is quite a thick paste. It behaves similarly to the Plasti Dip™, and should be applied with a spatula as described above. The paper-glue method is described on page 63.

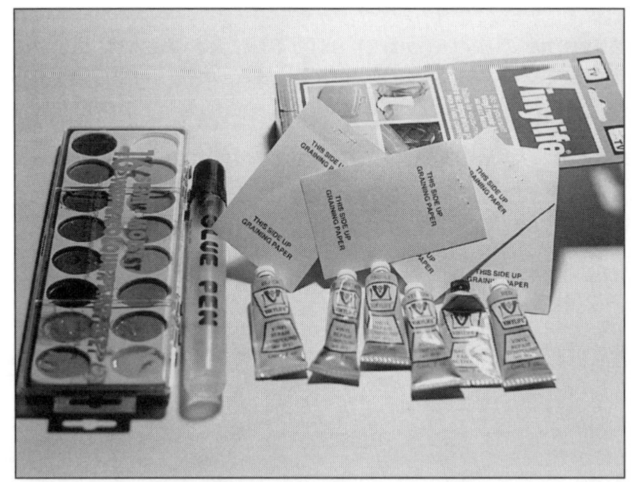


*2.3: Vinyl repair kit.*

### Method 2

Many bellows constructed from multi-layers can be saved by recovering them with a new outer skin. The example I'm using to illustrate this discussion is from a Kodak Folding Pocket No.3-A Camera (photo 2.4). The following procedure is applicable to bellows with flaking outer layer and exposed ribs, but only if the inner liner is still in fair shape. If both layers are falling apart, the bellows cannot be saved.

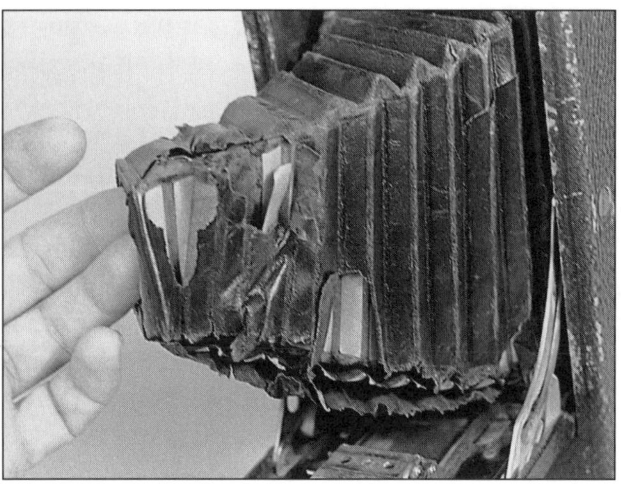

*2.4: Restorable bellows.*

Proceed as follows: Try to open up the seams dry. Dampen the seams with warm water if they refuse to separate. Use only as much water as necessary to open the seams but not enough to detach the cardboard ribs. Their position is critical. Flatten out the bellows.

Separate the outer skin and discard it. (If the outer layer is still good, see the instructions for Method 3.) Try to keep the ribs in place. If some ribs are missing or damaged, you can cut out new ones from a business card (see "Constructing Bellows").Model new ribs after the good ones. Using a steam iron, press the inside layer with the ribs still attached (photo 2.5).

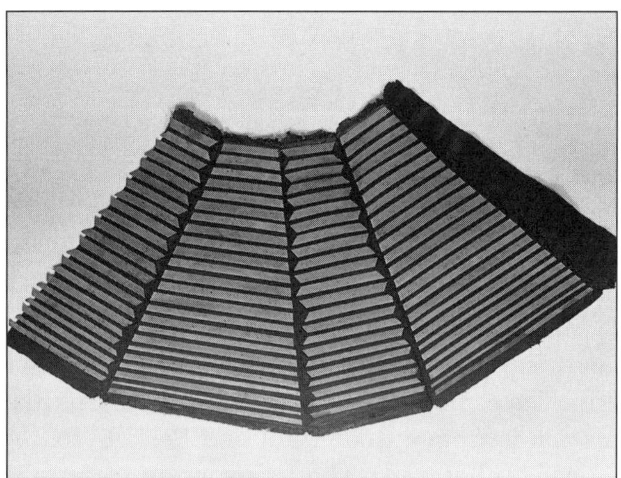

*2.5: Inner liner with ribs.*

Moisten the loose ribs, and glue them back on in their original positions. The ones still attached should be glued down securely as well. With a small paintbrush, apply water under the ribs, then press them down. Go over the complete bellows again with a pressing iron.

For the cover layer, use sheepskin or goatskin. One hide costs about $10 from your leather craft shop. Due to irregular shapes and holes, one skin seldom yields more than two or three medium sized bellows. Use the portions of the skin which are about .2mm to .25mm thick. Don't throw out the leftovers; they can be used for lens cap construction (see Chapter One). If you can't find the exact color you need, stain the skin. Leather stains are usually available from the same supplier.

Cut out the shape using the inner liner as a template, but keep in mind that the seam of the cover skin should fall beside the seam of the inner liner, not on top of it. Clean a smooth non-porous surface thoroughly before laying the skin on it. With a large soft brush, apply the stain liberally. Let the skin sit undisturbed for an hour before hanging it up to dry. After the skin is completely dry (at least 12 hours), if you're not satisfied with the color, you may apply more of the same stain or a darker shade to modify the color.

Once the skin is dry, buff it up with a soft shoe brush. I would talk you out of trying to enhance the sheen with some kind of shoe polish, wax, leather balm, or other product.

A bewildering variety of leather treatment products are available from leather shops, and shoe shops, but be careful when trying a new product. If you apply a polish with solid dye in it, the finish might become blotched. Anything that leaves an extra layer on top of the skin is no good. For one thing, it shows; for another, it might remain sticky for a long, long time.

Even clear shoe polish — which I often recommend — might soak into the skin and cause uneven discoloration. If you're determined to use a leather treatment product, experiment first on a fairly large piece of skin to see the effect. Other than for color and sheen, test for stickiness and handling as well. If handled, the finishing coat may crackle, peel, or rub off. Be careful; you can easily ruin your new bellows with some unfamiliar product.

For gluing the skin onto the original inner liner and rib sandwich, use clear liquid paper glue, such as Glue Pen. Since the glue dries fast, you must do the panels one after the other. At first, liberally apply glue with a Glue Pen to the top panel. With your fingertip, spread the glue evenly over the ribs as well as between the ribs. When the glue begins to thicken, lay the sheepskin on. The glue must be spread thin, otherwise it will discolor the skin by soaking through it. Press the skin down with your clean fingers or use a clean rubber roller for rolling the layers firmly together. Do the side panels the same way.

The seam of the inner layer must be glued up before gluing the skin over the bottom panel. You can do this flat on a table by folding the bellows onto itself. Conversely, you can use a corner iron or a two-by-two supported in a vise.

By paying attention to the original ribs and crease lines, match up the seam in the exact original position. The seam of the inner and cover layers must fall side-by-side and not on top of each other.

Glue down the bottom ribs in their original position after the seam is done. If the ribs are misaligned, it will be impossible to fold up the bellows properly. Once the inner seam and the ribs are done, glue down the cover layer one flap after the other.

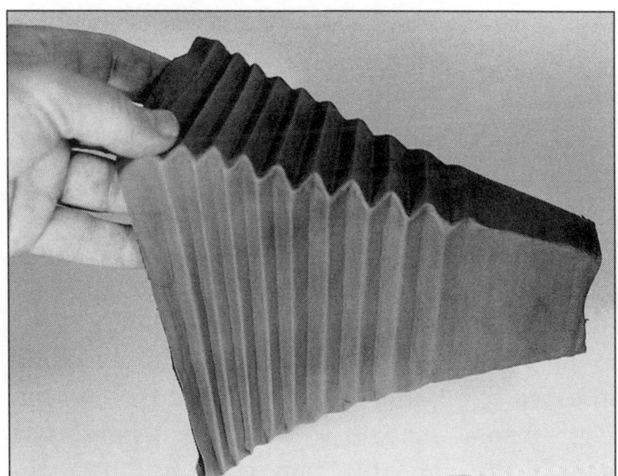

*2.6: Forming the folds.*

Before the glue dries completely, trim off the overhanging edges of the sheepskin.

To fold up the bellows, you can start forming the folds at either end. Work around and around going down towards the other end.

You can brace the one end against the table or against your chest, so you can work with both hands. Help the corners form with your thumbnail or with a flat blade while forming the folds from the inside as well as the outside (photo 2.6).

This is not difficult since the original creases and the ribs inside are there to guide you. However, if the ribs have been carelessly positioned, the job will be more difficult. Press the folded bellows down flat, and put a heavy book on top of it.

## Method 3

The discussion below is illustrated by a Kodak Premoette bellows.

Some bellows just fall apart due to the glue drying out and releasing the bond between the layers. If the material is still good, it's possible to rebuild the bellows using the original layers. Start with separating the bellows from the camera.

In order to restore the bellows, place them into cold water and let soak for 30 minutes. Separate the seam carefully. The upper layer might be quite flimsy, especially when wet. Roll it back slowly, helping the glue separate with a pointy tool such as tweezers.

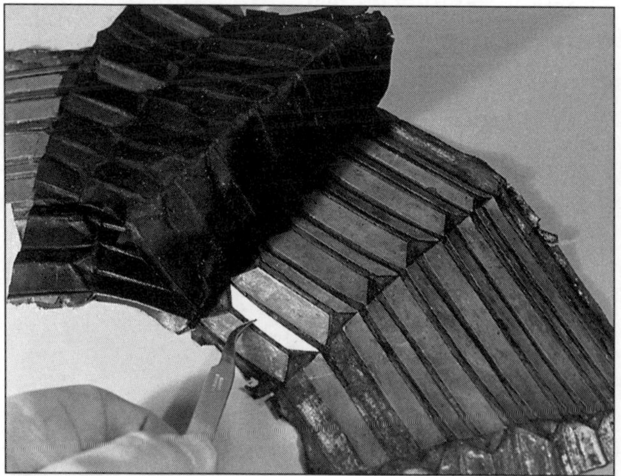

*2.7: Regluing the layers.*

**Warning:** Some old bellows might be too frail and brittle to survive the wet method. If the seams come apart easily, you can try to do the restoration dry, using contact cement instead of paper glue. Unlike sheepskin or goatskin which will soak through, the upper layer of the Premoette bellows can be glued with contact cement.

Spread the bellows flat with the outside layer on top. Peel off the outside layer only at the portions which are already separating. Find the original place for every cardboard rib (photo 2.7).

Glue them down with extra paper glue if doing it damp or contact cement if doing it dry. Once the ribs stay put, spread a coat of paper glue over the ribs. Apply the glue first with a "glue pen" or a brush, then spread it evenly with the tip of your finger. (Contact cement, on the other hand, should be spread on top of the ribs only, not in-between.)

Let one side of the bellows hang over a corner, such as the edge of a table (photo 2.8), then fold the cover skin down precisely over the inner layer. If one layer has stretched more than the other, the layers might not want to overlap correctly. In this case, proceed carefully in smaller steps, especially when gluing up the seams.

The cardboard ribs leave permanent impressions in both the inner layer and the outer skin. Pay attention to the impressions, as they are your guide to matching up the layers precisely.

You might have to stretch one or the other end. Proceed with care and attention to all details. Roll the whole sandwich down with a rubber roller, or just pat it down with your fingers.

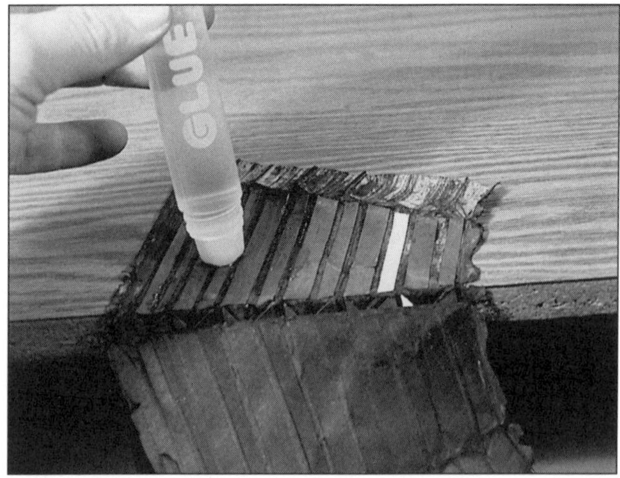


***2.8:** Hang the bellows over a corner.*

Let it firm up for 15 minutes, then glue up the seams in the original position. When gluing the seams, lay the two halves of the bottom panel over a wooden square or a corner iron. Do the inner layer first, then the ribs, then glue down the outer skin one flap at a time. Let it sit again for 15 minutes, then fold up the bellows as explained in Method 2 before it completely drys.

## Constructing New Bellows

**Note:** Before embarking on a construction project, examine the old bellows to see if it's repairable. Repairing even a hopeless-looking bellows is often easier than constructing a new one.

There are at least two different folding patterns for camera bellows (photo 2.9).

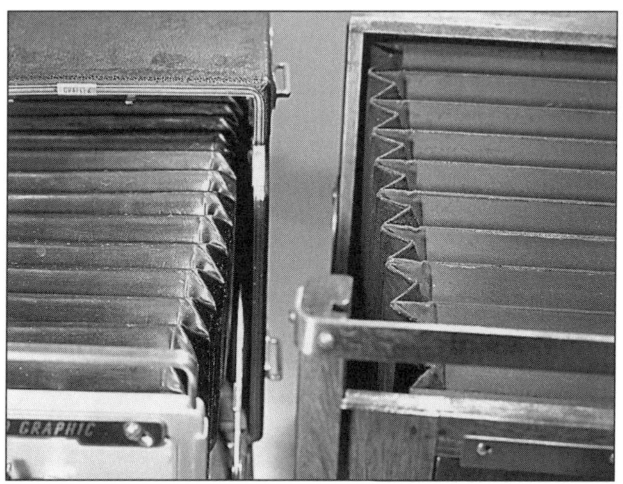


***2.9:** Square and octagonal bellows.*

One is the "modern" type where the ridges and valleys alternate on adjacent sides, and the corners are chopped off at a 45° angle — let's call these "octagonal." The "square" type is generally an older design. Here the valleys and ridges on adjacent sides line up. The ridges meet at 90° angle. The meeting points of the valleys support an extra triangular fold to provide flexible corners. In some models, these corner triangles all point in the same direction; while in others, the direction of the triangles alternate.

As to function, we distinguish between parallel and tapering bellows. Tapering bellows are usually found in older folding cameras. The parallel kind may be found in close-up attachments. View cameras may have either tapering or parallel bellows. The tapering/octagonal kind is the most difficult to construct.

## Materials

Most modern bellows and many older ones are constructed by sandwiching three layers. These are: a simple or coated fabric inner liner, a leather or leatherette outer skin, and shaped cardboard ribs between. The photo of the worn old Kodak bellows clearly shows the sandwich construction (photo 2.10).

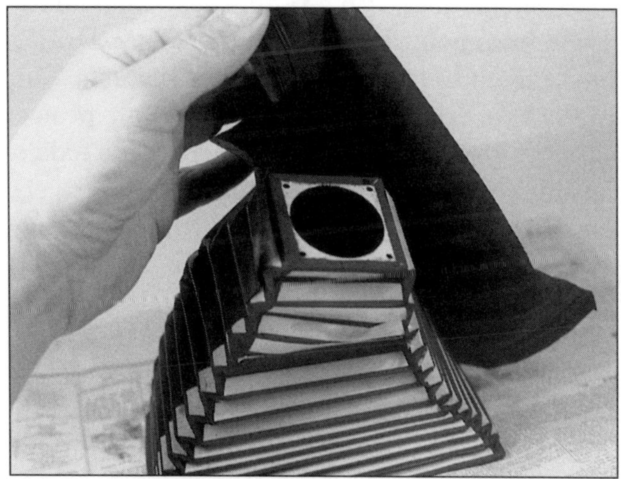

***2.10:*** *Sandwiched layers.*

Some applications call for ribbed sandwich construction, but for medium-sized bellows that are primarily for show, single or double-sheet material is perfectly adequate. Durability depends on the materials used and not so much on the construction method. Examine some old bellows and note the differences in wear.

Materials to consider: The right material must be stiff, not too rubbery. It should crease easily.

1. **Solid vinyl** wears the hardest. It comes in a variety of rich colors, but it's good at room temperature only and may be difficult to fold up. You can experiment with thin plastic sheets other than vinyl.

2. **Rubber-impregnated canvas** material is also long lasting. In fact, some of the older bellows made with such material are still in perfect shape (Lancaster & Son Merveilleux).

3. **Plastic coated paper** is easy to work with, comes in colored leather grain, but the plastic coating is not always durable.

4. **Paper-backed natural skin.** Glue a 20lb black paper sheet and goatskin or sheepskin together yourself. This material is one of the best for bellows. It's easy to work with, the color is always your choice, and durability is adequate (see above for instructions on staining).

The type of material you use depends on what you can find and on the type of bellows you're building. Medium-sized bellows are the most forgiving as to material. Large view camera bellows are heavy and tend to sag readily; thus, the best material for them is stiff and light. Large view camera bellows are mostly built by the ribbed-sandwich method from good quality materials. Small bellows, on the other hand, have finer pattern closer folds, thus the gauge, stiffness and flexibility of the material must be suitable for this more exacting application.

The instructions below are geared for single and double-sheet bellows, but once you know the principles involved and are familiar with the design parameters, you can build bellows with the sandwich method if you are willing to expend the time. If you want to successfully make bellows, I suggest you practice first using paper. Paper, in fact, is the ideal bellows material as far as ease of construction is concerned.

## Parallel-Square Bellows

These are the easiest to construct. To practice, take a sheet of paper, fold it up into an accordion by forming alternating parallel creases (photo 2.11).

Now smooth out the paper again and make one fold perpendicular to the accordion creases. Help each inside corner to lean in one direction while gently folding up the accordion. It's easy once you get the hang of it.

Using this method to construct parallel bellows is just as easy. Parallel-square construction allows all folds to be creased before gluing up the seam. Define the outside corners and the length (see tapering bellows below). The pitch of the folds are uniform and are defined by the inside corners (see Merveilleux in Chapter Six).

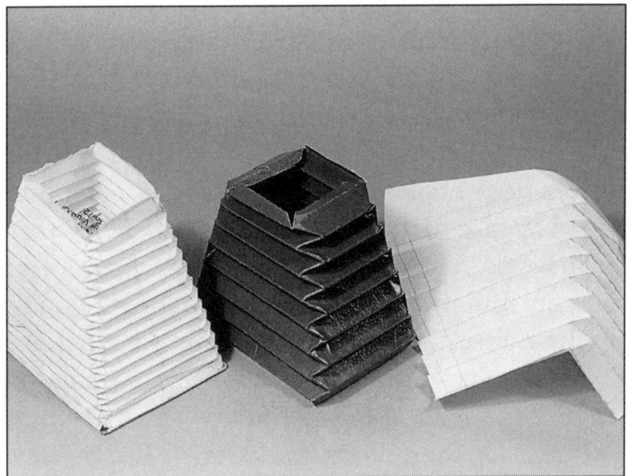

***2.11:*** *Practice on paper.*

## Tapering Bellows

Constructing tapering bellows from scratch is not quite as easy as it seems at first, but it can offer fun and educational opportunities.

The attributes to consider are the taper, the pitch of the folds, the longitudinal extension and the transverse extension. We will address these variables at the design stage.

The building consists of four steps: 1. designing and drafting the pattern, 2. scoring, 3. gluing up the tube, and 4. folding.

**1. Draw the Pattern** on the outside of the material. If this is your first time, practice on an ordinary sheet of writing paper.

If you have a sample bellows you want to copy, cut it up lengthwise alongside the bottom just where you find the original seam. You must draw in not only the exact outline but all the crease lines as well. Notice that in tapering bellows the distances between alternating folds are different. Every other one is wider than the ones in between to allow for the taper (see below). The corner zigzag is also asymmetrical. Leave an extra 5mm on one side for overlap where the seam will be glued up. Be precise; otherwise, the finished bellows might not fit, might not look good, or might even refuse to fold up properly. Study the sample pattern ( diagram 2.13). That should give you an idea of how the pattern should look.

**Designing Your Own:** If you don't have an old bellows to copy, here is what you do. (To draft the pattern, a rudimentary knowledge of geometry will help.) Since the seam is at the bottom side, place the top side at the center of the sheet. Determine length "a" by measuring from the focal plane to the back of the lens standard. Multiply that measurement by 1.4 to prevent overstretching the bellows.

Draw the long axis "a" first, then lines "c" and "b" at each end perpendicular and symmetrical to "a". Add "e" to each end of "b" at the front; add "d" to each end of "c" at the rear. Draw a circle section from point A with a radius of f/2, and another one from point B with a radius of g/2. Draw a line tangent to both of these circle sections. This line is the axis of the side panel. Now project points A and B symmetrically across the axis of the side panel and call them A1, B1 respectively. Connect points A with A1, and B with B1 to complete the side trapeze. Repeat this for the left hand side as well.

The letters denote:

***a*** = focal length at closest focus times 1.4

***b*** = minimum width available at the lens standard. This is usually the outside diameter of the rear lens group.

***c*** = minimum width available at the film gate. This is usually the width of the film gate.

***d*** = the width available beside the film gate. This is the gap the bellows fold into. Remember that in folding cameras, the struts may get in the way and must be cleared.

***e*** = the available width beside the lens if there are restrictions at the front. If there are no restrictions, then this length is given by the pitch of the folds which is your choice (see below).

***f*** = the minimum height of the bellows at the front. Again, this is usually the outside diameter of the rear lens group, but often it's larger.

***g*** = the minimum height of the bellows at the rear. This is the height of the film gate.

Since the seam is joined at the bottom, the bottom panel will be divided equally between left and right. Attach the bottom panel to the side panel by the same method we just used to attach the side panel to the top panel: Using a compass draw a circle section from point A1 with a radius of (b/2)+e and another from point B1 with a radius of (c/2)+d. Draw a line tangent to both of these circle sections, and call it "h". Draw lines through A1 and B1 such that they are perpendicular to line "h". The other half of the bottom panel goes on the other side of the pattern the same way. Attach a 5mm glue flap to one side. Attach a 5mm wide mounting flap to both the front and rear of each of the panels (see pattern). When mounting the bellows, the glue flaps may point in either direction (in or out) as required (diagram 2.13).

**Warning:** Pay close attention to pitch and taper as outlined below; otherwise, your bellows is not going to work.

With the outline completed, we have to fill in the crease lines. To some extent the pitch of the folds are given by "e" and "d". If "e" and "d" are of equal length, we have constant pitch. Often, however, the room inside the camera body is so cramped that the rear of the bellows must have finer pitch for the folds to fit into the body.

Many medium and small Kodak bellows feature variable pitch. A variable pitch gives us a little extra work but not enough to worry about.

The pitch of the folds are your choice, within limits. Larger pitch is easier to do, but requires more room inside the camera frame.

Smaller pitch is, perhaps, more pleasing aesthetically. I'd suggest choosing a larger pitch that still has room in the frame, especially at the rear portion. Extremely large folds, aside from mechanical considerations, might cause optical interference if hanging inside the path of the light

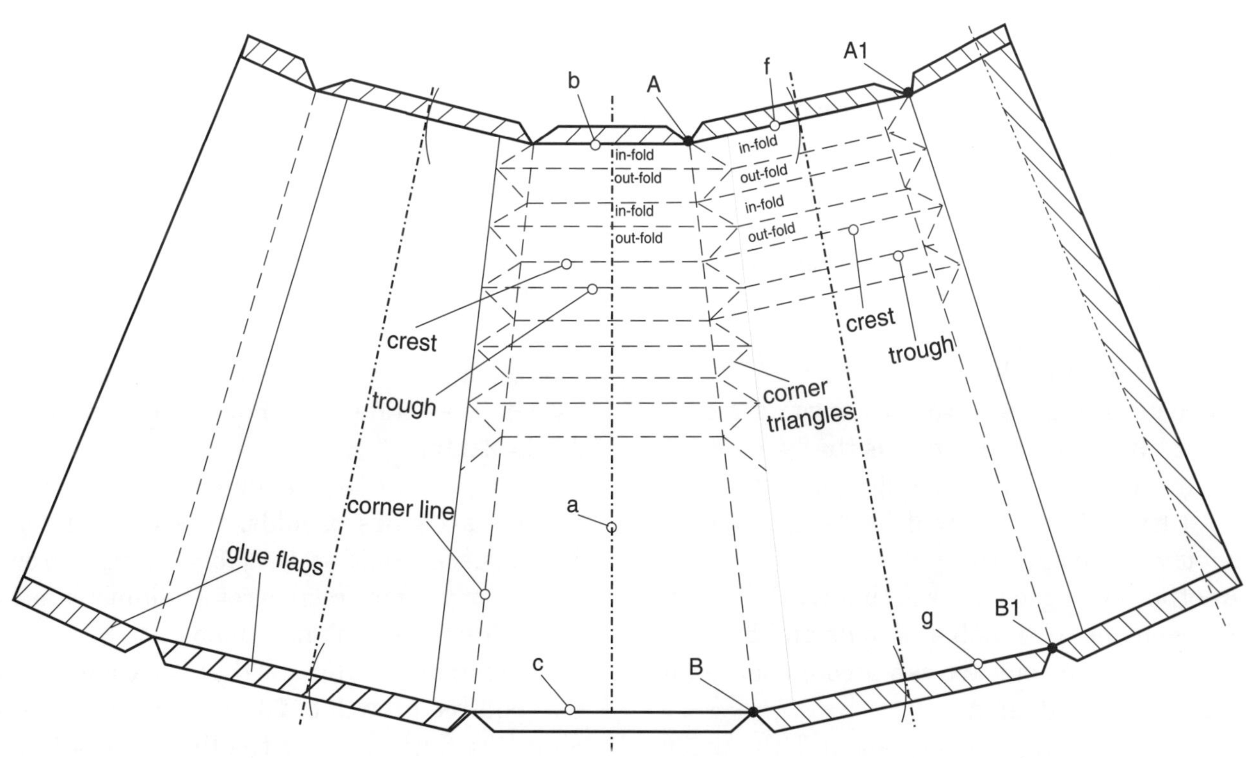


***2.12:*** *Tapering, constant pitch square bellows.*

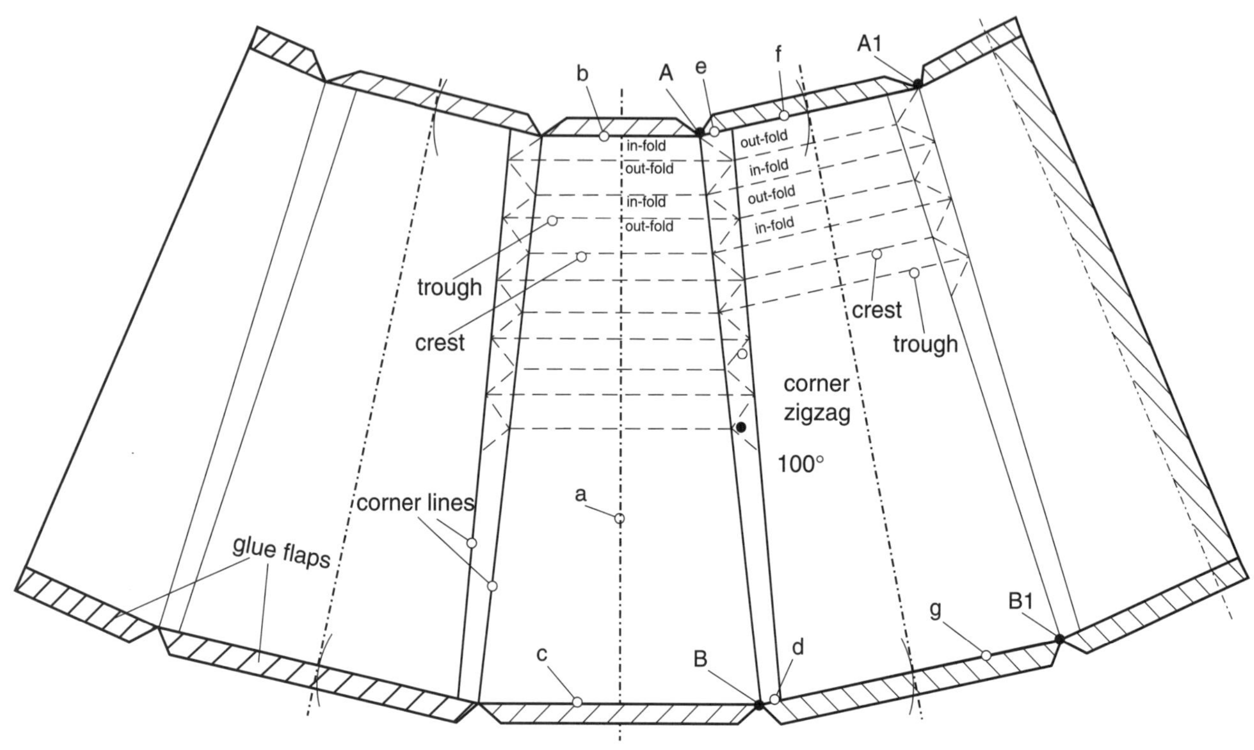


***2.13:** Tapering, variable pitch octagonal bellows.*

rays. (If you followed the instructions so far, you will have no problem.) Even though we have drawn the corner lines already, we still have a little leeway for the pitch. If you have no sample to copy, a 20mm stretched-out pitch is a good figure for small/medium bellows.

Since in the example e>d, we are going to have variable pitch. The good news is that we have to calculate the crease lines for the top panel only, and all the other sides will be defined by the geometry of the pattern.

Another bit of good news is that we don't have to worry about the number of folds and how the last one will come out. We can accommodate the last fractional fold later.

What we do have to worry about is the taper. The folds on top must accommodate 20mm of taper or growth ((g-f)/2=20). We calculate taper allowance (sideways displacement of the folds) for the top only, which accommodates the taper of the sides (diagram 2.14). This is quite apparent from the diagram and from studying an actual tapered bellows.

There is some tolerance as to the pitch. This means that we can stick with round numbers. The pitch is given by the distance between the corner lines times 1.9. For the first pitch, it's dx1.9=22mm.

This goes into "a" six times since we are going to have six pairs of folds. In a constant pitch design, each would yield 20/6 = 3.33mm growth. Don't worry about fractions of a millimeter as long as the fractions don't accumulate.

The important thing is that you come up with the required growth of 20mm from front to rear. Since the first pitch for the first pair of folds is 20mm, let the in-fold be 9mm and the out-fold 13mm (growth = 4mm). To cut down on the arithmetic, we can use the same numbers for the next pair of folds: 9 and 13 (growth=4mm).

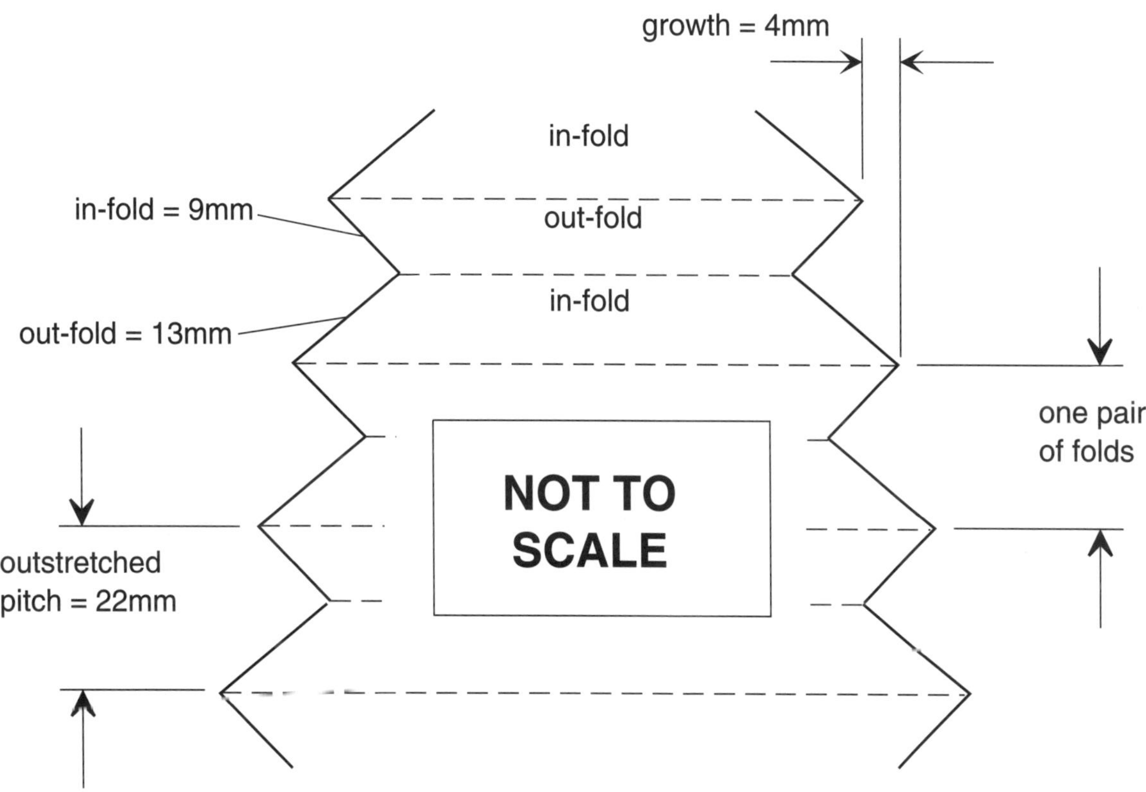


***2.14:*** *Taper growth.*

The next pitch is 10 x 1.9 = 19; this yields 8 and 11 for the folds (growth = 3mm). Let the next fold be again 8 and 11 (growth = 3mm). For the next pair 8 and 10 (growth = 2mm). From here on, we can just keep on drawing the lines with the same pitch until we reach line "c". We then have to draw parallel lines at points measured from line "b" at 13, 22, 35, 44, 55, 63, 74, 82, 92, 100, 109, 116, 125 and 132mm.

Use a sharp pencil, and draw the lines parallel to line "b". Do a precise job. Starting from the front, the wider folds project outward and the narrower folds project inward. The first line spans the inside corner lines; the next, the outside corner lines, and so on alternating.

The exact figures would be different for closed and opened bellows and at every point in between. That's the reason why the corners as well as the crease lines move and why we don't worry too much about being exact. That's why the material has to be flexible and hard wearing. If we'd construct bellows out of metal plates with metal hinges, the bellows would not budge from the designed position!

The rest can be done with a pencil and ruler. Draw in the parallel lines at the remaining panels such that they begin where the crease lines intercept the previously drawn corner lines and end on the opposite corner line.

This too must be done precisely You will notice that the wide and narrow folds are interchanged on the adjacent panels. The reason is that the peeks and valleys are interchanged between adjacent panels.

With the parallel lines done, draw in the corner zigzag. The zigzag simply joins all the intercept points on the corner lines. Study the diagram. If the corner zigzag is drawn incorrectly or without care, the bellows will not fold or will wear faster due to too much strain on the tips.

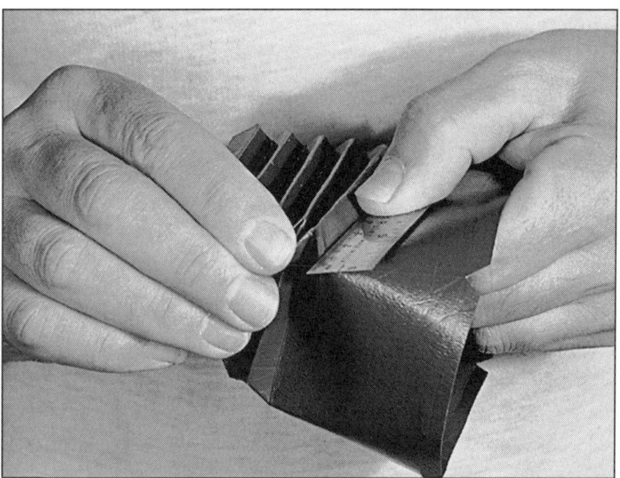

*2.15: Folding tapering/octagonal bellows.*

The zigzag angle should be about 95° to 100°. With this figure you can double-check the positions of the crease lines. At any rate, the zigzag angle is a compromise.

If you study a bellows closely, you'll notice that as you extend or compress the bellows the corners move slightly sideways, changing the zigzag angle as they move.

All this geometry sounds a bit complicated, but the only simplification possible is to stay with constant pitch and parallel or square bellows. This design is the most common in the class of cameras that collectors are interested in.

**2. Scoring:** Once you've got the pattern all drawn, you have to score it before folding. A good scoring wheel may be made from a single-wheel carbide glass cutter. Hold the carbide wheel at an angle to a spinning grinding stone. The stone rotates the carbide wheel and blunts it at the same time so it will score but will not cut.

Place the pattern on a firm, but not hard, surface, such as three or four sheets of typing paper. Using a ruler and the scoring wheel, score along the crease lines, pressing the wheel fairly hard. The lines must be visible as well as fold easily. The corner zigzag must also be scored, but not the straight corner lines.

Once you have gained some experience you can score the crease lines directly without drawing them first (once the outline is drawn.) Either the score lines or the pencil lines must be visible from the outside to aid you in folding correctly.

**3. Gluing the Seam:** After scoring, but before folding, the tapering tube must be glued up. Smear contact cement on both sides of the open seam and let it dry for 20 minutes. Fit the edges up precisely, *then* press the edges together hard.

**4. Folding:** Now it's time to crease the material along the scored lines. This may be relatively easy or difficult, depending on the material, the dimension, and on the precision you achieved when drawing and scoring.

Start from the small end crease along the scored lines. The short lines end up on top of the crests; the long lines end up at the bottom of the troughs. Progressing from the front toward the rear, the wider out-folds must project outward, and the narrower in-folds must project inward. (That's how the growth occurs.)

When forming the folds, it's important to apply pressure from the front. You can do this by holding the small end with one hand and pressing it gently down to the table while forming the folds with the other hand. Use your thumb nail at the corners to crease the zigzag.

Another good way to apply pressure is by bracing one end against your chest. That way you can use both hands to form the folds. Fold the opposite straight lines first one way, and then the adjacent sides the opposite way. You may use a straightedge to help the long creases buckle inward (photo 2.15).

Once you've succeeded in constructing paper bellows, you can try your hand at the real thing. The procedure is the same only the material is different.

If you're using material that is somewhat flexible, i.e. tends to unfold even when creased (vinyl), you'll have a tougher time than with paper. You will have to backtrack often and redo the folds already done.

If you're having difficulty finishing the whole bellows in one go, stop half way, and weigh the folds down for an hour to prevent them from unfolding.

Another problem with solid vinyl is that the scoring tool won't leave much of an impression on it. Use permanent ink to draw in the crease lines to guide you visually.

Once you've got the whole accordion finished, you have to press it. Do this by weighing it down overnight.

If you're using material that is not black on the inside, spray a light coat of matte black enamel or acrylic on the inside of the material before gluing.

Constructing tapering bellows is an exacting and time-consuming job, but the finished result is well worth the effort in terms of beauty, functionality, and satisfaction. Once you're familiar with tapering bellows construction, parallel bellows will be a cinch.

For parallel bellows, use the instructions above, but forget about taper and variable pitch. The crease lines are equidistant from each other; the corner lines are parallel, and the corner zigzags are symmetrical.

The square type is even easier to construct. Use diagram 2.12 in drafting the pattern for a square tapering bellows.

# Chapter Three

# Restoring a Camera Stand

If you find an old camera stand, it's certainly worth restoring. A large view camera on a wooden stand is an impressive sight (photo 3.1).

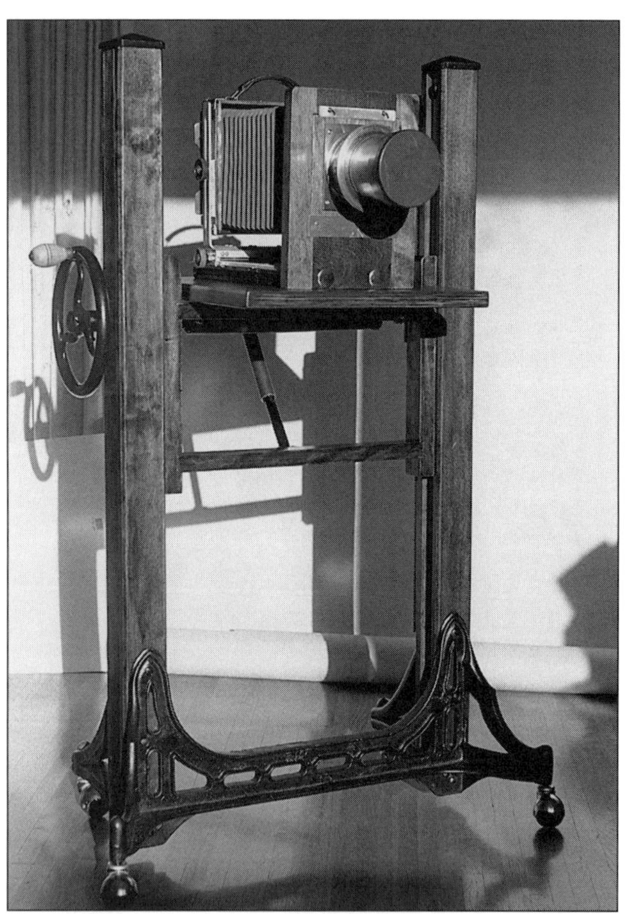

***3.1:*** *View camera on a stand.*

The one I acquired was made by the Century Camera Co. With its massive columns, cast-iron base, double rack-and-pinion elevator, and large cast iron handle wheel, this camera stand is formidable.

## What You will Learn

You will learn how to: fabricate missing parts out of wood; design parts to match the style of the original; repair existing wooden parts; and clean up and refinish rusty iron parts.

## Assessment

One of the cast-iron bases is missing; the table top is missing; the iron parts are rusty; the wooden parts are warped, and almost all the joints are falling apart.

Start with fabricating the missing parts in order to stain and finish them together with the restored originals. The table top must be solid and should not warp.

This means either plywood or "butcher block". If you don't have a woodworking shop, stay with plywood. Have the lumberyard cut off two boards of 1/2" plywood 17"x20" each. Ask them to be precise, so you won't have to rasp and sand much at home.

The table is constructed as seen on diagram 3.2. A 1/4" nut is recessed into the bottom half of the table at each of the three positions. The two halves are glued together with the nuts sandwiched inside.

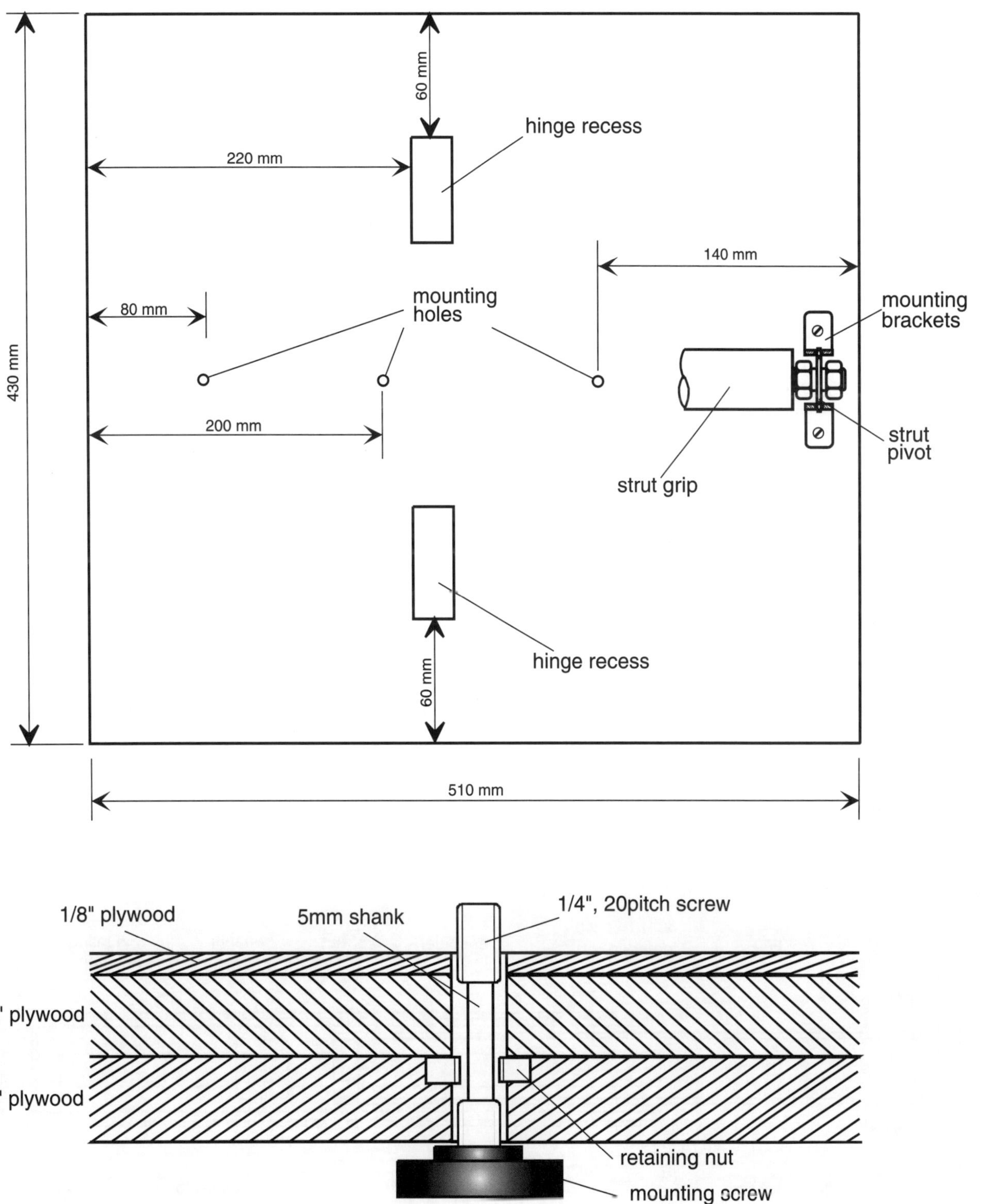


***3.2:*** *Table construction.*

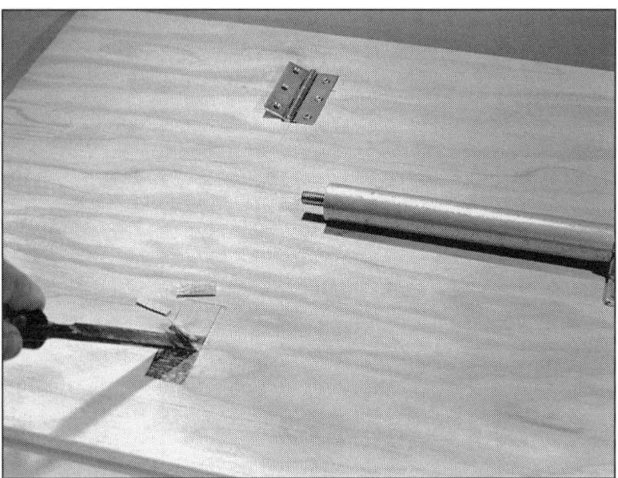

*3.3: Mounting the hinges.*

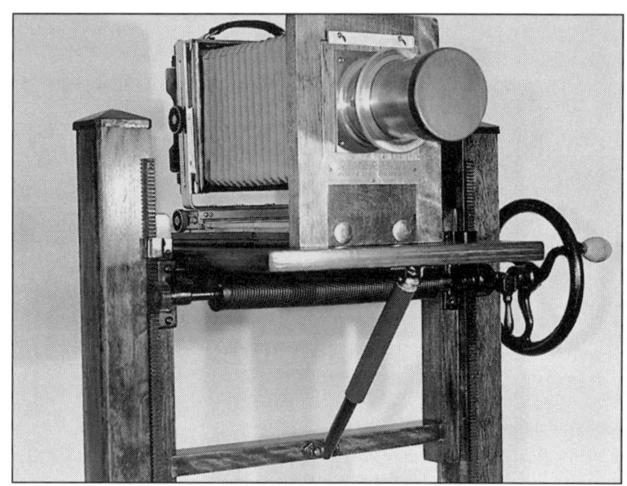

*3.4: Expandable strut tilts the table.*

You can buy good quality plywood for the top board or glue either veneer or an extra layer of door skin on top.

The hinges are recessed into the underside of the top. If the hinges are missing, buy them first and mark out their place so that the pivot point falls 220mm from the front edge. Rout or chisel out the hinge recesses. Cut around the contour with a sharp utility knife before using the chisel (photo 3.3).

The back edge of the table is supported by an adjustable strut. As the strut is expanded, the table tips forward allowing the camera to point downward. If backward tilting is necessary, the stand should be turned around and the camera pointed the other way. If the strut is missing, a replacement may be made from two loose-fitting metal tubes with a nut and a threaded rod inside them (photo 3.4).

The strut must be able to pivot at either of its ends (diagram 3.5). By undoing the lower pivot, the table can be positioned vertically for storage (photo 3.6).

In this position, the stand takes up little room; it can be carted on its own castors and stored against a wall or in a broom closet.

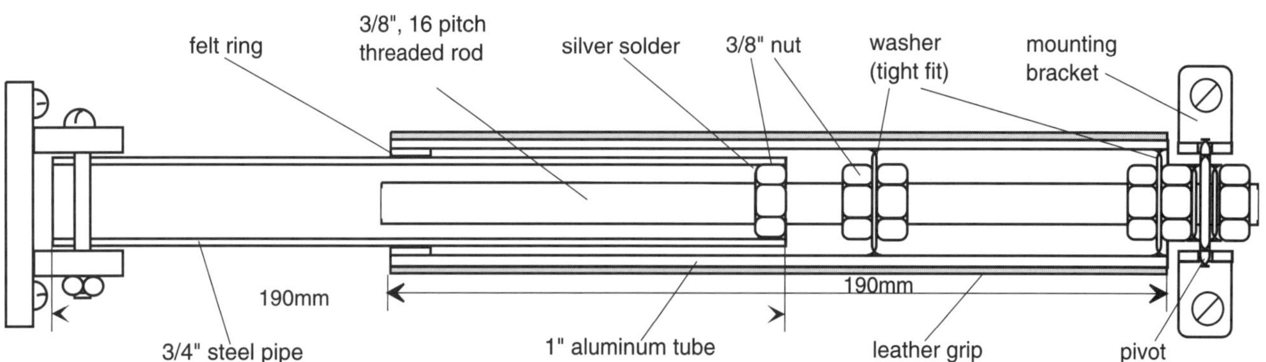


*3.5: Expandable table strut.*

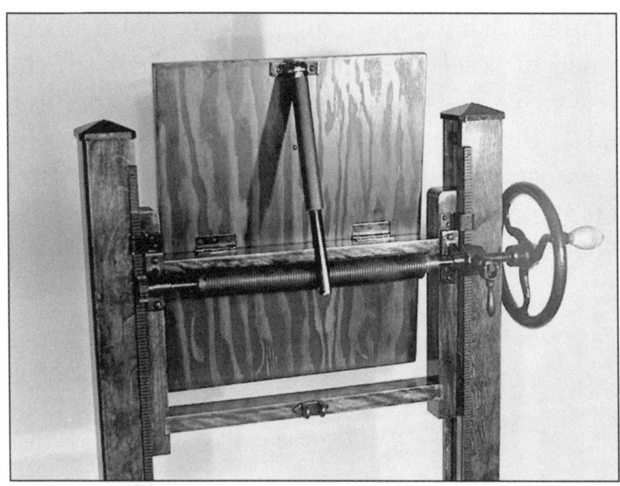

***3.6:*** *Vertical table position.*

Since one of the bases is missing, we have to provide a replacement. It's possible to have another base cast using the existing one for the pattern. The problem is, the metal shrinks 3/16" for each foot, leaving the new cast 1/2" shorter than the pattern.

This, however, is not a big problem if the screw holes are plugged up before casting, and drilled out later at the proper positions.

If you have to have any pattern work done, the cost goes up; you may be looking at anywhere between $150 and $500.

You would like to use iron for weight and rigidity, but brass or aluminum is also a possibility, though more expensive.

At any rate, I opted for wood. The design should look old-fashioned but not too fancy. Don't make lion-claw legs carved from solid oak. The new legs must look somewhat austere befitting an industrial environment.

You can make suitable legs out of wooden slats bent and glued together to form a stylized triangle. You may either buy the wooden slats or have the lumberyard slice them from a two-by-four or from a sheet of door skin plywood.

You'll need ten 42-inch lengths of 2x1/8" slats. Cut each one into two 12" and two 9" lengths by scoring both sides with a utility knife, then snapping them off.

While a form is desirable for the controlled bending of wood, it is not necessary for short pieces. Paint white glue on eight pieces, except the outside of the first and last one. Bundle one more piece on both sides, without gluing, to protect the wood from damage by the clamps. Hold one end of the bundle in a vise. Bend the bundle little-by-little while placing clamps on at one-inch intervals (photo 3.7). Having an extra hand makes the job easier.

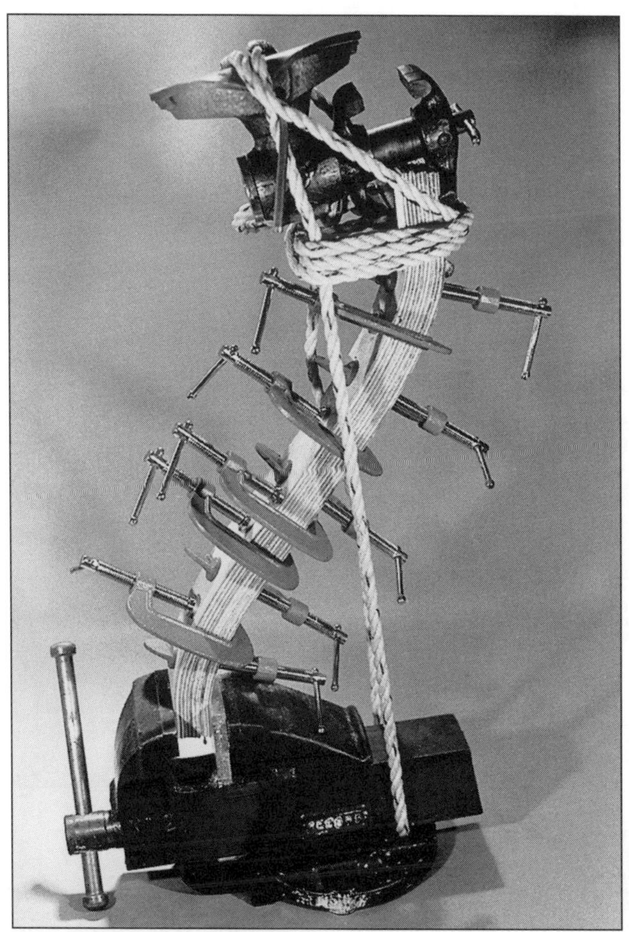

***3.7:*** *Gluing a double-curved member.*

Once the bundles are dry, plane their sides smooth, then round them off using coarse sandpaper. Glue the outside tips together, and reinforce the joint with two wood screws.

All this must be done precisely if you're using the original bolts for mounting the new legs (see the finished legs on photo 3.8 and 3.9).

Once the new pieces are done, examine and repair the original components of the stands. In my example, the column components were all warped. I had to knock them apart and plane each piece flat to be able to reglue them properly (see

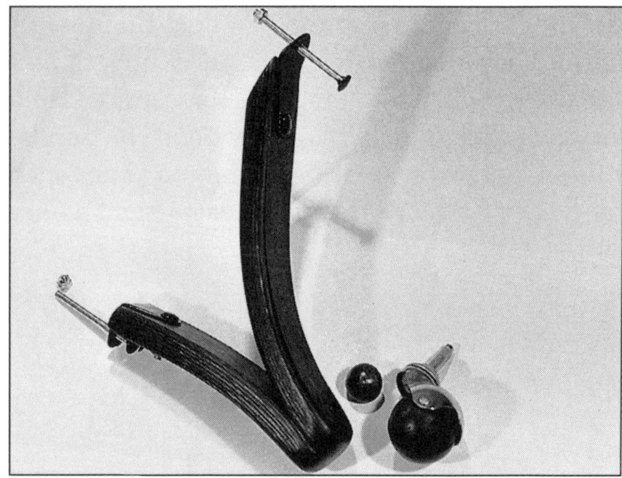

***3.8:*** *The finished leg with hardware.*

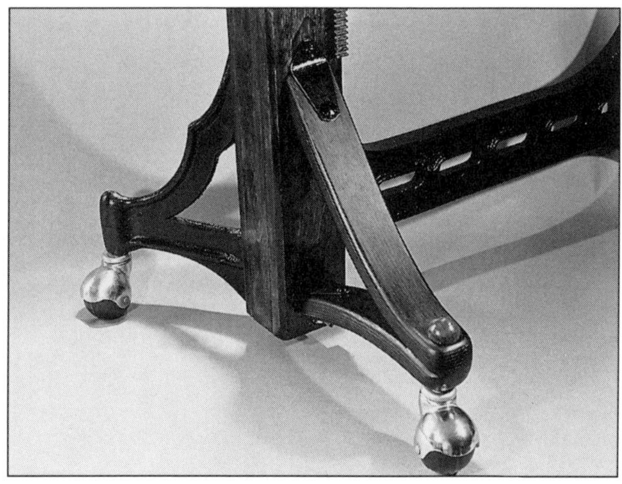

***3.9:*** *The new leg mounted.*

photo 3.10). If there is old varnish or paint on the parts, you will have to strip them first. Stain and finish all the pieces as described in Chapter Six.

Since the cast-iron parts are quite rough originally, one thin coat of black enamel applied with a paintbrush will yield an adequate result. Using a pad of steel wool and detergent, rub off the heavy rust and dirt before painting. All other iron parts, including the screw heads, as well as the new metal hardware, should be painted black. I left the casters chrome, but you can paint those black also.

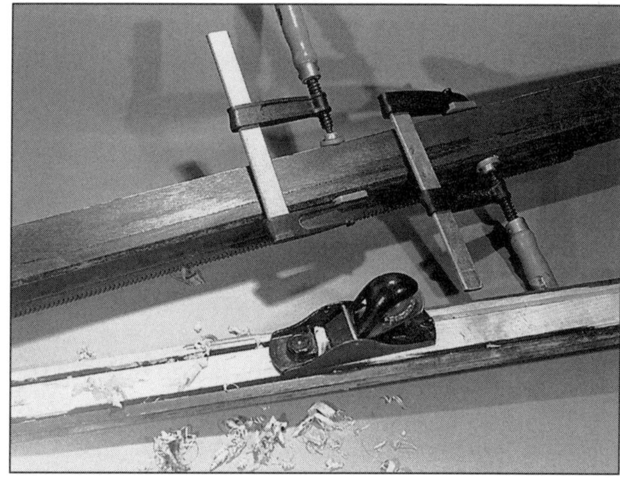

***3.10:*** *Repairing the columns.*

Lubricate the sliding surfaces between the columns and the elevator bracket with soap. Lubricate the rack and pinions with automotive grease and the bushings with heavy oil. Before mounting the base casting(s), install the elevator bracket 10" from the top of the columns. Make sure the mesh with the racks is the same on both sides. Mount the base casting(s) now. Make sure the columns are parallel before tightening the bolts. You can install the table and the rest of the hardware once the columns are secure in the upright position. Photo 3.1 shows the restored stand.

Chapter Four

# Lenses and Lens Shutters

## Lenses

Many older view camera lenses are constructed along similar veins. The main barrel and aperture rings are usually made of brass; the lens mounts are either brass or aluminum (photo 4.1).

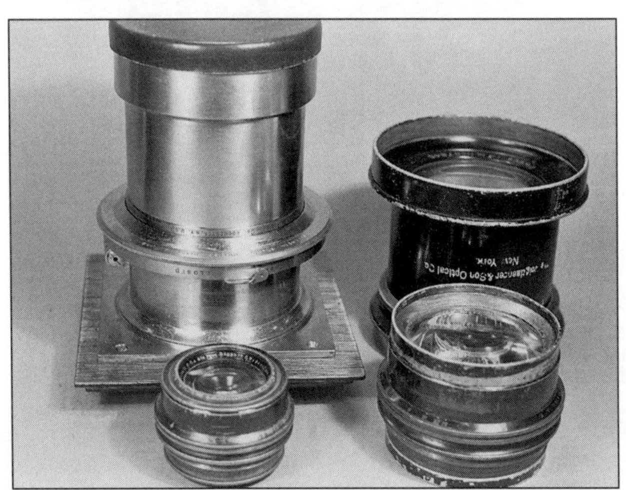

***4.1:*** *An assortment of lenses.*

Regardless of size and make, these lenses often come apart in like fashion. Unscrew the front and rear lens groups. The cover sleeve over the main barrel is pressed on and can be pulled off, although some of them are tight. A position screw in the side of the barrel keeps these sleeves from turning; nevertheless, they should come off by hand without any tools. If you must, pry it off with the flat of a screwdriver blade (not with its corners). At the largest setting of the aperture ring, a slot in the ring lines up with the screw head. In this position, the ring can be pulled off the barrel. With the aperture dial off, the connecting screw in the side of the diaphragm ring inside the barrel is accessible. Now you can shake out the blades and the diaphragm rings (photo 4.2). Notice the huge number of blades in this Bausch & Lomb lens.

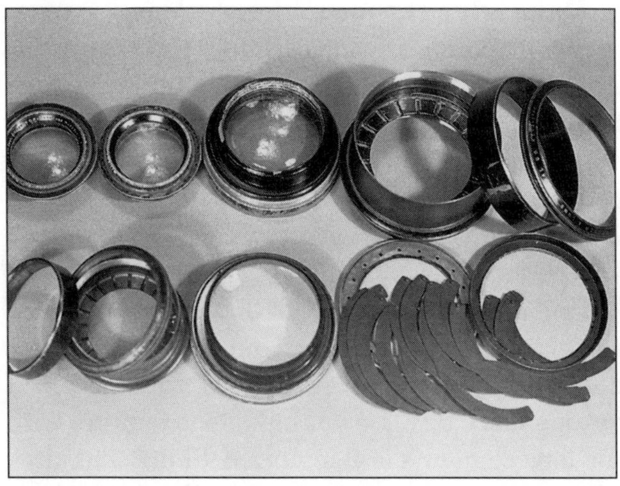

***4.2:*** *Parts of a lens.*

The outer surfaces of the lens groups can be cleaned easily; cleaning the inside, however, may be difficult or next to impossible. Many of the lens elements are secured in their mount by a metal rim. The fold of this rim must be opened up before the element is free. (The procedure is described in Chapter Five, Kodak Six-20.) Be very careful not to damage the glass.

A loose brass ring is often placed over the diaphragm ring inside the barrel. This ring is not threaded. If it's tight, you can pull it out with a wire hook. Pull alternately at opposite points of the ring. These rings, as is the case with most other parts, tend to be snug in these brass lenses. The wire hook should be made of stiff piano wire or bicycle spoke.

Many of these brass lenses are painted black by the factory. If you prefer the brass finish, paint varnish remover over the black paint, then rub off the paint with steel wool and detergent. If the lettering is engraved, you can fill them in with black paint as described in Chapter Ten. If the lettering is nickel-plated over brass, you must be extra careful when cleaning off the black finish. Plated numbers can be rubbed off easily.

Some of the factory blacks are extremely tenacious; stripper will not touch them. Use #400 wet and dry paper followed by steel wool to strip a really tough black finish. Do this only if the letters are engraved, as plated letters won't survive the sanding.

Quite often the mount for the lens groups is made of aluminum even though the rest of the parts are brass. In this case, the aluminum must be painted black. If the original is still good, just wipe it off with an oily rag; otherwise, you must put it through the full treatment: stripping, sanding, masking, and spraying.

You can always achieve a tougher paint by baking it on. Bake acrylic at 300°F for two hours. Let enamel dry for a day, bake it at 150°F for a day (approximately eight hours), then at 200°F for one more day. Do not bake lens mounts with the lens elements still mounted. Short of baking, let any fast-drying paint dry for at least two days, and slow-drying enamel for at least a week before handling the part.

## Voigtlander Heliar No.6

A large 14", f/4.5 monster, this lens is constructed differently from the standard lens as described above. It has a brass main barrel, but all other barrels, including the lens mounts are aluminum. The rear lens group is stuck solidly in the aluminum mounting ring. As it often happens with these older lenses, the naked aluminum threads cold-weld together, never to come apart again (see Chapter Seven). If you encounter this problem, don't try to force the barrels apart; it will not work and you might ruin the lens in the process.

If the diaphragm cannot come out of the main barrel backwards after the rear lens group is removed, all is not lost. In this case, it's possible to get to the blades from the front. Unscrew the front lens group first. You'll see a serrated retaining ring in the bottom of the barrel. It is threaded and should unscrew counter-clockwise. If it's stuck, drill or mill two small holes or notches into the ring, and then use a metal tool to unscrew it. Once this retaining ring is out, the diaphragm ring and blades fall out forward (photo 4.3).

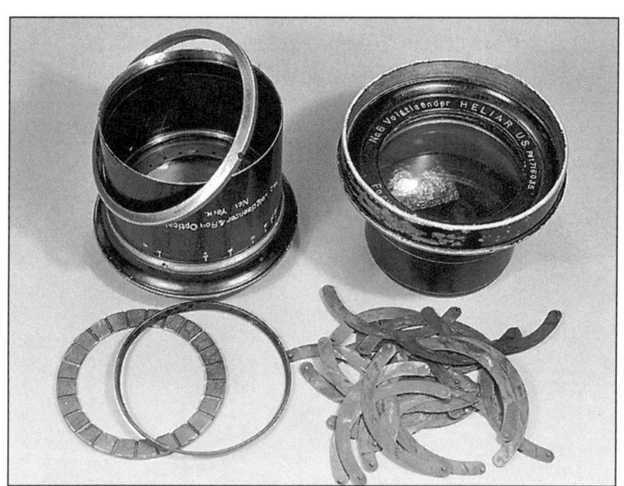

***4.3:*** *Voigtlander Heliar No. 6 disassembled.*

If, on the other hand, you are successful in unscrewing the rear lens group, remove the connecting screw from the side of the aperture dial. The dial is threaded, and can be undone counterclockwise. Remove the two screws you find under the dial. Knock the complete diaphragm assembly out backwards. It's tight, but it will come out.

## Bausch & Lomb Iris Diaphragm Shutter

The early shutters with their heavy brass bodies and twin nickel-plated pneumatic cylinders decorating the face of the assembly are considered true works of art by today's collectors (photo 4.4).

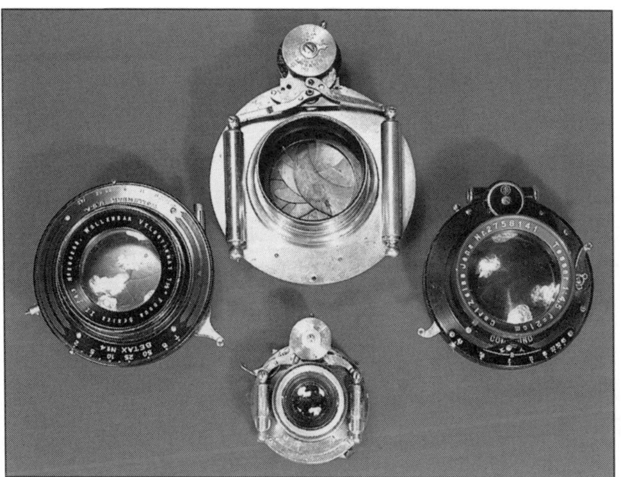

**4.4:** *Bausch & Lomb shutter.*

Bausch & Lomb created fine shutters beginning in 1889. Some of their earliest models had only one set of blades as opposed to two sets — one for shutter, one for aperture — in later designs. The iris diaphragm shutter construction is unique and somewhat rare. This particular shutter is large, measuring 4 and 1/4 inches on the outside. While it has only a fraction of the parts count of today's shutters, the Bausch & Lomb iris shutter is not exactly an easy mechanism to figure out, repair, or restore.

If lens groups are mounted on the shutter, just unscrew the barrels from the shutter body.

The control mechanism is somewhat tricky. Pay close attention and take notes during disassembly (photo 4.5).

The numerous washers you find there play important roles as well. Remove the T-I lever first, then the shutter-speed cam (each held by one screw in its center). The long latch lever and the escapement lever come off next.

These last two levers connect with the pneumatic cylinders. Remove the cylinders as well; only one nut holds them from the other side of the shutter housing.

While you're at the back of the shutter, remove the third nut as well. In order to free the escapement lever, pull the brass crescent out of the shutter-speed hub.

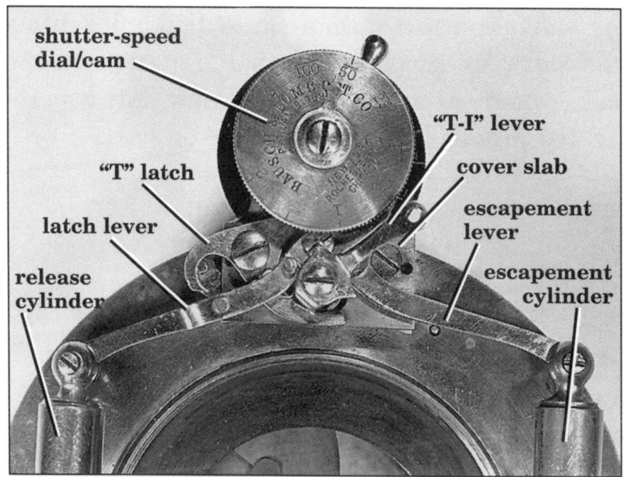


**4.5:** *The control assembly.*

With those parts out of the way, you may remove the whole control unit. First, remove the cover slab only (one screw). The control unit is still supported by two register pins. Now the interaction between the blades, the operating cam, and the aperture dial can be studied (photo 4.6). You may expect to repair any malfunction in this shutter only if you familiarize yourself with every aspect of its operation in minute detail.

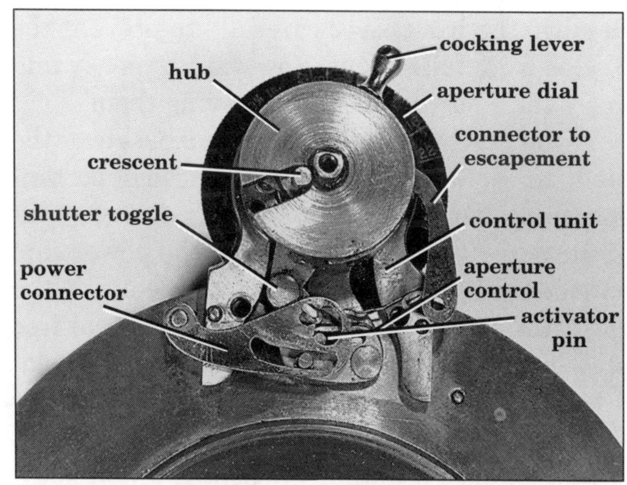


**4.6:** *The pin should stay in its slot.*

In my example, the little auxiliary arm that connects the brass crescent to the escapement lever was broken. Luckily the broken pieces were still there so I could copy them. I ground a new lever out of a saw blade. When fashioning parts from hard steel, use a thin grinding disk. Do not let down the steel. Depending on hardness, you may have to use a carbide bit to drill holes into a new part. In my case, the shoulder rivet had to be knocked out as well, and the new part was re-riveted. Photo 4.7 shows the broken part.

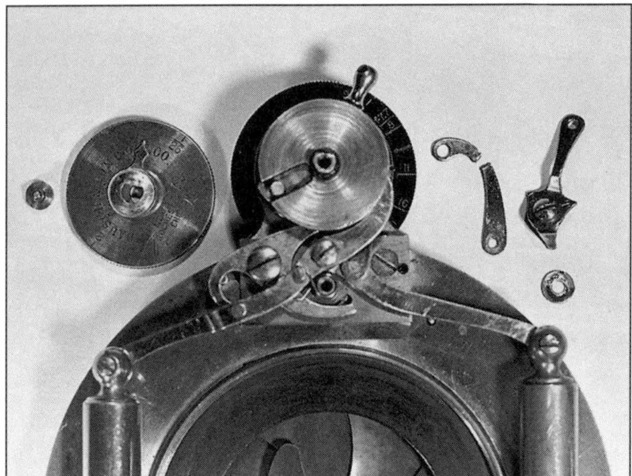

***4.7:** The broken part.*

The blades in this shutter are made of plastic sheet which tends to warp from heat strains as well as misuse of the shutter. You can get to the blades by removing the three screws and three slotted nuts from the back of the shutter unit. Remove the back cover carefully to prevent the blades from falling out. You want to study and mark their position before removing them.

If you find one or more small washers over the blade hubs, note their position. These important spacer washers are there to take the free play out of the activator ring. Notice how the power cam outside the base cup connects with the pin on the activator ring. If there is too much vertical free play in the ring, the pin may pop out of the slot in the cam (photo 4.6).

The blades are made of thermoplastic and can be straightened beautifully in boiling water. You'll have to make a simple jig in order to do so. Using shears, cut two 23x70mm rectangles out of a 1/32" aluminum sheet. Drill a 3/8 inch hole in one corner of both rectangles where the brass hub of the blades will go.

Sandwich each blade between the two halves of the jig and squeeze it gently between parallel pliers (photo 4.8). Immerse this sandwich into boiling water. Hold it in the water for two minutes to let the heat soak in thoroughly. Pull it out and hold it in the air for another minute and a half without waving it around.

You want the assembly cooled to room temperature slowly to avoid strain building up in the structure of the plastic. Do not hurry the cooling in any way or the blade may warp again over time. If your jig is of heavier stock, you would have to soak it and cool it proportionally longer. Once the jig is only lukewarm to the touch, you may remove the blade.

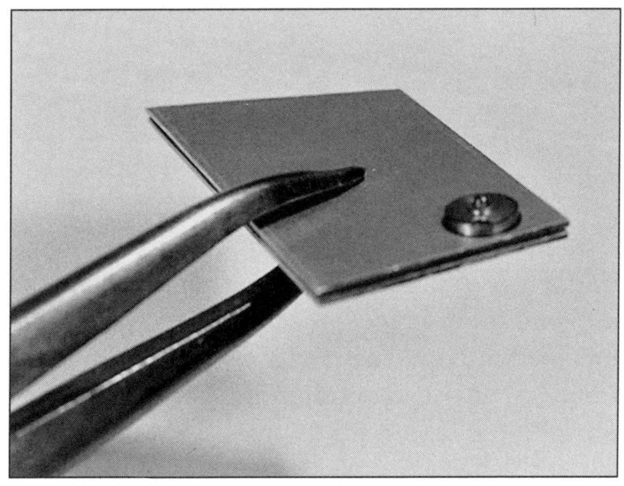

***4.8:** Jig for straightening the blades.*

Do the next blade the same way. There might be slight differences in the diameter of the brass hubs. If one doesn't fit the hole in the jig, you have to enlarge the hole to accommodate the hub. Do not force the hub into the hole; it must fit loosely. Don't touch the hub either while the jig is hot. The plastic blade becomes very soft in boiling water and can be damaged easily if not handled with care.

The first and the last blades are mounted on a common hub. In order to straighten them, you have to separate them. Notice that this hub is constructed of three disks. The two outer ones are just pressed onto the shaft. Pry one of them off carefully to free one blade. The other may stay on the hub.

Once the blades are straightened, place the front half of the shutter housing in front of you with the control disks up top, away from you. The blade activator ring goes in first with the activator pin poking through the hole in the housing. Install the blades next. Notice that each blade is displaced vertically by a one blade thickness from the one before it. Each blade has its own place in the shutter assembly. Also notice that the blades are rotated by a linear, up-and-down movement of the operating ring, not by a rotational movement as in modern shutters.

Before installation, carefully examine the hub of each blade and line them up in the order of disk thickness (photo 4.9). Install the blades in that order. Place the blade with the shallowest bottom disk to the 9 o'clock position. Both pins on the bottom of the hub should fall into their respective holes (one in the base cup, the other in the operating ring).

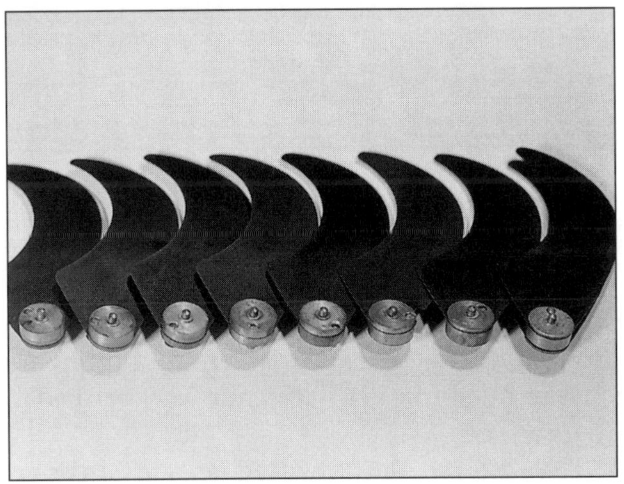

***4.9:*** *Line up the blades.*

The next blade goes clockwise on top of the first and should stand only one blade thickness higher. In this fashion, install the rest of the blades (photo 4.10). Last, the double blades go to the 7 o'clock position and should hug the bundle of blades on both sides. Thread them in deftly; it's not difficult.

Don't forget the spacer washers over the hubs up top, nearest to the control disks. Once the blades are installed properly, place the cover half onto the bottom cup. Now install the three screws to hold the two halves together.

The activating pin sticks out through the front top of the lens housing. With your tweezers, pull the pin up and down. The blades should open and close. Attempt to move the pin vertically to the shutter housing. There should be a minimum of free play. If there is too much play or the blades don't move freely, the shim washers I mentioned before might be missing or improperly placed.

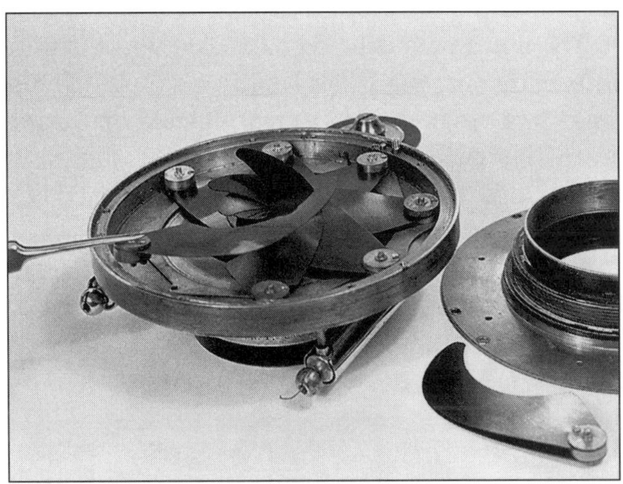

***4.10:*** *Install the blades clockwise.*

## Wollensak Iris Diaphragm Shutter

The Wollensak shutter follows the same general principle as the Bausch & Lomb we discussed above, but it is much simpler and a lot easier to restore. The blades are made of the same plastic material as in the B&L shutter, but they have no hub.

If they are bent, you can straighten them in hot water sandwiched between two aluminum plates (see above), but since the blades have no hub, there is no need to drill a hole into the plates.

First, unscrew the lens groups from the front and rear of the shutter, then remove the screw from the face of the aperture dial. Unscrew the dial counter-clockwise. The ring above it with the inscription, "Wollensak Optical Co. Rochester, N.Y. U.S.A." will be forced off when the dial is being unscrewed. This ring is just pressed on.

Pull off the aperture cam next, and remove the five screws from the face of the cover. One of these screws provides the dial stop; mark its position. With the cover off, the shutter mechanism is accessible.

Unlike in the B&L shutter, the blades here are all similar to each other and are suspended on pivoting arms. The arms are rotated by the center disk, quite akin to the way modern shutters work. Removal of the blades is easy. You don't have to mark the blades; they are all identical.

The outer ring is held by five screws. With the outer ring out, the inner ring is also free. Under those two rings are the spring-loaded operating levers. Note the positions of the levers as well as the springs before removing them (photo 4.11).

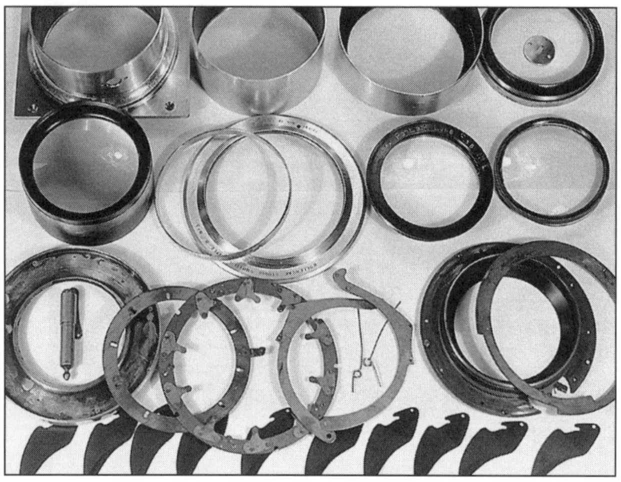

***4.11:*** *The shutter disassembled.*

That's all. There is no escapement or any mechanism to govern the shutter speeds. Presumably, the shutter speeds are controlled either by the operator manually or by an external mechanism. I would remove the pneumatic release cylinder from the back of the shutter assembly in order to be able to operate and test the shutter by the pin sticking out there.

Clean the inside of the shutter base as well as the parts before reassembly. Rub dry graphite powder onto the sliding parts. Clean the blades as well. The blades must be clean and dry; no lubricant. Don't use any oil or grease inside the shutter assembly on any of the parts.

The blades go back easily. You can start at any point and place one blade on top of the other in a clockwise direction. The last one goes on top as well (photo 4.12). You don't have to interlace them akin to diaphragm blades in a modern shutter. Yes, there is quite a large gap remaining between the first and the last blade where light has a chance to leak in. This is probably why this type of shutter has not been pursued. Clean the cover plate, and make sure each of the blades are sitting on their pins properly before refitting the cover.

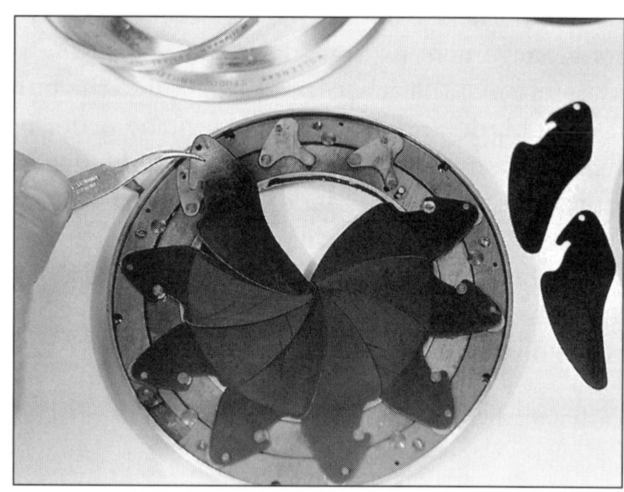

***4.12:*** *Refitting the blades.*

While the barrels are apart, clean them and strip any paint with varnish remover. Rub all the outer surfaces thoroughly with an SOS™ pad and rinse them with running water and a soft brush. After that, the engraved letters and numbers must be filled-in with black paint as described in Chapter Ten.

The restored shutter fitted with a Vitax portrait lens is seen in photo 4.1 and in Chapter Six fitted onto the Rembrandt Portrait camera.

## Packard Ideal Shutter

This shutter has only three blades in a unique arrangement. You might find this type of shutter retrofitted in old shutterless view cameras. It is operated by a pneumatic cylinder. The pneumatic pressure opens the shutter blades without help from any springs, and suction closes them.

Housed in a flat square metal box, this shutter unit is quite drab as it's intended to be mounted either inside or behind the lens standard where it is hidden from inquisitive eyes. Being simple, it seldom breaks down, except for the cylinder seizing up or the cover plates binding the blades.

The remedy is simple: after the mounting screws are removed from the 4 corners, remove the 3 screws from the face of the unit. The two halves of the housing can be pried apart (photo 4.13).

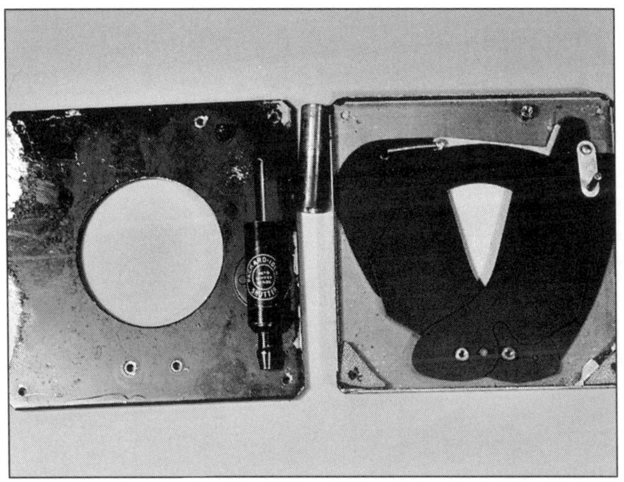

***4.13:*** *Pry off the cover plate.*

The blades are made of plastic in this unit. If they are damaged or broken, it is possible to cut out a substitute from a suitable plastic sheet. If bent or distorted, you can straighten them the way it is described above (see Bausch & Lomb.)

Turning the unit over, you will observe a hole at the 11 o'clock position in addition to the screw holes. This hole accommodates a pin that, when inserted, disengages the control cam from the large crescent blade and allows the opening and closing of the shutter in one compression stroke (photo 4.14).

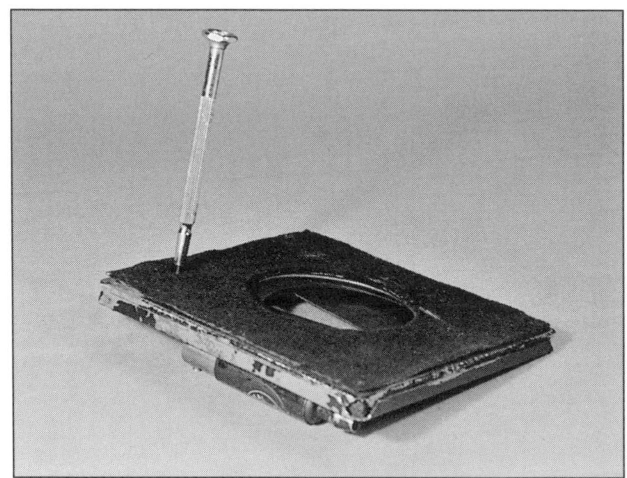

***4.14:*** *Insert a pin to change to "I" mode.*

By squeezing the bulb slower or faster, different shutter speeds can be achieved, typically from 1/25 sec to a number of seconds. The pin is inserted from the front of the camera through the lens standard or lens board.

If the pin is withdrawn, a "B" action is achieved, i.e. the blades open by compression and close by suction.

The pneumatic piston and cylinder must be clean and smooth. Lubricate them with fine graphite powder. Rub the powder on, and blow off the dust. Lubricate the blades with graphite as well. The pneumatic bulb must be fairly large and of good quality. It should provide good suction to close the blades in the "B" mode, or reset the shutter in the "I" mode.

Chapter Five

# The Folding Camera

## Disassembling the Body

Complete disassembly of the body may be required only if the bed, the folding mechanism, or the body itself is damaged or requires new parts. Kodak leather-covered folding cameras may have metal frames but wooden sides. In order to disassemble the body, the sides must come off first. That, in turn, requires the removal of the leather cover.

The leather comes off easily from the metal backing but not from wood. In fact, you'll find many of these with some of the leather pieces missing from the body because the glue has dried out and lost its grip on the metal.

In order to remove the leather from the wood, however, the glue must be dissolved. The glue most often used is ordinary bone extract which will dry and crack with age especially on non-porous surfaces. This glue dissolves in water no matter how old it is.

There might be fittings that should be taken off first, such as the film advance key or film reel spindles. These may be secured by screws or by retaining tongues through the wood. Straightening the tongues might require a special crowbar-like tool you can make by bending the tip of a screwdriver 90°.

To soften up the glue, dip a paper towel into cold water, and spread the wet towel onto the leather. Cover it with a plastic sheet to keep the water from evaporating. Leave it soaking for about three hours. Once the leather has fully soaked through, and the glue has softened, just lift off the leather (photo 5.1).

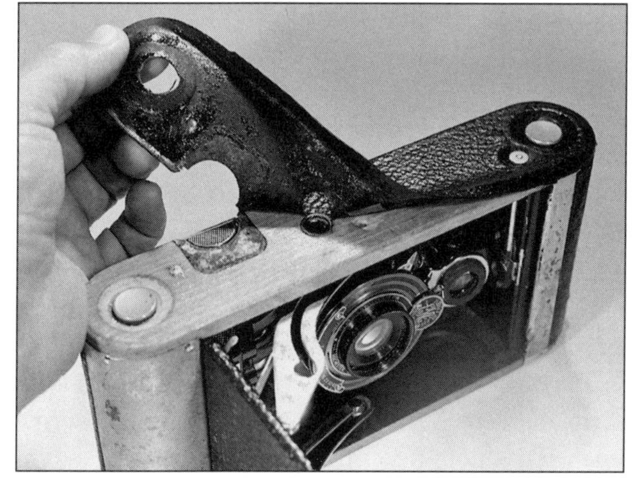

***5.1:** Removing the leather.*

Depending on the tanning process and the age of the leather, soaking it in water might actually expand the leather, but it will inevitably shrink when dry. If you try to prevent the leather from shrinking, such as by clamping it down, it will tear itself apart. If that happens it's too old and brittle and should be replaced with new leather.

Once the leather is off, the method of fastening the body parts together becomes obvious. There may be screws or tongues through the wood that are folded over on the outside.

In Kodak folding models, pull out the nails from the tip of the tongues that stick through the wooden sides. Pry up the tabs, straighten them as much as you can; otherwise, the tongues will not pull through easily. Remove the screws as well from the top and bottom of the metal housing, and just pry the sides off the body (photo 5.2).

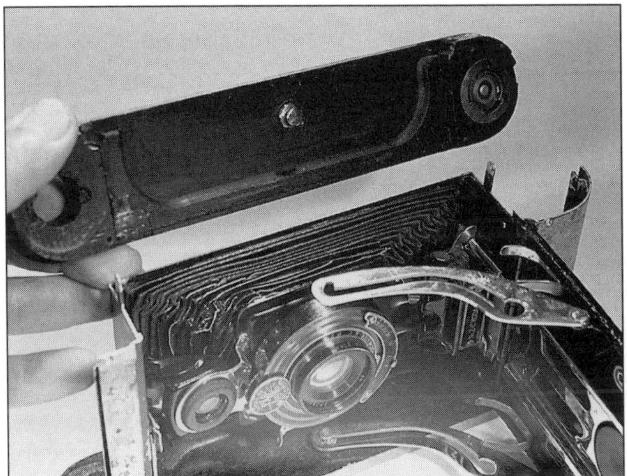

***5.2:*** *Removing the sides.*

Try to pull off the sides by hand. Prying under the wood with a metal tool might damage the wood or the soft aluminum frame.

If the frame is bent, straighten it perfectly before reassembly, as the edge of the metal must fit into the slots in the wood.

With the sides off, you can remove the folding bed, the struts, and the bellows easily. In order to remove the bed, just push out the hinge pin. With the bed loose, the struts can be disengaged as well (photo 5.3).

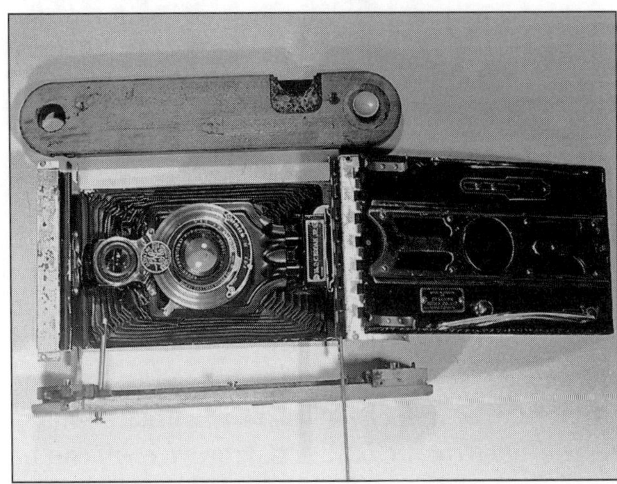

***5.3:*** *Disengaging the bed and struts.*

## Copper Oxide Blisters

If there are brass screws or brass fittings under the leather, the green copper oxide corrosion forming on the brass will build up over the years and push the leather higher and higher, forming little hills over every screw head and brass fitting. These blisters are in fact a regular feature of many old leather covered models (photo 5.4).

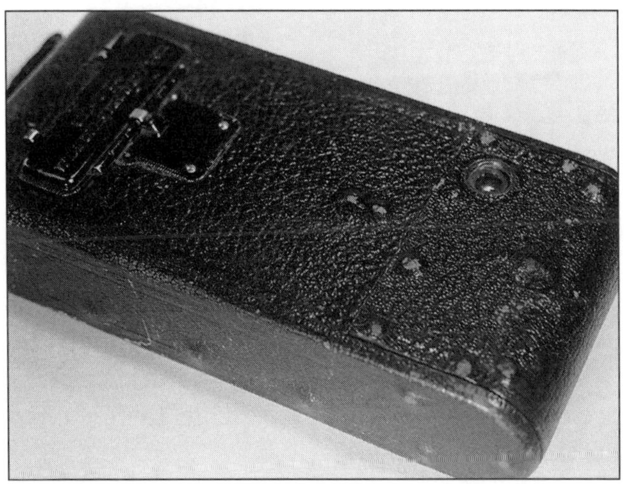

***5.4:*** *Copper oxide blisters.*

If you had to remove the leather anyway, just scrape the green oxide off. Whether sticking the old leather back on or replacing it with new, the bumps will not show any more.

If you want to eliminate the blisters without pulling off the leather, slit a cross into each blister with a sharp knife. Fold the four lobes up and scrape the green oxide off from the metal and the back of the leather as well (photo 5.5). Blow out the remaining dust. (Avoid breathing the dust.) Feed contact cement under the leather with a small screwdriver, and then press the four lobes down hard with a smooth blade. Take care to fit the edges together perfectly and not smear the glue on the outside. Don't worry, for now, if the lobes don't stay flat. Let the glue set for an hour, then press the lobes down again. Press them down again after another couple of hours.

The Welta Welti provides a good example of the copper oxide blisters caused by a brass body. Welta cameras were produced by the Welta Kamerawerke Company in Germany beginning

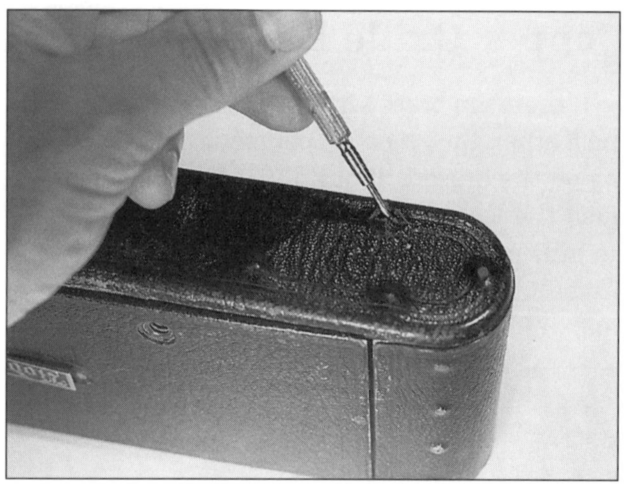

*5.5: Repairing the blisters.*

in the 1920's. The Welti is a folding, self-erecting 35mm model in a class with the folding Retinas (photo 5.6). Even though the brass body plates are nickel-plated, they have been roughened up for the glue to grab better. As a result, the brass is exposed in places and is able to form the inevitable green oxide.

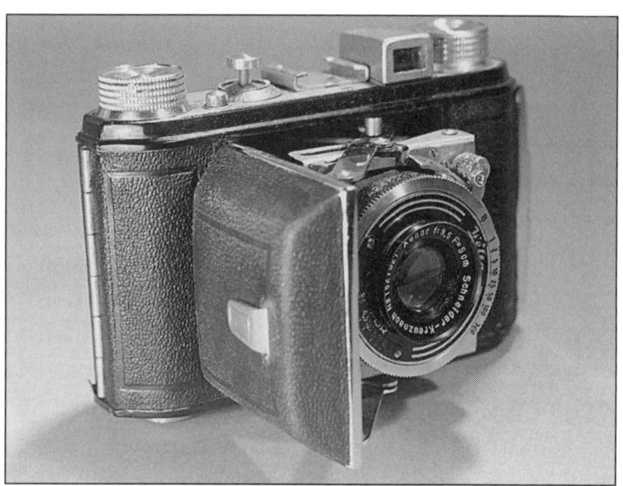

*5.6: Welta Welti.*

The leather must be peeled off and the brass body cleaned. You will not be able to dissolve the glue as in the case of the Kodak cameras. Use a sharp utility knife and methodically separate the leather from the metal by carefully applying the knife at the contact line between the leather and the metal. Scrape the cement residue from the metal, and clean it with a damp tissue. Clean the reverse side of the leather with detergent and a stiff toothbrush. Blot up the excess water from the leather by pressing it between folded paper towels. Reglue the leather while it's still damp. Spread a thin, even layer of white glue on the leather, and then press it onto the metal. You can position the leather throughout the drying process. Even though the leather may stretch from soaking, don't trim it. Compress it with a smooth blade to fit the metal. Damp leather is easy to shape. Keep watch over the drying leather, and press it down again occasionally with a smooth, flat tool. When completely dry, apply shoe polish to blacken the faded areas. Buff it up lightly, then rub on a little oil to dampen the gloss.

## Struts

The strut guides (mushroom studs) are eccentric in many wooden models to facilitate adjustment of the bed perpendicular to the body. You need a narrow wrench to get between the strut and the side of the body to complete this adjustment (photo 5.7).

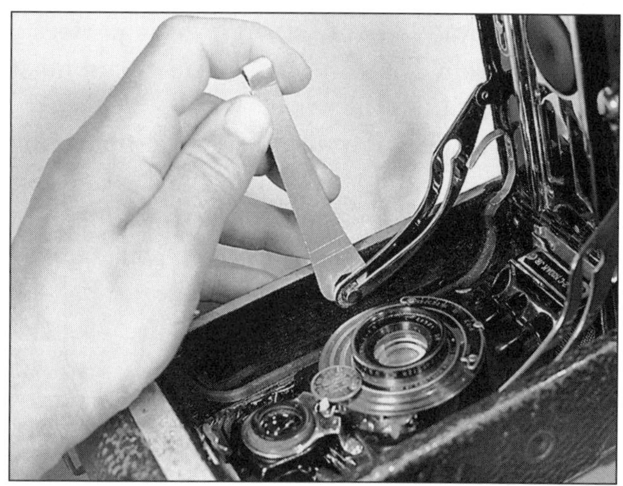

*5.7: Adjusting the strut guides.*

The same wrench may be used to unscrew these mushroom studs completely. Unscrewing the studs will free the bed from the sides. The bed can now be dropped 10° or so, allowing the lens standard to be freed from the body without removing the sides (photo 5.8). A narrow wrench can be made easily from a mild steel plate or by grinding down the sides of an existing wrench.

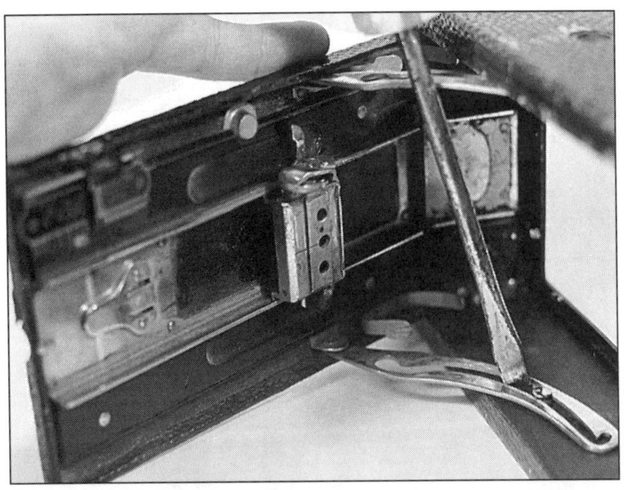

*5.8: Spreading the strut with a screwdriver.*

With a little force the struts can be freed without removing the guide studs. Fold the bed half way up so the guide is in the middle of the strut slot. With a large screwdriver, spread the slot in the strut to let the head of the guide through (photo 5.8). You can install the strut again the same way. The metal is flexible; it will not spread permanently. When spreading with a screwdriver, find a blade that's almost as wide as the slot in the strut. Pry with the flat of it, not with its corners, to avoid damaging the strut.

## Screws

In old cameras, screws are made of either brass or nickel-plated steel and have a straight slot. Brass is not very hard and can be damaged easily by blunt screwdrivers. Damaged screws must be replaced with new ones, but rusty nickel-plated steel screws can be restored.

Unfortunately, the regular screws you find in hardware stores are too big, and the straight slot is out of fashion these days. Obviously, you cannot use Robertson or Phillips screws in your antique. Likely sources for suitable screws are your local marine accessory supplier, hobby shops, luggage and leather shops, and clock parts suppliers (see Appendix).

Nickel-plated screws are hard to find, but the color of stainless steel is close to that of nickel. Stainless steel screws may be substituted for nickel-plated ones if they are otherwise suitable. Your regular camera repair shop cannot help unless they specialize in antique restoration. If you want to stock up on antique screws, you might be able to find specialty houses catering to restorers. See the Appendix and also browse through the ads in *Shutterbug* and other photo publications.

If you want to restore the original rusty screws, pour liquid rust remover (available from auto accessory suppliers) into a small cup, and dump the rusty screws into the acid. Let them soak with occasional agitation as long as it takes to dissolve the rust and turn the screws to steel gray.

Depending on how heavy the rust is, and on the concentration of the acid, this may take from several hours to several days. Really heavy-duty rust removers may do it in minutes, but they are not readily available.

Once the rust is gone, you can brighten the color by rubbing the heads with steel wool (SOS™). Unless you want absolute perfection, you can use polished, unplated steel. Otherwise, have them nickel plated. You will have to do a bit of phoning around because "everybody" does chrome-plating, but not many places will handle nickel-plating. If you go that route, save up as many parts to be plated as you can, because the plating cost will probably be the same whether you've got ten or fifty pieces (unless they are very big pieces).

It's also possible to either buy or rig up your own plating vat. For power, all you need is 12VDC or less with only a few Amps of current capability. The necessary accessories and chemicals are available from your local jeweler's supplier.

## Cleaning the Optics

**The reflex viewfinder.** The only viewing system on many of these folding models is the small triangular reflex viewer by the shutter assembly. The triangular shape comes from the reflex mirror placed at a 45° angle and the convex lenses in front and on top of the unit. Any of these viewers will swing 90° for either horizontal or vertical orientation. Many of them incorporate a combination hood and cover. Since these viewers always sit right up at the front of the camera, they must be perfectly clean.

Some units will open up to facilitate cleaning the mirror. Most of them are easy to remove just by unscrewing the front retaining ring. In some cases, however, the hinge pin must be knocked out in order to remove the unit. Be careful not to rub the mirror off when cleaning a front-surface mirror or polished metal.

As with most other parts, I would scrub the whole unit with liquid detergent (Fantastic™) and toothbrush, rinse it thoroughly under running water, and blow it out. Make sure no water remains behind the mirror. Then warm up the whole unit with a hair dryer. The nickel-plated case or hood of the viewer should be rubbed down with an SOS™ pad. Do not use Brasso™ for cleaning or polishing anything on a camera (not even brass parts).

Whether on a front or rear surface, corroded mirror coating cannot be remedied short of replacing the mirror. You can either find a good mirror in a parts camera (unlikely) or cut out a new one from a Polaroid mirror (see Abstract). The Polaroid mirror can be used with coating forward or back. The mirror in the viewer is often held in its casing by metal tabs which must be unfolded to remove the old and carefully pressed down again to secure the new mirror.

## Vest Pocket Autographic Kodak Camera 1915-1926

### What You will Learn

You will learn how to: repair trellis struts; restore engraved plaques; make a bellows tool; and remove bellows from a folding camera. You will practice constructing small tapering bellows, and study a Kodak ball-bearing shutter.

### Assessment

With this camera, the lens standard is suspended by trellis struts instead of rails on a folding bed. Grab the finger tabs at the side of the standard, and pull the front out.

The end of each strut is anchored by sliding shoulder rivets inside a long slot. The struts and rivets are easily damaged. If forced, the rivets might come loose and fall out, or the struts might bend. In order to perform work on the folding mechanism or on the bellows, remove the two screws from the bottom of the camera body, and pull out the inside mechanism from the cover housing (photo 5.9).

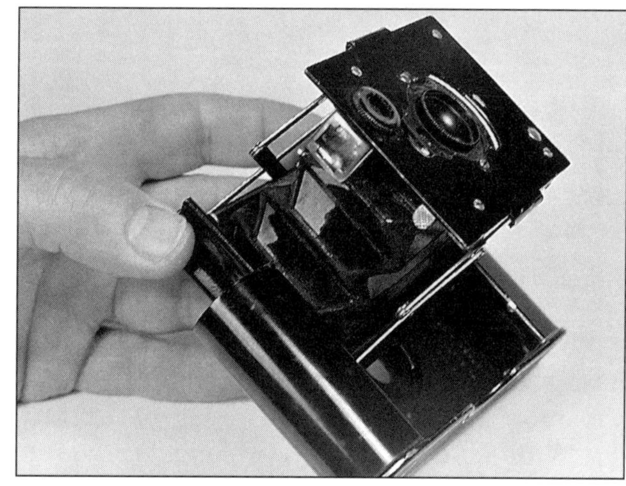

***5.9:*** *Pull off the cover.*

In my case, one shoulder rivet was missing, but luckily I found it stuck between the base of the bellows and the housing. Always be on the lookout for loose or broken parts, and save them if you can. It's often easier to repair or refit the original part than it is to make a new one from scratch. Even if the original is not repairable, you at least have a sample you can copy.

Re-riveting the shoulder pivot is not too difficult. Find a stock about ⅜" square. Hold it in a vise. Remove the front plate from the camera in order to make room for the vise. Insert the rivet and squeeze the square stock under the rivet head pushing the bellows aside. If the bellows must be replaced anyway, you can remove it before the riveting job is performed to provide more room (see below for removal of the bellows).

Spread the tip of the shank with a center punch (photo 5.10) and flatten the rivet directly with a light hammer. This part may end up stronger if you countersink the hole before inserting the rivet.

In order to clean the viewer, unscrew the retaining ring from the front of the lens standard. Unclip the viewer frame from the top of the triangular unit. Clean the mirror and the lenses with plenty of liquid detergent, rinse the whole thing in running water, then blow it out. (See "Cleaning the Optics" above.)

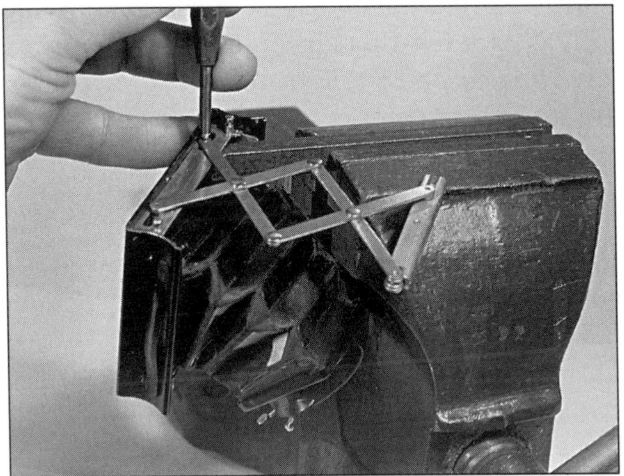

*5.10: Repairing the strut pivot.*

The shutter is a simple "ball bearing" type (printed on the name plate). To remove the shutter unit, pull the complete mechanism out of the cover housing. (See above.) Reach in from behind through the bellows to remove the retaining ring from the reverse side of the lens. Remove the two screws from the front of the standard on both sides of the lens.

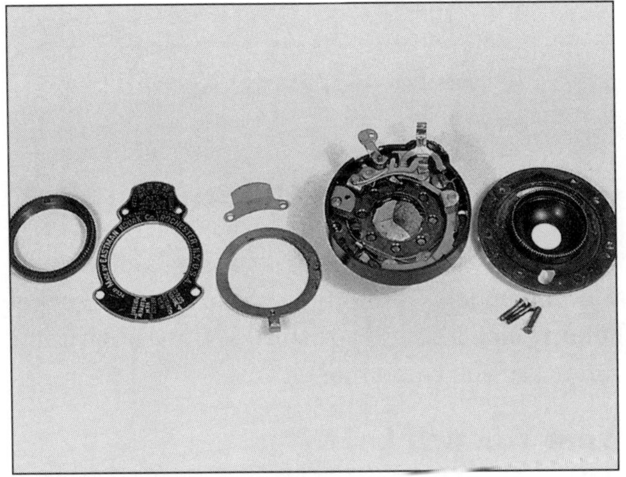

*5.11: Parts of the shutter.*

The front cover plate on the shutter is secured by three screws from behind. The shutter is functional with the cover plate removed (photo 5.11). The cams and levers may be repaired or adjusted without further disassembly. The mechanism is simple and reliable. A flood-cleaning job is probably all that's required. (See Abstract.) Many of these shutters have never been serviced, yet they work reliably after almost a century.

Should the blades need removing, lift out the inner base. It's secured by three screws inside the shutter. Don't remove the threaded lens barrel from behind the unit; it retains the bearing parts (steel balls and crescent spacers). The shutter is a concentric three-bladed type with an inertia timer. The blades are made of mild steel, not spring steel as is the case with modern shutters. Therefore, you should be careful handling either the shutter or diaphragm blades; they bend easily.

With the shutter unit out, the front of the bellows is free. In order to remove the bellows, the rear must be freed as well. Unfortunately, there is no easy way to fold up the tabs that secure the skirt of the bellows. You have three options:

1. Cut off the bellows and get to the tabs from the front. (I don't recommend this because the bellows may be repairable or needed for the pattern.)
2. Grind off the tabs with a thin grinding disk through the film gate. (Do a precise job, try to do as little damage as possible.)
3. Make a special tool for the job. Start with a pair of small curved-tip pliers. Using a propane torch, heat the tip of the pliers to cherry red, and bend the tip about two or three millimeters inward. Grind the tips wedge shaped, so they will be easy to force under the tabs (photo 5.12).

With this tool, reach inside the film gate. Force the tips of the pliers under the tabs, and fold them up, out of the way (photo 5.13).

Fold up the tabs just enough to clear the bellows as they break off quite easily. Don't worry, though, if some of the tabs break off; just grind the edge smooth, and use the other tabs to secure the bellows. If too many break off, you can glue in the new bellows with contact cement, and forget about the tabs.

How to repair or make new bellows is described in Chapter Two. In case the old bellows is missing, use the following figures to substitute into the formulas in Chapter Two (all measurements are in millimeters): a = 110, b = 23, c = 42, d = 6, e = 8, f = 36, g = 69. The crease lines measured from line "b" are at: 9, 15, 24, 30, 39, 44, 52, 57, 65, 71, 79, 85, 92, 98 and 104. Don't forget, as you progress from the front toward the rear the wider out-folds project outward and the narrower in-folds project inward. The glue flaps at the rear may project either inward or outward. Use any of the materials recommended in Chapter Two. Try a thin sheet, but definitely not thicker than .25mm.

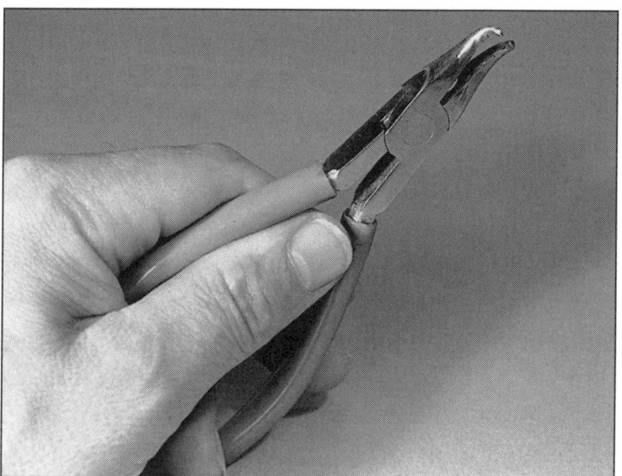

***5.12:*** *The bellows tool.*

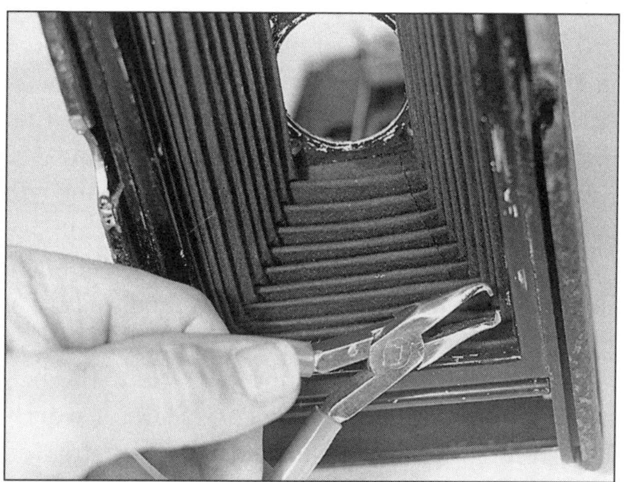

***5.13:*** *Unfold the tabs.*

### The Front Plate

If the front plate is corroded, you can restore it easily because the frame and lettering are raised over the background. First make sure the plate is perfectly straight. Then all you have to do is sand the face of it with #600 sandpaper. Glue the sandpaper onto a plastic or wood backing. Sand lengthwise only, never across.

If required, touch up the black background with a black felt-tip marker. For this, choose an extra fine tip and permanent ink. A good pen for this job is the Steadtler Lumocolor 313. Once the ink is dry, clean off the plate and spray clear lacquer onto its face.

If the background color is mostly gone, spray black paint on the complete plaque. Let it dry thoroughly (one day for quick-drying paint), then sand it as described above. If done properly, this will be a stunning feature of the restored camera. (See the finished camera on photo 5.14.)

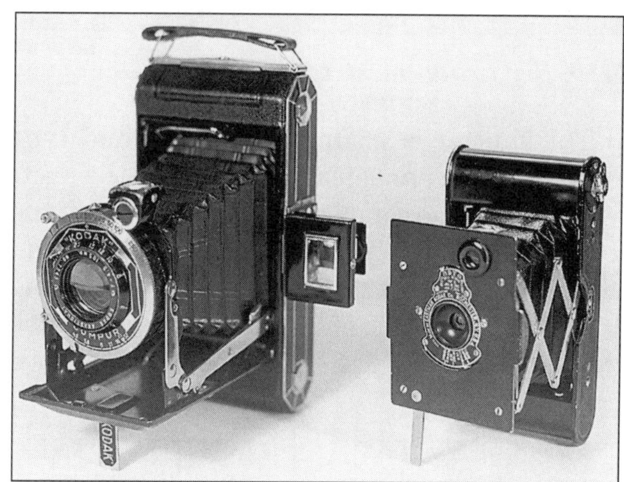


***5.14:*** *The restored Vest Pocket Kodak.*

## Kodak Folding Pocket No.3-A

You have three examples of the same or very similar models (photo 5.15). Two are the Pocket Folding No. 3-A, and the third is the Autographic version of the same model.

### What You will Learn

In this section, you will learn how to: strip and combine parts from damaged examples to create two good cameras out of three bad ones; repair metal parts; re-skin hopeless-looking bellows; make red number windows, and disassemble and repair the B&L Automat shutter.

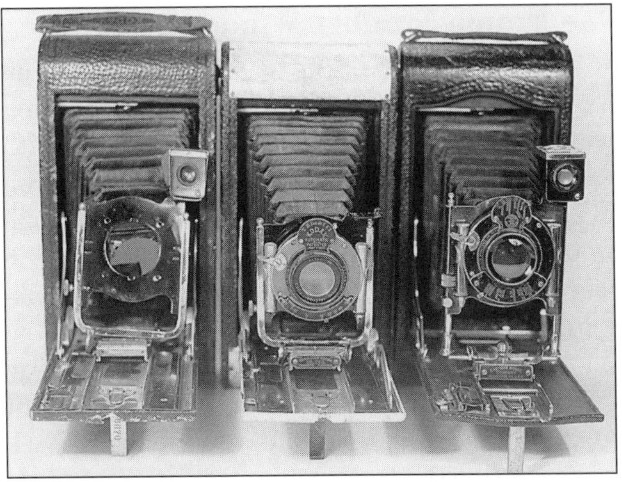

*5.15: Three folding models before restoration.*

## Assessment

The Autographic model is complete and in good shape, only its bellows is somewhat frayed. Only one of the three has good bellows. You will use that to replace the one in the Autographic. The other two models are identical. You will pick the best parts from each, and put them together in the brown body.

## Re-skinning the Bellows

The third bellows is in very poor shape (photo 5.16), but you will be able to keep the inside liner and the ribs, and recover the outside with red sheepskin. The original was actually red in this model according to *McKeown's*.

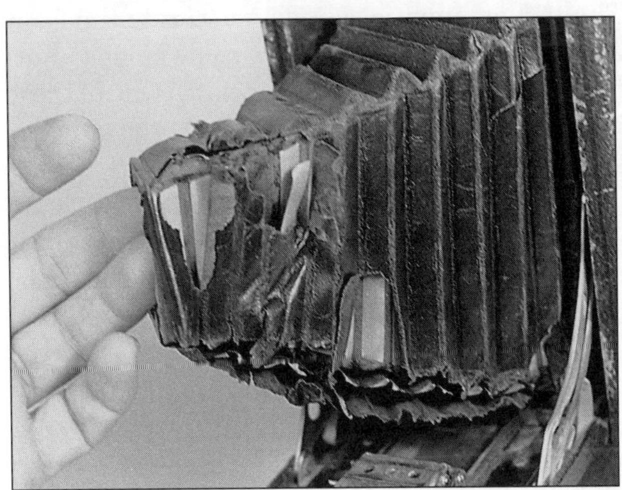

*5.16: This bellows must be re-skinned.*

You can also ascertain that the bellows was replaced at least once in the past by scrutinizing the fastening tabs inside the film gate. Since this model was produced from 1903 until 1915, it's not unreasonable to assume that the original bellows wore out a long time ago. This also means that the tabs will probably break off when unfolding. In fact, some of the tabs on our sample model are already broken.

It's important to remember that the bellows in many old models are often not original. This means that you can look for models that originally came with colored bellows but now have black ones. It is perfectly legitimate to restore the original red-bellows condition.

A major restoration of a bellows is always exciting, so we'll start there. Luckily, you don't have to start from scratch. Remove the bellows from the body. Using the tool described previously (Kodak Vest Pocket), fold up the tabs in the film gate. The plate inside the front of the bellows is riveted to the lens standard. Pull out the lens standard half way, and grind off the inside flare of the tube rivets carefully. Extricate the rear of the bellows from the housing. Try not to be impatient lest you damage the bellows.

Peel off the bellows material from the front and rear frames. If required, you can apply cold water locally to soften the glue, but don't soak the body of the bellows. Avoid damaging the inside liner, but the fate of the cover skin is of no interest, since it will be discarded. Scrape the glue off the mounting flaps with a blunt knife. For further instructions on replacing the cover skin, see Chapter Two where other methods for restoring bellows are also described.

## Body Restoration

One of the strut guides have been substituted by an ordinary screw. To replace it, use one of the originals from the spare body. You need a skinny wrench to reach the hexagonal screw head between the strut and the side of the body. Grind or file one out of a mild steel plate, or grind down an existing wrench to fit inside the narrow gap (see photo 5.7). You can also remove the strut from the guide stud by spreading the slot in the strut with a large screwdriver (see photo 5.8). The mushroom heads of the guides are eccentric. By rotating them with the skinny wrench you just made, the bed and the camera body can be adjusted to enclose a precise 90° angle when the bed is locked down in the taking position.

One lens-support fork has been disfigured by filing. In the other example, the same part has broken off its stand and someone has tried to glue it back on. Scrape off the glue carefully to avoid scratching the nickel plating. Use the special rivets from the other camera to re-rivet the base.

To recover the rivets, take a square stock and drill a hole into it as large as the head of the rivet. Hold the stock in a vise. With a 1/16" punch, punch out the rivets. Use the rivets to fix the other lens-standard base (photo 5.17).

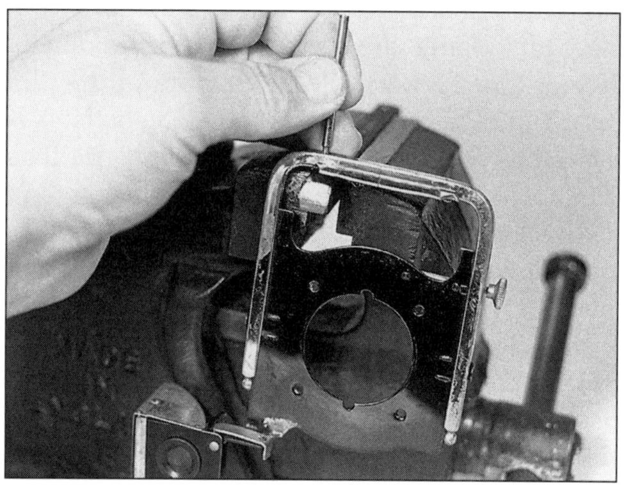

***5.17:*** *Fixing the lens standard.*

The locking screw of the standard is also broken. Unfortunately this screw often breaks due to the deep, coarse thread on a brittle brass shaft. Find a 6-32 x 1/2" screw with a fairly big head. Re-tap the hole in the locking knob with a 6-32 threading tap. File or saw a notch into the side of the screw head to accommodate the little stud on the underside of the standard base. This will keep the screw from turning. When assembling the unit, don't forget to insert the lopsided washer over the screw on top of the base plate.

**Reminder:** The vertical lens movement knob must be pulled out for adjustment as it is locked in the home position.

## The Frame Number Window

Two of the three backs have lost the red number window. If you can't find one in a scrap camera, you can make one easily enough. Start with a red plastic sheet of sufficient thickness (not cellophane). You can try plastic shops, but you will probably find a suitable red plastic sheet right in your home. Toys and stationary items, even packaging material, may be useful sources. (The red plastic I used, started its life as a label sleeve in a loose-leaf binder.) Cut off a square about 20x20mm. For the template, use a camera back that's missing the leather cover, or drill a 1/2" hole into an aluminum plate. Place the red square over the round hole for the number window. Hold this over the kitchen range turned onto low heat. When the plastic begins to curl, press the plastic sheet into the hole with your thumb.

This action will force a spherical bubble into the hole and at the same time presses the overhanging rim flat around the periphery of the hole. Trim the edges off leaving only a millimeter or two for a flange. Lift up the leather on the back of the camera, and slide the red window plastic in-between the aluminum and leather with the convex side facing inward.

## The Shutter

Folding Kodaks are fitted with a variety of shutters. The 3-A folding model is fitted with a Bausch & Lomb Automat, 1906 type (photo 5.18). The two pneumatic cylinders decorate the front as opposed to the sides as on some Kodak shutters of the same period. (See below.) One of these is the trigger cylinder; the other is the shutter-speed escapement.

This shutter is easy to disassemble for cleaning or repair. Remove the screw from the center of the shutter-speed dial, and pull off the dials. Some of the mechanism is visible under the dial in the chrome cup.

You can remove either of the pneumatic cylinders (two screws) in order to clean the cylinder and piston. If you have to get inside the shutter, undo the retaining ring from inside the bellows in order to free the complete shutter assembly. Remove the three screws from the back of the unit to free the front cover (photo 5.18). If you want to flood-clean without disassembly — in case the shutter works but it's slow or sticky — unscrew the front and rear lens groups, and just squirt lighter fluid onto the blades. Work the shutter, then blow it out.

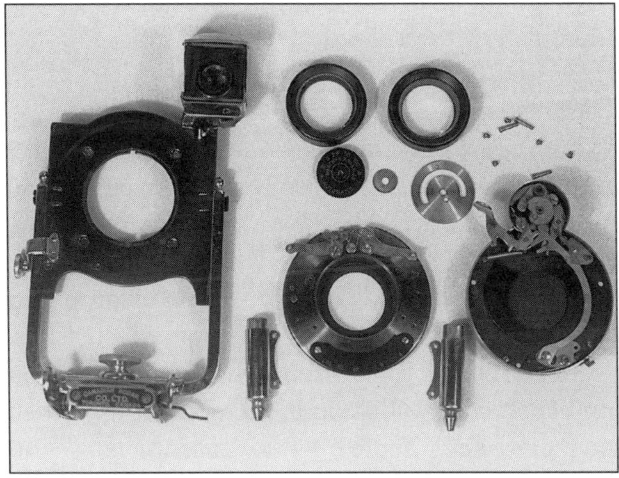

***5.18:** Bausch & Lomb automat.*

The Kodak Automatic shutter is almost as simple. Here the cylinders are mounted on the sides of the unit and are secured by two screws, each from behind. Disassembly is from the front. Unscrew the lens groups.

Remove the aperture scale from the bottom of the shutter, then the four screws from the periphery of the cover plate. There is no need to remove the shutter-speed scale or the release lever. Pull off the cover plate.

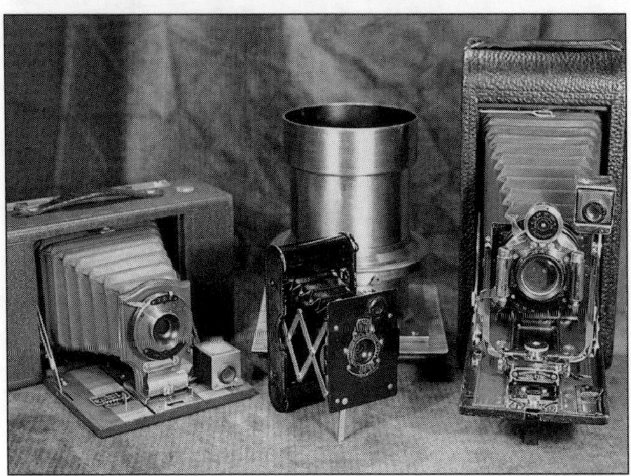

***5.19:** From left to right: Folding Brownie, Vest Pocket, Wollensak, Folding Pocket.*

Again, if the shutter is slow or sticky, you can flood-clean it without further disassembly. Insert the four long screws into the front plate perpendicular to the plate; otherwise, they can easily miss their threaded hole. If you want to brighten up the face of the unit, rub down the cylinders and all screw heads with SOS™. Treat the dials and plates at the face of the unit as described above at Kodak Vest Pocket, page 42. If the shiny parts on the body need polishing, rub them with a soft cloth or chamois dipped into Silvo™. Whenever you use Silvo™, make sure no traces of it remain in the cracks. The parts may have to be disassembled and rinsed off under running water to get rid of the white abrasive powder completely. Silvo™ removes tarnish and polishes the nickel, unless it's rusty, flaking, or pitted. If those problems exist, remove the parts, and rub them down with a wet SOS™ pad. Rinse them with a soft toothbrush under running water. The restored No.3-A is seen in photo 5.19.

## Kodak No.3 Folding Brownie

With a horizontal brick-shaped body and red bellows, this is a handsome camera (photo 5.20).

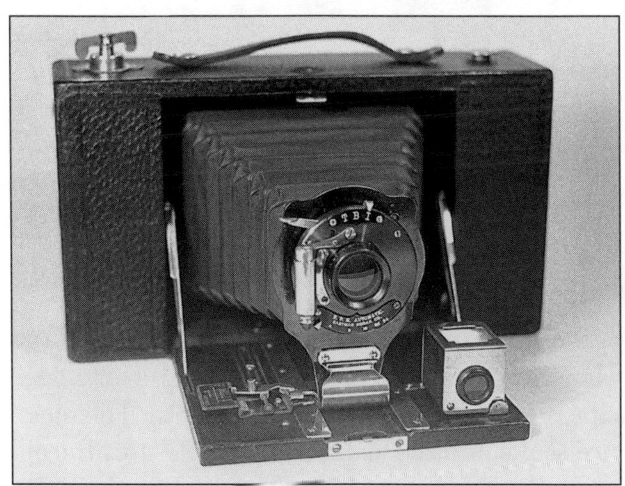

***5.20:** No. 3 Folding Brownie.*

### What You will Learn

You will learn how to: restore the color of faded red bellows; clean and polish the metal parts and the viewer, and buff up the leatherette.

### Assessment

In the sample I acquired, the bellows are faded to a pale orange color (a regular feature of red Kodak bellows); the shutter doesn't work; some of the screws are loose, and it's quite dusty and dirty.

Using the tool described on page 41, undo the mounting tabs from the skirt of the bellows. The tabs, being steel, won't break off as easily as aluminum tabs; nevertheless, don't fold them farther than required to release the bellows.

The lens standard can be pulled all the way off the rails now with the bellows coming with it (photo 5.21). Four screws hold the lens standard to the front of the bellows. You can undo those from inside the bellows to separate the bellows from the standard.

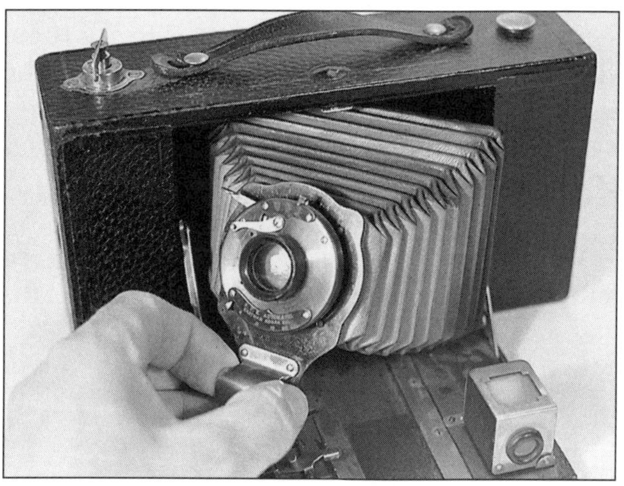

*5.21: Removing the bellows.*

### Bellows

It's amazingly simple to restore the rich red color from the faded orange. All you have to do is wipe off the outside with a damp cloth. The moisture soaks into the leather and reactivates the old faded dye. While wet, the color may be quite dark, but it will brighten considerably after completely dry. Once dry, buff up the bellows with a soft brush. If you're not happy with the color, be careful when trying to improve on it. Remember that any stain that soaks into the leather may come out too dark even after it's dry. Any substance that cannot penetrate will sit on top of the leather, causing a blotchy, and perhaps sticky residue. If you must, experiment on the bottom side of the bellows.

The Kodak original in this particular model is made of good quality leather. Other than being faded, the bellows should still be good. If it's frayed, damaged, or missing, see Chapter Two to find out how to proceed.

### Fittings

Turning to the body, remove all the fittings from the inside (photo 5.22); they are attached with wood screws. Brush out the inside with a stiff brush, then blow it out. You can wipe out the body with an oily rag, followed by a clean paper towel to eliminate any liquid oil from all surfaces.

Since the bed is covered with leatherette, you can brush shoe polish on it then buff it up. Wash the distance scale with toothbrush and Fantastic™. Rub the rails and struts with SOS™. Straighten the rails perfectly before refitting them.

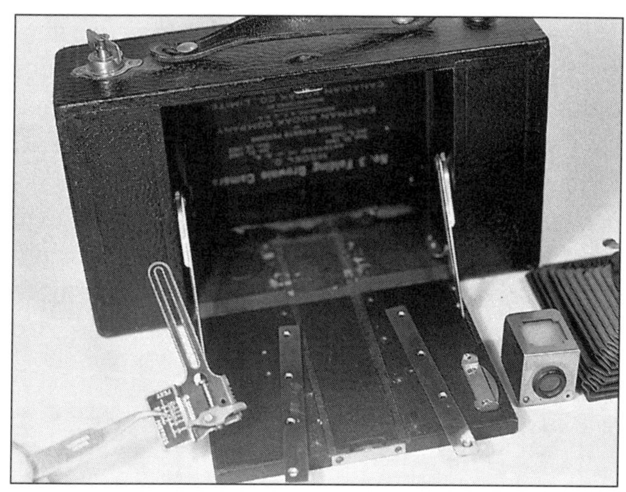

*5.22: Remove all the inside fittings.*

Clean off any traces of glue you find on the parts. Some of the screw holes might be stripped. Don't glue in the screws. Plug up the enlarged holes with wooden pegs and white glue, then either pre-drill with a smaller bit, or use an awl to punch a new hole.

### Viewer

The viewer unit comes off easily. Remove the flat spring (2 screws), then pull out the hinge pins from both sides. Remove the two screws from the front and rear of the viewer to free the cover frame. The mirror will probably have to be replaced. The front surface mirror in a reflex Polaroid is a good replacement. Cut out a 21mm x 25mm piece.

You'll get an image no matter which way the mirror is inserted, but the image might be sharper one way than the other. Glue in the mirror lightly as well as the ground glass on top of the unit. Brighten up the metal parts by rubbing them with SOS™.

You can try a metal cleaner instead, for example Silvo™ or toothpaste, but do not use any cleaner recommended for brass. The steel wool will not damage the part, but abrasives in a cleaning agent might. Rinse the parts after they are cleaned in order to remove all residue. Rinsing is more difficult with the parts still in the camera.

Clean the screw heads as well. (See "Screws" this chapter.) The screw under the viewer unit is for adjusting it to the horizontal.

## Body

Buff the outside of the body vigorously with a soft brush. If it doesn't come quite clean, you can rub shoe polish in with a soft cloth and brush it up afterwards. It's better to brush a grainy surface, than it is to buff it with a cloth because a brush penetrates deeper into the grain.

If the leatherette is peeling, glue it down carefully with clear paper glue. If the glue runs over the edges, wipe it off with a damp cloth. Hold the edge down with your finger for at least 20 seconds while the glue sets.

If the corners of the body are damaged, you might want to round off any ruggedness, and then touch it up with a satin black paint such as acrylic enamel. It's difficult to replace small portions of the leatherette.

First, you wouldn't find the exact grain pattern unless you could salvage some from another body.

Second, unless a complete panel is replaced, the patch will definitely show. See below (Model A) to re-skin the body completely.

## F.P.K. Automatic Shutter

Remove the unit by unscrewing the retaining ring inside the bellows. If the shutter works all right, just wipe off the outside with a mild detergent (Windex™) and leave it alone. If it doesn't work, remove the pneumatic cylinder first (two screws), then the aperture plate at the bottom of the unit.

Remove the three screws at the rim of the face. The cover plate comes right off exposing all the mechanism inside the cup. The shutter can be repaired without further disassembly (photo 5.23).

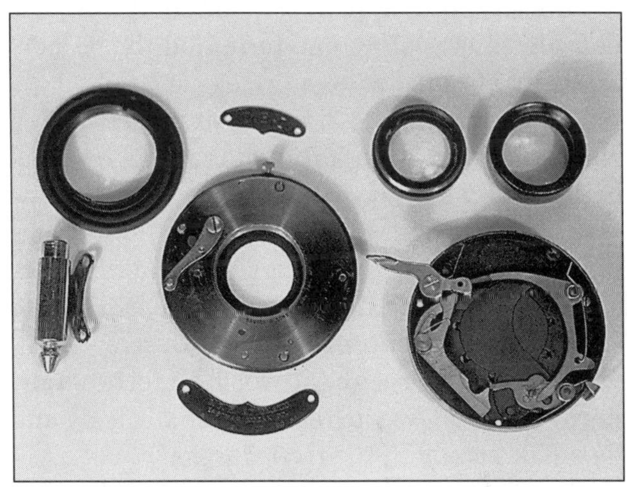

***5.23:*** *F.P.K. Automatic.*

The numbers on the aperture and shutter speed plates are probably black with age.

The white (or gold) paint inside the engravings have been chemically altered and cannot be cleaned. Using a sharp needle and a magnifying glass, scrape out the old paint from inside the engravings.

Paint some white enamel over the letters. The paint should penetrate down into the engravings. With the edge of a cardboard spatula (a business card), scrape most of the paint off the top of the plate, but leave it inside the engraved lines. Let the paint dry for an hour or so.

Moisten the business card with a little solvent, and wipe it over the plate to remove most of the remaining paint from the top of the plate.

Using the last method, finish the clean up the next day when the paint is dry. Photo 5.20 depicts the restored camera.

## Kodak Model A Folding Brownie

This model is slightly different from the model above.

### What You will Learn

You will learn how to replace the leatherette on the body of a camera. Repairing the wooden frame will also be included.

### Assessment

This example is in very poor condition; the leatherette is peeling and torn, and the corners are badly abraded.

The body must be stripped and the wooden frame repaired. In addition, since the original leatherette cannot be salvaged, the body must be re-skinned with new leather.

First, all the metal fittings must be removed, including hinges and pieces from the bed (photo 5.24). Some of those are fastened with screws; others are riveted through the wood. Unfortunately, there is no good way to reach inside the body and file off, or grind off, the rivet flares).

The ones you can reach from the inside, such as the door latch rivets at the back edge of the top, you can knock out with a punch. Otherwise, reach under the plate the rivet holds, and pry up the fitting together with the rivet. A slight damage to the wood is of no concern.

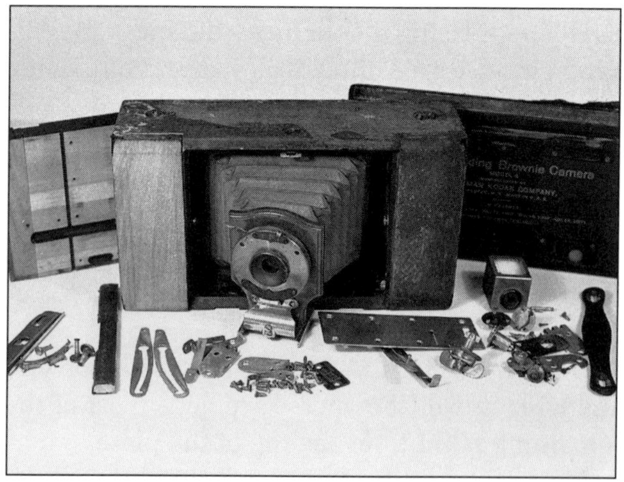

*5.24: All fittings removed.*

Another problem is that the rear of the bellows is retained in the body with wood strips. It is impossible to free the bellows without prying the strips and causing damage. If the bellows is in reasonable shape leave it in.

The lens standard is held by four screws from behind and comes out easily. (If the bellows must be replaced, pry out the retaining wood strips, and repair the damage later.) Leave in the tripod sockets as well. Knock out the hinge pins from the hinges to separate the bed, but leave the hinge plates on.

Once the fittings are removed, rip off the leatherette. You can help it by applying warm water at the contact point. Soaking the outside doesn't work well because the leatherette is water tight. Only the little water that seeps through the cracks and around the edges can work on the glue. Try to get one edge going, then pull the leatherette off slowly in one piece.

Examine the body integrity. If panels are loose, glue them back on, using white glue (see Chapter Six). Using wet-and-dry coarse sand paper and warm water, sand off all sides, the back door and the front flap. Be careful not to damage the inside of the door where the model information is printed in red.

If some of the original glue doesn't come off, don't worry, just sand over it later when the wood is dry. Round off the front/top and front/bottom edges on the body and both long edges of the back door. Leave all other edges sharp. If the corners are worn off, you can build them up with epoxy putty, or ordinary wood filler. If the door corners are worn off, glue on a piece of wood or use epoxy to build up the corners.

We are going to cover the outside with leather. Depending on the cover material you find, the original method of overlapping the panels and folding them over all the edges may not work.

If you find suitable leatherette, sheep or goatskin, you could try the overlapping method but only if the sheets are .2mm thick, which is very unlikely.

Sheepskin usually varies in thickness between .2 and .4mm and it tends to be quite uneven. I opted for thicker, sliced pig skin. This kind of leather is easier to work with and is much more durable. With 1.2mm thickness, this is almost like a board compared to sheepskin.

The panels will be butted at the short outside edges and folded around the long horizontal edges you rounded off earlier. This leather is somewhat stiff; it doesn't take a sharp bend.

Turning to the bed (front lid), even though the inside was black originally, you can strip and sand the black paint to produce a natural wood-grain finish. You might have to sand quite a bit to get rid of all the black penetration (photo 5.25).

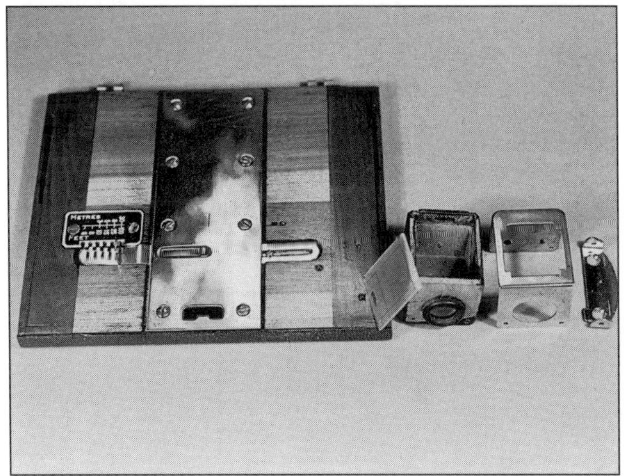

***5.25:*** *Sand off the black paint from the bed.*

Finish the side-edges of the lid in natural wood-grain as well (see how to refinish wood in Chapter Six).

Cut out a piece of leather 125x116mm to cover the front and the upper edge of the front lid. Smear an even layer of white glue onto the wood. Press the leather on, and slide it back and forth to enhance the bond. Line up the rear side where the hinges are.

If the leather overhangs the other three sides, you'll trim it later. Smooth the leather down evenly. Put the lid leather-side-down into a corner where a horizontal and vertical surface meet so that both front and top folds of the leather are supported.

Place a heavy object onto the wood until the glue drys. Once the glue sets (about three hours), trim the overhanging edges using a sharp utility knife (photo 5.26).

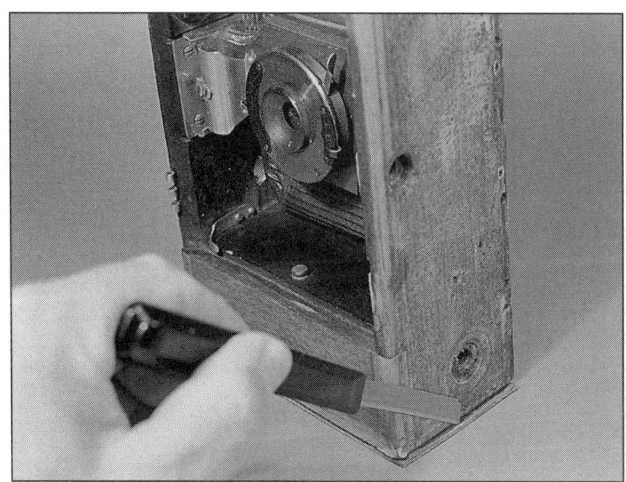

***5.26:*** *Trim with a knife.*

Cover the sides of the body the same way. When trimmed off, the leather piece is exactly the size of the side panel: no folding, no overlapping. Before gluing on the right-hand leather piece, press the leather into the tripod socket with your thumb in order to impress its position into the leather. With a 10mm circle-punch, punch out the hole for the tripod screw. Place the leather onto a soft plastic support and hammer the tool. Glue on the leather. Find a 12mm ring in your junk-box. A thimble or a battery cover from a Pentax ME will do. After the glue is dry, press the rim of the ring into the leather concentric with the tripod socket. Tighten a C-clamp over it. Leave the clamp on for at least an hour.

Cut off two 8x110mm strips. Glue these strips into the front sides of the front opening. When cutting the leather, use a straightedge and a sharp utility knife (not scissors) to ensure that the cuts are straight. Press the straightedge down hard to prevent the leather from sliding while cutting it.

The top, front, bottom, and back leather will be of one piece and will be flush with all the edges of the side panels. If the corners of the door are broken or worn down, now's the time to repair them. Once the corners are repaired, cut off two strips 3x120mm each. Glue these onto the outside edges of the back door.

Cut out the pattern shown on diagram 5.27 (see next page). The inside rectangle should be exact, but leave a millimeter or so on the outside

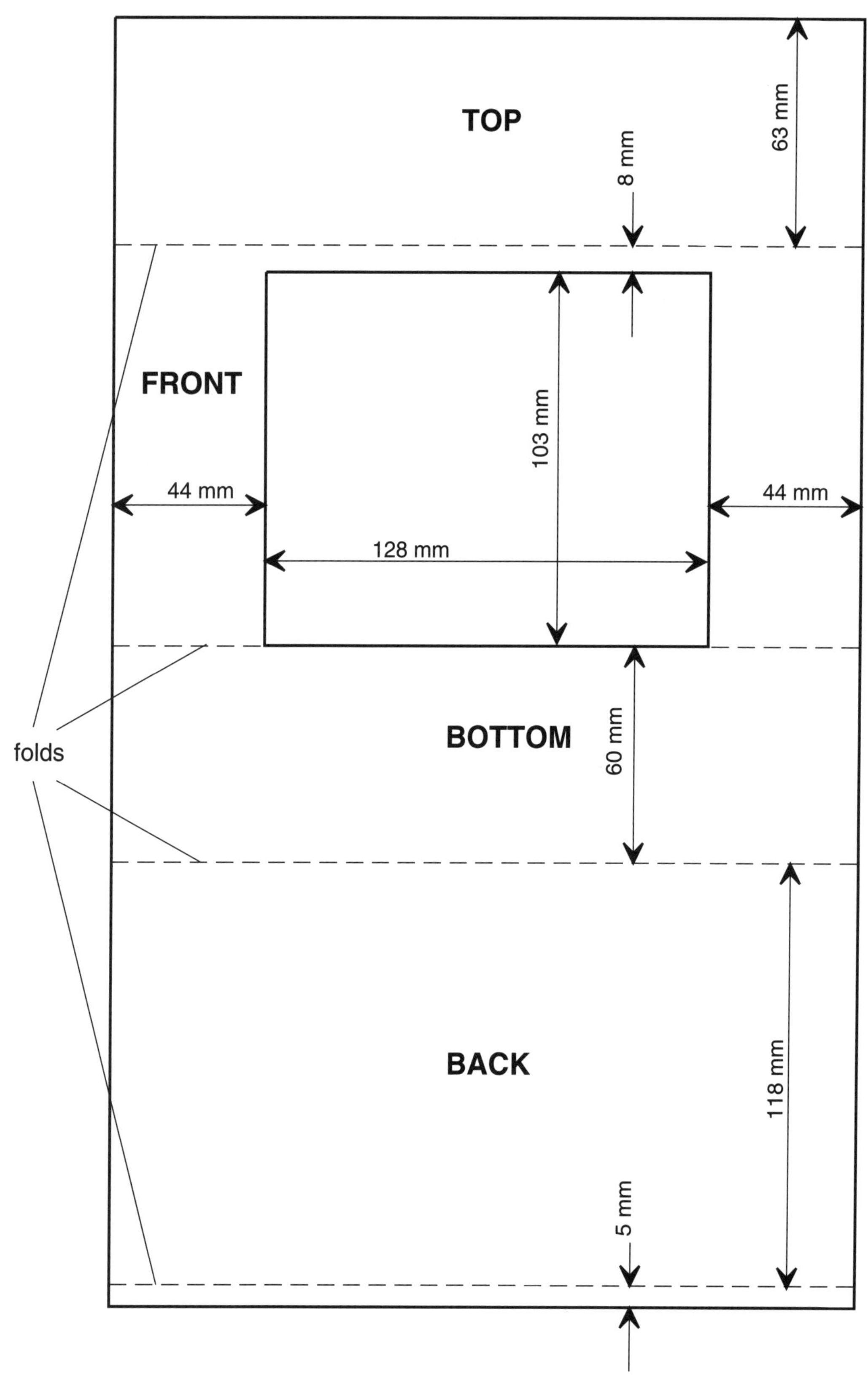


***5.27:*** *Model-A, body cover pattern.*

edges for trimming. Don't use my figures, though. You must take the measurements off the actual camera you're restoring, as there may be slight differences from one example to the next.

To glue this large piece on, start with the front. Line up the center cut-out exactly. Weigh it down and let it set for thirty minutes.

Before gluing on the top flap, transfer the two spindle hole outlines to the leather, and punch out the holes. You can drill out the other holes later. Insert the bed release knob into its hole. When applying the glue, leave a clear circle around the bed release button and around each of the spindle recesses. Leave about 10mm clear of glue behind the latch spring recesses. Don't get any glue into the spindle recesses or into the recesses for the door-latch springs.

Before gluing on the bottom flap, take an impression, and punch out the holes for the tripod socket and the spindles the same way as on the top. It's easier to impress the serial number now than after gluing. It's possible to buy a kit for punching numbers, but just for one time use on leather, an acceptable result can be achieved by using homemade wire numbers. Form the numbers out of mild steel wire. Glue or solder the wire numbers onto a metal slab (photo 5.28).

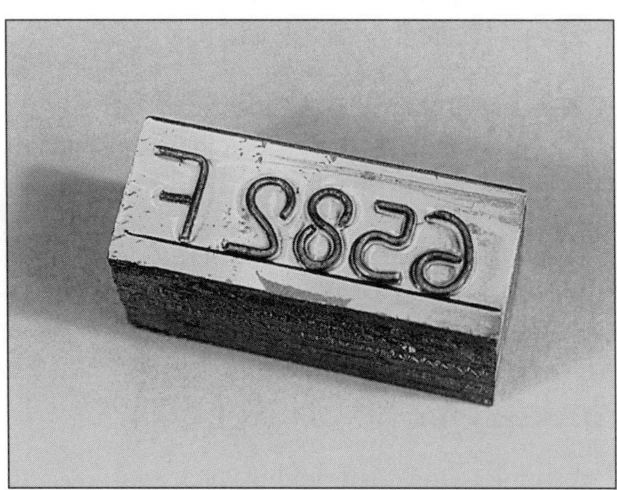

***5.28:*** *Homemade number punch.*

For one-time use, white glue is adequate. When gluing up the numbers, turn them around to obtain a mirror-image alignment, and make sure the numbers are flat against the back slab. Place hard wood or plastic on the reverse side of the leather, and place the number stamp on the finished side. Clamp the sandwich with a C-clamp. Leave the clamp on for an hour (longer if you're not in a hurry). When gluing up the leather keep the spindle recesses free of glue (photo 5.29).

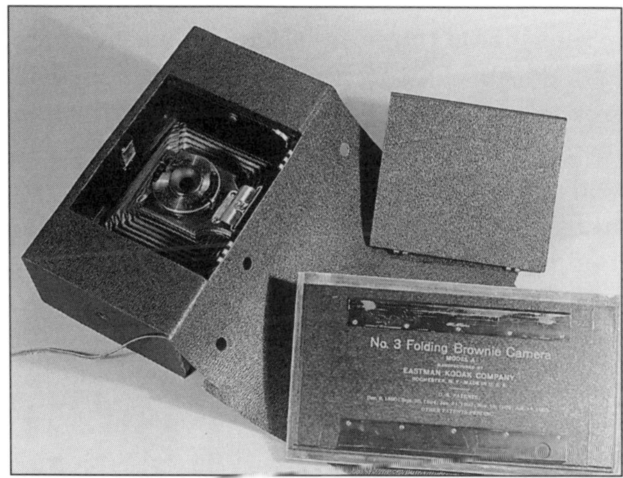


***5.29:*** *Gluing on the cover skin.*

Before gluing on the back door, make sure the bottom and top outside edges are sanded round, the corners are repaired, and the edge strips are glued on. Trim the corners of the edge strips to follow the contour of the rounded edges.

Close the door; fold the leather over it, and press the leather into the number window with your thumb. If you can't see the impression, wet the edge of the hole slightly, and try again.

Punch out the viewing hole with an 18mm circle punch. Press a 22mm ring around the hole the same way it was described above. Insert the door into its recess before gluing on the leather. Let the glue set for 30 minutes, then fold the leather over the top edge of the door and glue it on. Weigh it down to keep the leather in place. Let it all dry overnight before trimming the edges.

Stain the trimmed edges with either leather stain or unfilled wood stain. (I used Minwax™ Wood Finish 2716 Dark Walnut.) Score in the decorative lines.

You can use double lines as on the original, but single lines are also acceptable. A good scoring tool is described in the bellows making section, Chapter Two.

Make sure that all the lines are the same distance from, and are parallel with, the edges of the camera. Press the scoring tool hard into the leather. Go over the lines several times until the impression is deep enough (photo 5.30). The circles around the spindles can be done now. Find a ring of suitable size.

Such metal rings can be found among camera, lens, or binocular parts. You can press the ring in with a C-clamp (photo 5.31), or heat it up to about 150° with a propane flame. Hold the ring with a pair of pliers while heating it. Press it hard into the leather. If doing it cold, tighten the C-clamp hard over the ring, and leave it on for at least an hour.

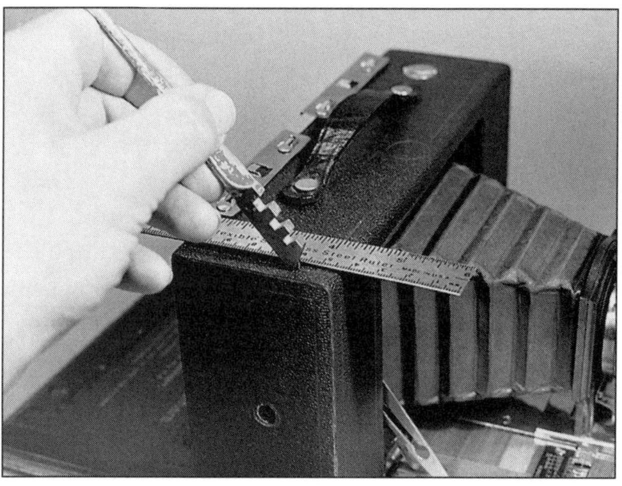

***5.30:** Scoring the lines.*

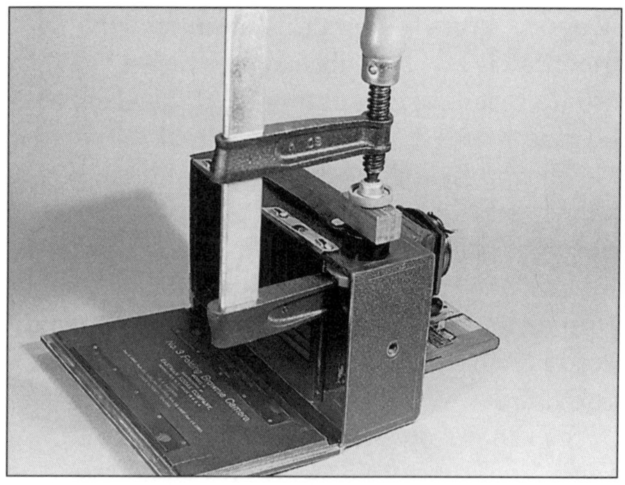

***5.31:** Impressing decorative circles.*

Drill holes for the door latch and handle rivets. You can find the original holes by sticking a needle up through the hole from inside of the camera. Insert the latch springs into their recesses under the leather. File or grind off the flairs from the original rivets, and use 5-minute epoxy to glue them in.

If the latch rivets don't stay put, place wood or plastic over the pair of them, and clamp it down lightly with a C-clamp. The latches may need bending to lock and release the door reliably. Let the glue set overnight before bending the latches.

### Shutter

Remove the shutter from the standard by undoing the retaining ring from behind. You can wipe off the standard with furniture polish or light oil. Don't leave any traces of liquid oil anywhere on the camera.

Wipe it clean, and buff it up afterwards. The shutter-speed and aperture scales are printed onto the metal instead of being engraved as on other models. Gently wipe it down with oil if the print is still visible.

If the print is completely gone, you can try to substitute stick-on characters such as from a Letraset™ or Geotype™. Applying stick-on letters must be done perfectly or not at all. Practice first on a metal piece.

The rest of the restoration steps are the same as for the previous model. Treat the faded bellows with water. Use a soft paint brush to apply the water instead of a damp cloth.

Rub all metal fittings with SOS™ and warm water. The viewer is also similar. Restore it the same way as described above.

## Kodak Six-20 Model C

A lavishly nickeled, folding bed, self-erecting 620 format camera, it sports a handsome art-deco design on its sides and on the front of the shutter. The shutter is a good quality Compur.

You can expect copper-oxide blisters all over the body. How to treat these ubiquitous pests is described at the beginning of this chapter.

If any of the metal fittings are oxidized (probably the door latch on top of the body), first try Fantastic™ applied with a toothbrush. If that doesn't help, rub it down with SOS™, then rinse it off with clean water.

Blow the latch out thoroughly, and dry it gently with a hair dryer. If the fitting is clean but dull after this treatment, you can rub a little wax on it then buff it up. Apply wax sparingly so it doesn't get into the crevices.

To clean the reflex viewfinder just remove the two screws from the sides, lift off the top frame and the viewing lens. Lift out the mirror and clean it carefully: it's a mirrorized brass plate. You can clean the front lens of the viewer without removing it.

The shutter is of standard design. In order to open it up, remove the stop screw from the side of the focusing ring, and unscrew the front group. Find a small screw at the face plate just under the f/22 number.

Unscrew this carefully; it can be damaged very easily. In fact, if this screw is still undamaged, there is a good chance that the shutter has never been opened before. Turn the plate counter-clockwise about 10°, and pull it off. Then pull off the shutter-speed cam as well (photo 5.32).

If the shutter works, but the escapements are slow or hesitant, you can probably fix it just by brushing a tiny amount of oil on the escape wheels. A drop is too much.

If the blades need cleaning, unscrew both lens groups, remove the shutter assembly, and flood the whole assembly with lighter fluid a number of times. The original oil and grease are of a different composition than what we are used to; they are harder to dissolve. Be aware that with the shutter-speed cam off, the shutter doesn't work properly unless the B and T levers are manually disengaged.

The escapements are easy to lift from the assembly. The shutter-speed escapement unit is held by three screws. Mark its position before removing it as both ends are adjustable. The self-timer escapement is held by two screws, one of which constitutes the main spring anchor. Once the unit is out, you can flood the escapement with graphite and lighter fluid solution.

When refitting the master ring, pull the escapement levers aside, let the ring seat properly. When refitting the shutter-speed cam, turn the ring from end to end to help the levers fall into place.

It's quite likely that the compound lens elements show signs of separation. If that happens, you can reglue them, but first you must pull the lens from its mounting. This might be difficult as the lens is secured by the edge of the barrel being rimmed over the glass. You must unfold the rimming. Take a sharp but strong knife, and force the rim aside by running the point of the knife between the glass and the brass rim (see photo 5.33).

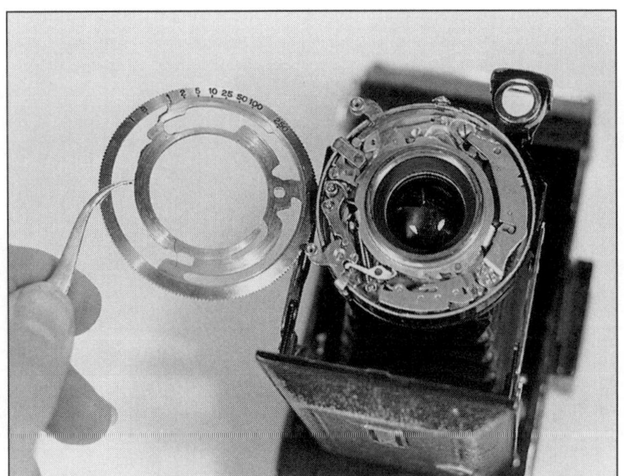

***5.32:*** *Removing the shutter-speed cam.*

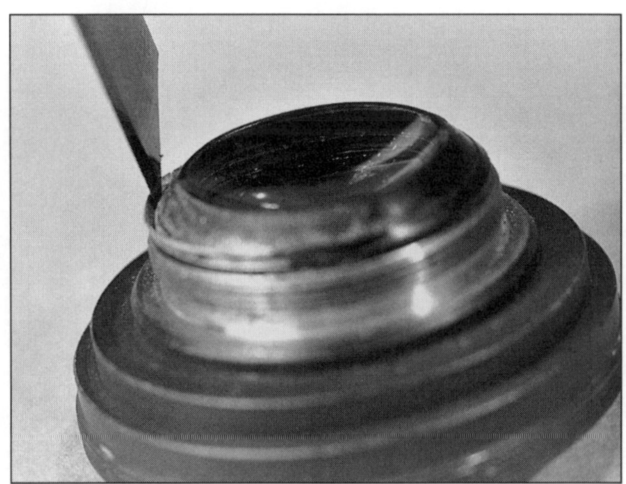

***5.33:*** *Unfolding the brass rim.*

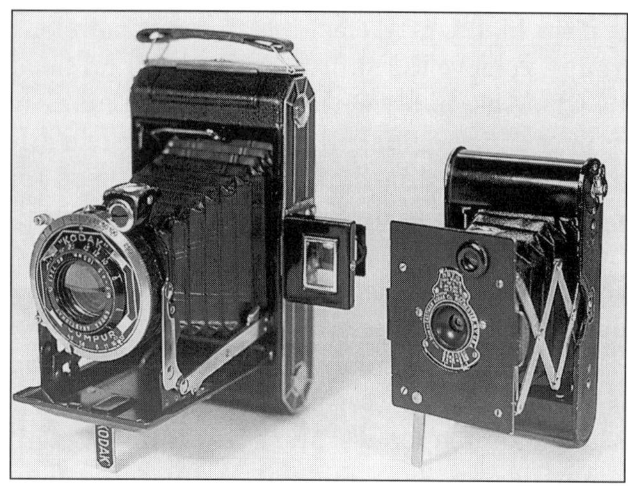


***5.34:** The Kodak Six-20.*

I know this sounds scary, but as long as you don't twist the knife trying to pry the glass out, it will not damage the glass.

Go around a number of times, carefully and gradually opening up the rim. Next, soak the assembly in Acetone™. This will dissolve the paint and Canada balsam that might glue the glass into the brass mount.

Now, try to push the glass out with your finger. If the glass doesn't budge, you must carefully apply some force to it. Make sure the rim is fully opened.

Support the rim of the brass mount in a vise, take a plastic or wooden rod, and a fairly large hammer. Alternately tap the glass at one side, then the other, with the rod.

Watch it closely to see how the glass is progressing. Always tap the side that is higher up. Put a soft cloth under the lens to catch the glass when it falls out.

Once the lens is out, soak it again in Acetone™. The two halves may separate. If the Acetone™ doesn't cut it, heat the elements with a hair dryer (see Abstract). The restored camera is seen on photo 5.34.

Chapter Six

# Wooden View Cameras

## Eastman 5x7 View Camera No. 33A

### What You will Learn

You will learn: to completely disassemble a wooden view camera; repair and refinish the wooden pieces; make a wooden lens board, and repair and restore the Bausch & Lomb Compound shutter.

### Assessment

The example I acquired has been "restored" with a spray can. As such, it's a good candidate for a complete strip down and rebuild.

As most of the fittings are fastened by wood screws, this camera is easy to disassemble as well as to reassemble. If you're worried that you won't remember how the parts go back, make notes, draw diagrams, and label the parts. The screws must go back where they came from. Use adhesive tape to stick the screws to a sheet of paper and write under them where they belong. This is one situation, though, when you can just remove all screws as you come to them until all the parts are free (photo 6.1).

The front and rear skirt of the bellows are glued to a square wooden frame. The front frame in turn is screwed to the lens standard by four wood screws, and the rear frame to the inside of the body frame by eight screws. You will have to pull the bellows aside a bit to see the front screws. If the bellows is still good, just brush it down vigorously with a soft, long-haired brush or a large paintbrush. If the bellows is damaged, see Chapter Two on how to restore or make a new one.

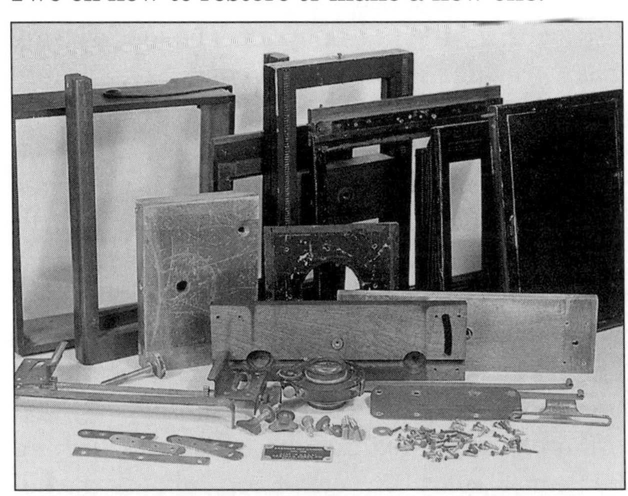

***6.1:** Complete disassembly.*

The body pivots are riveted on, and unless you file off the flared ends on the inside, you cannot remove the pivots or the metal brackets. Leave them on if the metal is in good condition.

### Refinishing the Body Parts

Strip the old paint and varnish one piece at a time. Brush a generous amount of varnish and paint remover onto the wooden pieces. Let them sit until the paint wrinkles up, or five minutes at the longest. Use a scraper or a knife to scrape off most of the paint. Get the varnish and dirt out of the grooves with a screwdriver. If after one coat, some of the original varnish is still hard, apply another coat of stripper, and let it sit a little longer (about 10 minutes). Scrape the piece again. Before the remover dries, rub off the remaining residue with steel-wool and liquid detergent (Fantastic™). Or use steel wool impregnated with soap, such as SOS™ and water. Make sure you obtain a uniform color by rubbing the darker areas longer. Rinse the piece under running warm water using a stiff brush. Do all this fast to prevent the remover from drying or the wood from soaking up too much water. Wipe off the pieces with paper towels, and let them dry overnight.

Use #220 garnet paper to cut back the raised whiskers. When sanding dry, the paper will clog-up fast. Replace the sandpaper with a new square often. Always sand along the grain, never cross-grain.

If any of the joints are loose, you can reglue them with white glue or epoxy. The long-setting epoxy provides the strongest bond. Five-minute epoxy is not nearly as strong. White glue is strong but requires clamping and works best on clean wood that is not contaminated with varnish or old glue.

You can get the glue into small cracks with a thin blade, but sometimes it's better to break off the cracked section, and reglue it properly. Making the crack completely accessible makes the job easier rather than more difficult. Or you can apply diluted white glue without knocking the frames apart. In a small cup, mix one part of water with two parts of white glue.

Apply this mixture to the cracks and loose joints liberally. Wiggle the loose parts in order to enhance capillary action. The mixture will seep into the cracks. Either clamp the glued parts or tie them down with string. Let the glue set for at least six hours. Try not to smear the glue onto highly visible section of the wood since the glue will soak into the wood preventing the stain from penetrating. This will leave lighter patches wherever glue has been smeared. Never use nails in naked wood. Nails are seldom necessary, but they may be used under a leather finish.

The wood is often blemished with nicks, impact marks, or extra screw holes. Small nicks and screw holes can be filled-in with wood filler. Look for stainable filler; otherwise, you'll have a hard time trying to match the color of the repaired area.

Large holes or craters should be filled in with solid wood. To do so, enlarge the crater to give it a regular shape. Carve a plug from a similar wood to fit into the cutout. Orient the direction of the grain on the plug with that on the original piece. Glue the plug in with epoxy so that it sticks out just a little. Let the epoxy cure completely (24 hours). Sand off the repaired surface flush with the surrounding wood. Once it's smooth, you can use wood stain on the inset.

For retouching small spots, try water-based felt-tip markers. It's easy to work with markers. You can blend the colors at will, and wipe it off if not satisfied. You will have to experiment. On larger insets try water color.

Staining the complete body is optional. You apply stain to darken the wood, change its hue, or seal the grain. Stain comes in two basic forms. One is quite watery with only a small percentage of solids. This type penetrates deeper and leaves the original grain structure readily visible (Minwax Wood Finish™). The other contains a large percentage of solids. It's more like a thick paint and surfacer. This will seal open grain more readily, but covers some of the wood's original beauty (FLECTO X-3D™). If you find other brands, you will probably have to buy the can as the label will give little help.

I recommend Minwax™. Apply it to the prepared case with a paper towel or rag. Use paint thinner to dilute the stain for a lighter effect. You don't have to premix. Just dip the rag into the stain, then into the solvent.

Do not overstain, you want the grain of the wood to shine through. You can also mix different colors together to suit your taste. Again, you don't have to premix. Apply one color, then the other. Keep it wet by dipping the rag into solvent occasionally.

Experiment and see what you get. Wipe off the excess with a clean paper towel. Let it dry overnight, and then sand it off again with a #220 garnet paper.

Make sure no streaks or unsightly blotches develop while sanding. If the result is too light, apply more stain. If it's too dark, sand a little longer. Always sand with the grain. Wipe off the dust with a soft cloth, then blow off the fluff and remaining dust. Blow into corners, crevices, and channels For blowing use a foot pump (see Abstract).

## Finishing

There are several options for a top coat. A hard shiny finish is the easiest to achieve. A good varnish is Varathane Liquid Plastic™ clear gloss, but others work just as well. Dilute the first coat with 20% paint thinner. Brush on a thin coat, and let it dry overnight. Sand it lightly with #220 paper before applying the second coat. Try to finish each piece before the varnish skins over. Apply thin coats, and make sure it doesn't run. Check all sides of the piece for runs and varnish build-ups before putting it down. If not satisfied after the second coat dries, apply a third coat the same way.

When applying varnish or paint with a brush, the proper technique is to "brush it in, then lay it down". The brush-in part consists of hard back and forth short strokes, while the laying-down is done with long, smooth light strokes of the brush, in one way only (from left to right if you're right-handed.)

When painting a large piece (table top), always lay it down into the wet paint (i.e. you're progressing from right to left, but lay it down from left to right.) If you opt for a spray can, apply thin coats and sand between coats as described above.

## The Bellows

If the bellows has also been sprayed with black paint, it cannot be stripped with paint remover because the original top coat will most likely be stripped away as well. You can try solvents other than paint remover, such as lighter fluid, Acetone™, or lacquer thinner. You want to dissolve the paint, but leave the original finish intact.

Experiment on a hidden corner first. If none of these solvents work, all you can do is clean the bellows with a damp sponge. When dry, rub a little oil into it. Blow it off. If the bellows is frayed or otherwise need attention, see Chapter Two for ways to restore or build a new one.

## The Lens Board

If the lens board is in reasonable shape, treat it the same as wooden parts of the body (see above). If it's missing or cannot be salvaged, you will have to make a new one. The best wood for lens boards, and the easiest to work with, is 1/8" rotary mahogany plywood, known as door skin (readily available in lumberyards).

Most lens boards have staggered edges to serve as light trap. The hole for the lens should, in most instances, be stepped as well in order to accommodate the retaining ring. If you use door skin, you can create the steps easily by gluing two boards together.

Cut off a door skin square 114mm on each side with a 36mm hole in its center. Follow with another one of 108mm square with a 48mm hole. It's the neck of the retaining ring that should fit into the hole, not the neck of the lens itself. Perhaps the easiest way to cut out the hole is by using a hand jigsaw, but it can also be carved out with a sharp knife. Draw the desired circle on both sides and cut along the lines with a sharp utility knife. Break out the disk, and clean up the hole with tightly rolled-up coarse sandpaper.

Use white glue to bond the two pieces together. Make sure they are concentric. Clamp them for drying; don't use nails. Paint the rear of the board flat black. Finish the front as you did the body (see above). You don't have to strive to match the body color; the lens board can have contrasting wood and color.

If the lens has a register pin in its back, you have to drill a hole for it into the lens board. Otherwise, tighten the retaining ring sufficiently to keep the shutter unit from rotating.

## The Shutter Assembly

My example is equipped with a Bausch & Lomb Compound shutter. The pneumatic cylinder is at the outside top of the unit. If the shutter doesn't work, it's very likely that this cylinder is faulty. Not only can the inside be dirty, thus jamming the piston, but the piston itself, being made of aluminum, may be corroded, or pock-marked. Either way, you will have to remove the cylinder and pull out the piston.

First, unscrew the front and rear optical groups. Normally no tool is required for this. Just use your fingers. Remove the center screw from the shutter-speed dial. Pull off the dial and the cam. Cock the shutter first, then remove the three screws from the shutter cocking lever, and the four screws from the face of the cover plate.

With the shutter open, you can gain access to the two screws that fasten the pneumatic cylinder. Using parallel serrated pliers, unscrew the end cups from the cylinder carefully. Be careful and make sure the pliers don't slip or the cups will get marred. Clean the inside of the cylinder and the piston. See if the cylinder slides smoothly. If required, polish up the piston with #400 sandpaper (photo 6.2).

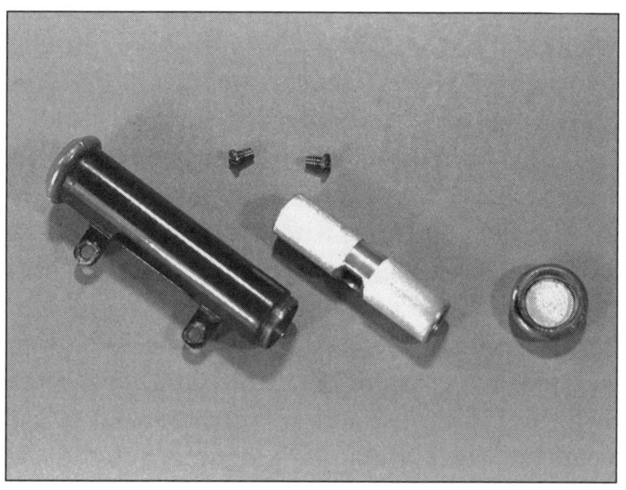

***6.2:** The piston & cylinder must be polished.*

These parts must be completely clean and free of dust or the escapement is not going to work. If it works all right but the shutter speeds are too fast, you can try a drop of oil inside the cylinder. Oil will slow down the escapement considerably. You can experiment with different viscosity of oil to get the shutter-speeds right.

If you have to get to the shutter blades, remove the four screws from the rear of the unit, and pull out the inside base (photo 6.3). Two of the blades are pivoting on pins, but the third is screwed down so it won't fall off.

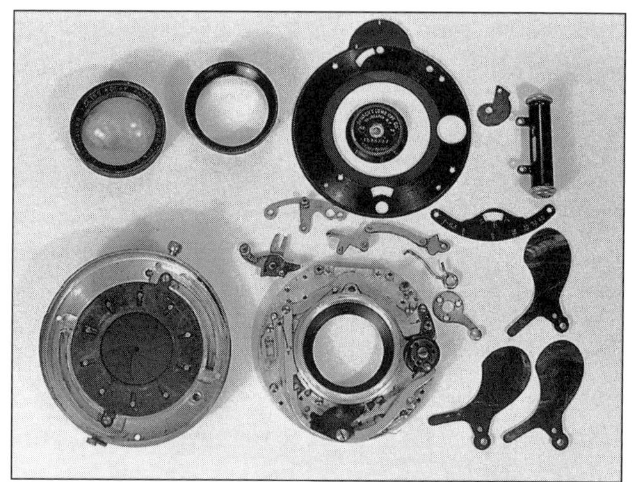

***6.3:** Bausch & Lomb compound shutter.*

If the nickel-plated control levers are oxidized, you can polish them up with SOS™ and warm water. With the SOS™ rub-down considerable improvement can be achieved even if the oxidation is quite pronounced.

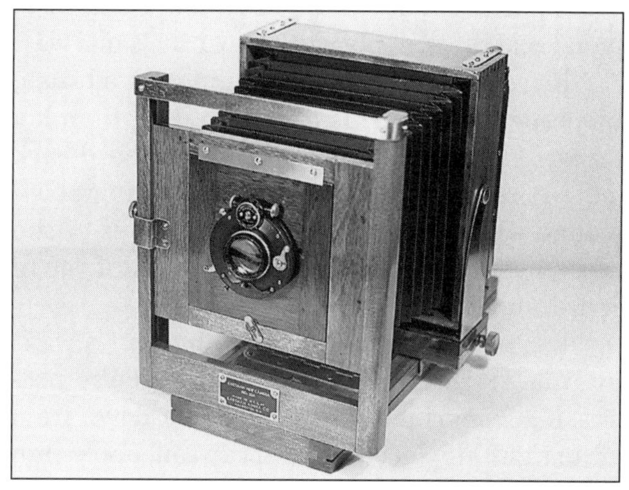

***6.4:** Eastman 5x7 View Camera No. 33A.*

The numbering on the face of the unit may need improving also. Unfortunately, the white paint inside the engraved lines has chemically altered and will not respond to any cleaning method. Try this: under a magnifying glass and with the utmost care, scrape the shutter-speed numbers clean with a sewing needle. As to the F-numbers, take a #600 sandpaper and very gently sand off the top of the numbers. Try to avoid sanding the background. You can touch up the background with a fine-tipped felt marker.

### The Front Plate

Touching up the brand name plaque is easy and should always be done. A sparkling plaque at a prominent position enhances the appearance of the camera. How to touch up the plaque is described on page 42 in Chapter Five. Photo 6.4 shows the restored camera.

## Lancaster & Son, Merveilleux

Lancaster & Son produced cameras from 1880 to about 1910. Many of their models are rare and valuable. Most of their models are view cameras, but there are others, such as a telescoping watch camera.

The Merveilleux is probably the simplest in the lineup. It has no shutter or rack and pinion for extension, just a ground glass focusing. It has a handsome teak body with brass fittings. The camera is small, measuring 6x5.5 inch on the outside. It's a cute little antique, yet quite affordable.

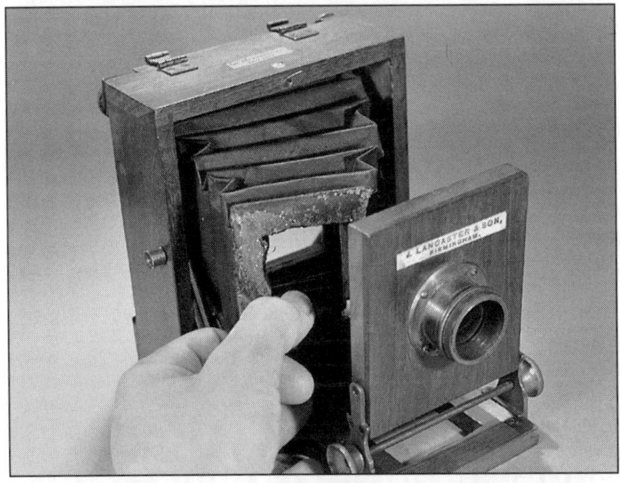


*6.5: Pry off the bellows.*

### What You will Learn

You will learn: to build a square bellows and substitute missing brass knobs.

### Assessment

The bellows is simply glued onto the lens standard at the front, and to the body frame at the rear. Just pry both ends off (photo 6.5). In order to make a new bellows, first read Chapter Two. Referring to diagram 2.12 (in Chapter Two), draw the pattern with dimensions: a=208mm, b=f=60mm, c=g=120mm.

Draw one trapeze, attach the side trapezes by drawing circle sections with radius of b/2 from point A and radius of c/2 from point B.

Draw one line tangent to both circle sections. Project point A and B over the tangent line. Complete the outline as shown in diagram 2.12 (on page 19).

Remember, the sum of the differences between infolds and out-folds provides a total growth of (120-60)/2=30mm from front to rear.

That means that since there are 8 folds altogether, one fold should provide 30/8=3.75mm growth. Since the pitch is 208/8=26mm (starting from the front), the in-folds will be (26-3.75)/2=11.125mm wide and the out-folds will be 11.125+3.75=14.875mm wide.

Draw in the crease lines. (See diagram.) Don't forget that the wider and narrower folds are alternating from front to rear as well as between the adjacent panels.

As I explained in Chapter Two, you don't have to split hair over decimals. Draw the lines as close to the calculated figures as you can, but don't drop the decimals completely either. One of the corner lines is given by the outside dimensions of the bellows; the odd numbered crease lines should intercept on that line. The other corner-line joins the interception points of the even numbered crease lines.

Study the diagram to figure this out. After scoring, you can crease all the lines before gluing up the tube. But watch your in-folds and out-folds. Make sure you fold them in the correct direction. Once creased, glue up the tube. Fold up the accordion as described in Chapter Two.

### Replacing Missing Knobs

Broken or missing knobs are quite common in old cameras. You will often be confronted with the dilemma of how to come up with replacements. In this book, the Thorton Pickard camera is missing its lens movement knob, the Graflex is missing the focusing knob, and the present model is missing both strut lock knobs.

If you have access to a lathe, you have no problem. You can make any round parts easily, such as knobs, wheels, rings, nuts and so forth. But most such parts can be substituted by "found" objects. Suitable serrated brass parts can be found in plumbing supply stores. Many electronic fittings: jacks, sockets, and adapters may be considered. Radio knobs are also strong candidates.

For a camera that features some original plastic parts, plastic radio knobs, wire-nut connectors, plastic jacks, and sockets may be adaptable. Even such things as bottle caps may be considered. Camera parts and accessories such as winding/rewinding knobs from old cameras, tripod or camera case screws etc. may be suitable as well. (See photo 6.6 for a selection of possible candidates.)

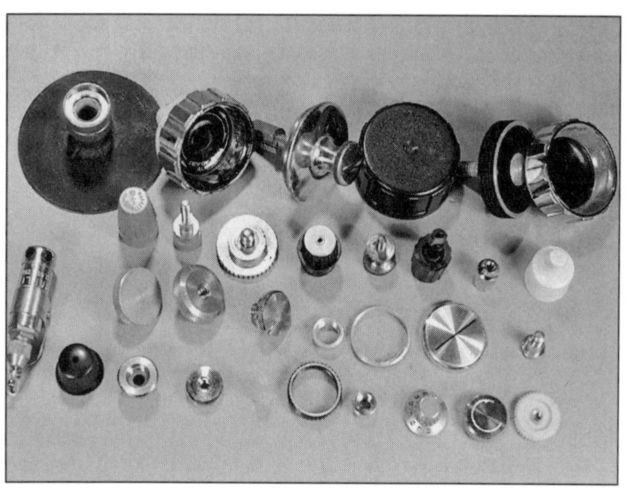

***6.6:*** *Selection of replacement knob.*

Chances are almost nil that any of the above will fit as is. You will have to browse through these objects, try to visualize how the item would look on the camera and how you can adapt it in a relatively easy way.

Start your search in your own junk boxes before laying out hard cash. Some of these items are bare brass, others may be chrome-plated, gold-plated or anodized aluminum. The color may be suitable as is, or you could sand off the plating, or rub it off with abrasive powder on a soft cloth. Sand-blasting is also a possibility.

If the original fittings are plastic or painted, then painting the substitute part may also be considered. An antique look can be achieved by painting a serrated knob, then wiping the paint off or lightly sanding off the top of the serrations. This way the paint remains in the deeper regions, but the peaks come out metallic bright as if rubbed off by years of handling.

The three Kodak Folding Pocket cameras we restored in Chapter Five yielded a bonus. The horizontal lens-movement locking knob from those models is a good replacement for the missing knob on the Merveilleux. All I had to do was drill up the hole, and tap it for a 4mm screw (photo 6.7).

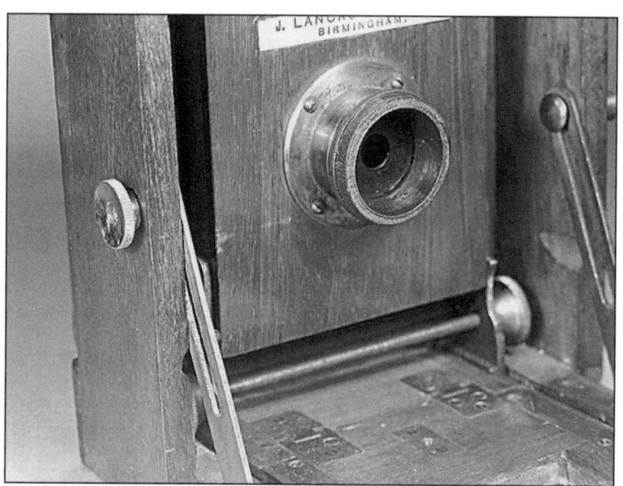


***6.7:*** *The new knobs fitted.*

If the screw is also missing, use a 4mmx17mm screw with an oval head. File off two sides of the conical underside of the head. This way, the flattened section fits into the slot in the strut preventing the screw from rotating.

## Rembrandt No.2 Portrait Camera, Burke & James, Inc.

This is a 5x7 view camera with a nice wooden body and red bellows. We will fit the Wollensak brass lens (see Chapter Five). onto this camera. The red bellows and the brass lens provide a stunning combination (photo 6.8).

### What You will Learn

You will learn to: repair distorted bellows; properly marry lens to body; and make a brass rail latch. You will practice refinishing a wooden body and making a large-sized lens board.

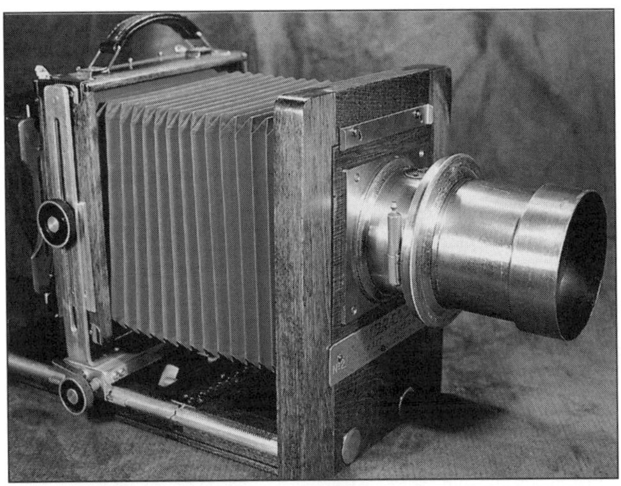

*6.8: Rembrandt No. 2 Portrait.*

## Assessment

Even though the body is in fair condition, there is really no good way to properly restore the finish without stripping it first.

The bellows are in fair, but by no means perfect, condition. Unfortunately, the camera has been stored for a long time with the bellows closed up wrong i.e. the body had been in a raised position when the camera was closed. (In this model, the body moves while the lens standard is stationary.) This caused permanent distortion to the bellows.

In addition, some of the corners are frayed and leaking light through pin holes (photo 6.9). Nevertheless, saving the present bellows is a lot less trouble than building a new one.

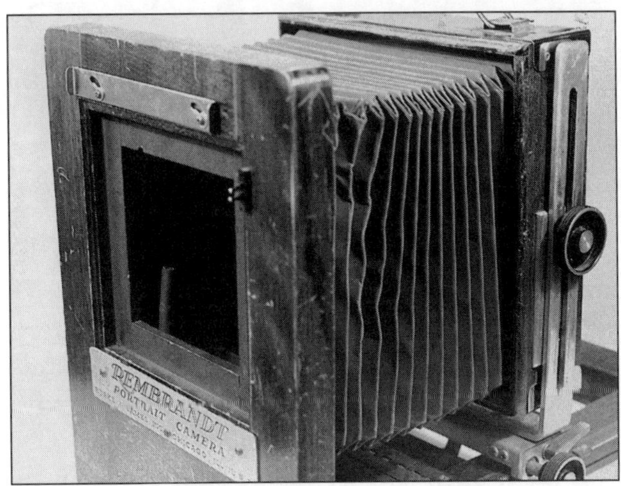


*6.9: Distorted bellows.*

The front of the bellows is held down, in addition to glue, by metal retaining strips and screws. The rear is fastened inside the housing frame by glue only. Remove the screws and the metal strips. Unfortunately, there is no good way to dissolve the glue. Stick a knife under the bellows material and pry it off slowly and methodically. The red vinyl side separates fairly easily, but the black fabric side is tough to pry off. Do your best; a little damage doesn't make much difference as the skirt of the bellows is hidden both front and rear. Once the front of the bellows is off, roll the frame back all the way off the track, pry off the rear skirt from inside the body frame (photo 6.10).

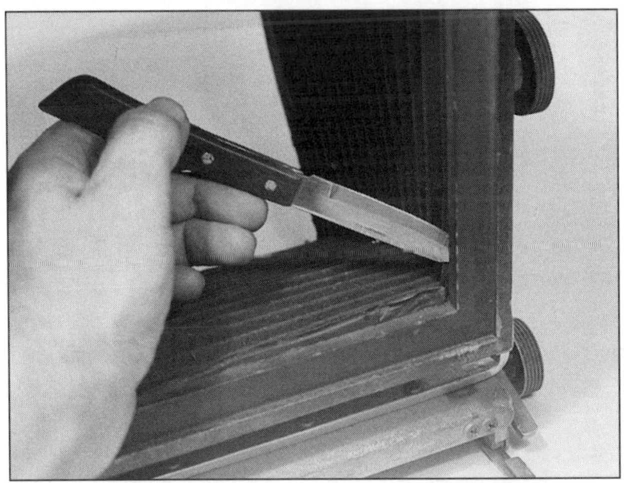

*6.10: Removing the rear skirt.*

Stretch the bellows straight. Vacuum the inside. Use warm water, liquid detergent, and a soft brush to wash the outside. Rinse off the detergent with clean water. At the portions where the bellows is distorted, moisten the inside as well. Blot the water off with paper towels.

Fold up and weigh down the bellows in order to smooth out the distortions. Since the corners are double layered, the straight sections must be built up for the press to be effective.

Cut off several strips of 160x10mm each from a cardboard shoe box or similar material. You need 17 such strips for each side in need of straightening. From the outside only, place one cardboard strip between each fold. Reach in between the folds with a blade, and smooth down the kinks. Once satisfied that all the folds are lying straight, weigh the whole sandwich down with a substantial weight (photo 6.11). Every day of the first week, open up the press and let the bellows air on the inside for at least an hour.

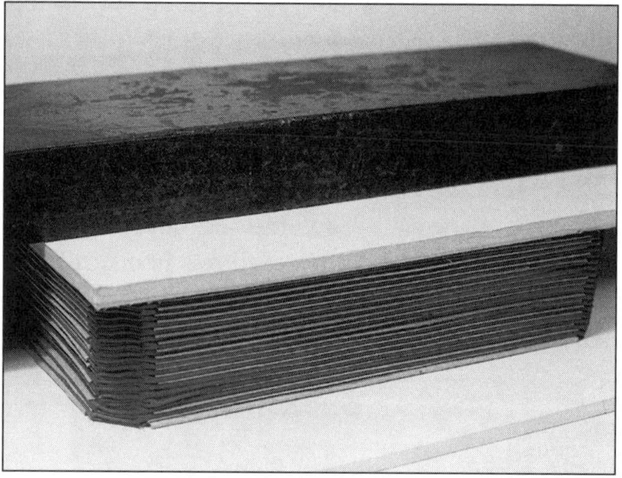

*6.11: Pressing the bellows.*

After the first week, just leave the bellows in the press undisturbed while you're working on the rest of the camera. Don't be in a hurry to install the bellows. The longer you leave it pressed, the better (a couple of months minimum).

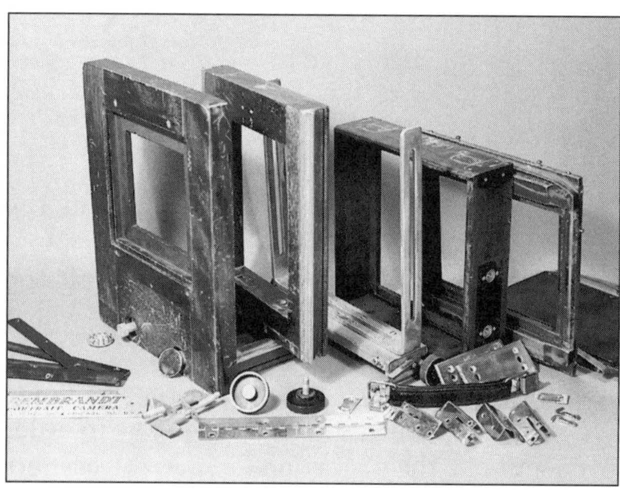

*6.12: Strip all components.*

Separate all the body parts. Strip all the components of their metal fittings (photo 6.12). See the instructions for refinishing the wooden parts at the beginning of this chapter. For this camera, I recommend the use of a dark walnut stain. I don't favor any reddish color for staining, as restorers seem to be hooked on "mahogany."

As a result, every restored camera ends up being red. Two coats of clear gloss varnish finish up the job nicely. Make sure to rub down all the fittings and screw heads with SOS™ before refitting them. If the screws are rusty, see "Screws" in Chapter Five.

After washing them in water and letting them dry, buff up the screw heads with SOS™ or with a wire brush in a Dremmel™. Don't begrudge this. Polishing 80 screw heads takes less than an hour and shiny screw heads do wonders for the appearance of the camera.

## Restoring the Viewing Hood

It is best to disassemble the rear unit to its components. The film holder has already been removed from the wooden frame (four screws). Open up the viewing hood and remove the four screws from the inside corners. The hood and the ground glass are separated from the cast-aluminum frame and can be cleaned comfortably (photo 6.13).

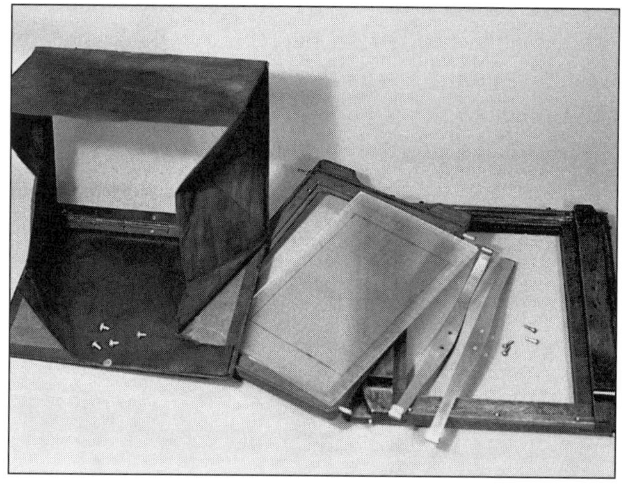

*6.13: Disassemble the viewing hood.*

Use Fantastic™ and a toothbrush to scrub the aluminum frame. Use Fantastic™ again, but with a soft brush, to clean the hood. The hood material is glued onto a thin steel frame. If this frame is rusty, separate it from the hood, scrub it with SOS™, and spray flat black paint on it.

If the hood is torn off the lid, glue it back using contact cement. Do a thorough job of it, or the hood may get loose again as the lid pops open. If the leatherette is torn from the outside surface of the lid, glue it down with contact cement, taking care not to smear the cement. Once clean and dry, buff up the outside surface of the lid with a soft brush such as a shoe brush (photo 6.14).

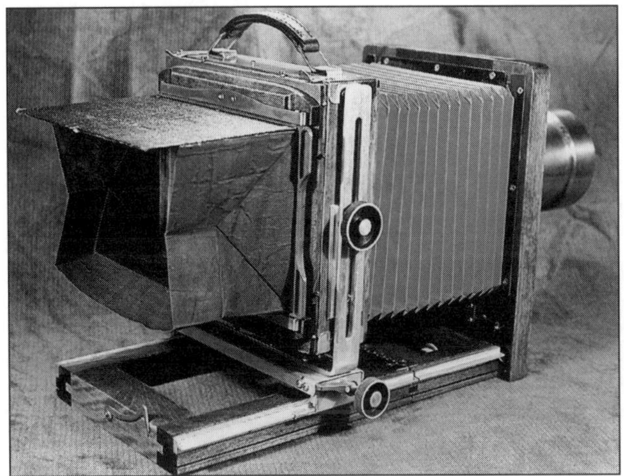

***6.14:*** *Viewing hood and rail latch.*

## Bellows

It's easier to touch up the frayed corners after the bellows is installed. Since in this camera the front and rear of the bellows is of the same dimension (parallel bellows), turn the better side forward. Probably the side that was forward before will go back into the body frame, and any ugliness remaining will be hidden there.

Use contact cement to glue the rear skirt of the bellows inside the body frame. Let it dry for at least a day, then glue the front end on as well, and install the metal retaining strips.

Extend the bellows half way. The frayed corners are easy to retouch. While we have at least three substances we could use to fix the corners, I recommend a mixture of paper glue and water color for this bellows.

The other two possibilities are Plasti-Dip™ and Liquid Vinyl™ (comes in a vinyl repair kit). These require precise color matching, and since they are not self-leveling and do not shrink, they require a very precise form of application with steady hands. They could be difficult to find, as well as being quite expensive. See photo 2.3 for the vinyl repair kit.

We can use another method that's a lot cheaper, and thus lends itself to experimenting. Start with a colorless paper glue such as Glue Pen™ (see photo 2.8).

If you find a different brand, spill a small amount on a plastic or glass sheet. Peel the substance off after completely dry. The dry glue should peel off in one sheet, should not be brittle, but should have a bit of a rubbery feel to it, not unlike a cellophane sheet.

Once you're sure you've got the right stuff, mix it with water color. If the mixture gets too thick, add a drop of water as well. Pick up a drop of this mixture with the end of a small screwdriver, and dab it onto the frayed corner of the bellows.

Work it into the material, but don't spread it. Just leave a small bead sitting there. This mixture is self-leveling and will shrink to a tight film. You can apply further beads if the coverage is not complete, or the color needs improving.

If you don't find the exact color to match the bellows, you will have to mix colors. The color must be exact. The repair is almost totally invisible if the color doesn't give it away. Strive for perfection. You can use other water-soluble colors such as Tempera, or Acrylic paint. Small jars of Acrylic paint, in every conceivable color, are available from arts and crafts suppliers, but they are likely to be expensive. The water color is easy to obtain, easy to apply, and inexpensive as well. After the corners are retouched, let the glue dry undisturbed for at least 24 hours.

Apply shoe polish with a soft cloth to the faded portions of the bellows. Buff it up thoroughly with a soft brush. The polish to use is either pale red or colorless. Don't use any polish with large amounts of solid dye in it such as Tana Leather Creme™ or similar products.

## Making a Lens Board and Installing the Lens

I described how to make wooden lens boards previously in this chapter. The difference in this case is that you stack a 1/8" board with a 1/4" one. The dimensions are 6" square for the 1/8" board and a shade under 5 1/2" square for the 1/4" board. Use white glue to glue the two layers together.

Make sure they are concentric. Don't use nails. Use clamps. Mark out the center and draw a 4" circle with a compass. Use a jigsaw or a rat-tail saw or a circle cutter to cut out the circle. Use a saw with fine teeth in order to avoid splintering the wood.

For a wider blade, you may have to drill more than one hole inside the periphery of the circle in order to be able to follow the curvature. The circle will have to be filed and sanded to make it smooth. To install the lens, use brass wood screws.

If you have a different lens, use the same board, but cut out the circle dimension that is required by your lens.

If the hole for the lens needs staggering to accommodate a retaining ring, cut the holes in the component boards separately before gluing them together. (See page 57.)

## Making a Brass Latch

The latch that holds the folding rails up is often missing or broken. The latches you find in hardware stores are made with drab steel wire, and are not suitable for a handsome antique camera. A more suitable latch can be made from brass plate. Hobby stores carry an assortment of brass strips that are suitable. Get 1/16x3/8" or wider. When designing the shape, aim for flowing curves rather than straight lines. Photo 6.15 shows two homemade brass latches.

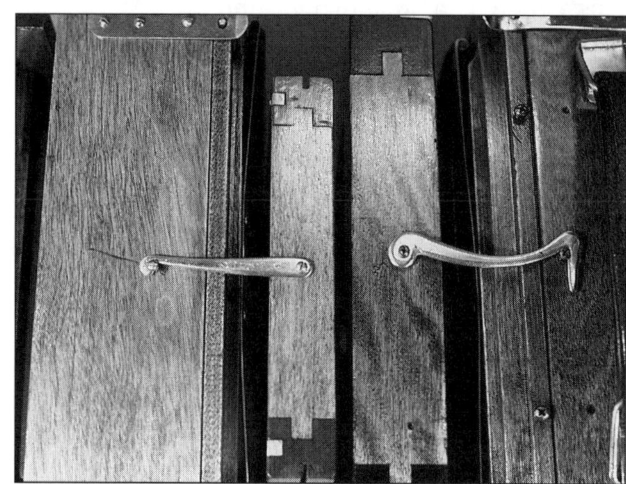

***6.15:*** *Brass rail latches.*

You can rough out the shape using a junior hacksaw. Refine it with files. Round off the edges. You can smooth it off thoroughly, or leave it somewhat rough to give the piece a wrought look. Finally, buff it up with steel wool. The length is given by the camera dimensions.

Chapter Seven

# Large Format Focal-Plane Shutter

Early large format focal-plane shutters follow two basic design philosophies. One design calls for two mechanically independent shutter curtains, plus the means to vary the gap between the curtains according to the selected shutter speed.

The other type of shutter constitutes a long strip of curtain material with fixed slots cut into it for each of the various shutter speeds (see diagram 7.25).

The models below provide examples for both of these designs, each of which can be found in either reflex or viewfinder cameras.

## Thornton-Pickard Duplex Ruby Reflex

This 5x3.5 SLR is equipped with a vertically running focal-plane shutter and an Aldis anastigmat lens (photo 7.1).

### What You will Learn

You will learn how to restore a large-format leather-covered wooden body. You will study an early focal-plane shutter design. You will replace the shutter curtains; restore the existing viewing hood; restore the reflex mirror, and substitute a missing knob.

### Assessment

The whole camera is quite shaky. The joints on the body are coming apart, and the viewing hood is in very poor shape. Some of the control knobs are missing. The mirror coating is all but gone from too much cleaning. The shutter doesn't work. The curtain material is dried out and cracked. Restoring this camera is an ambitious project.

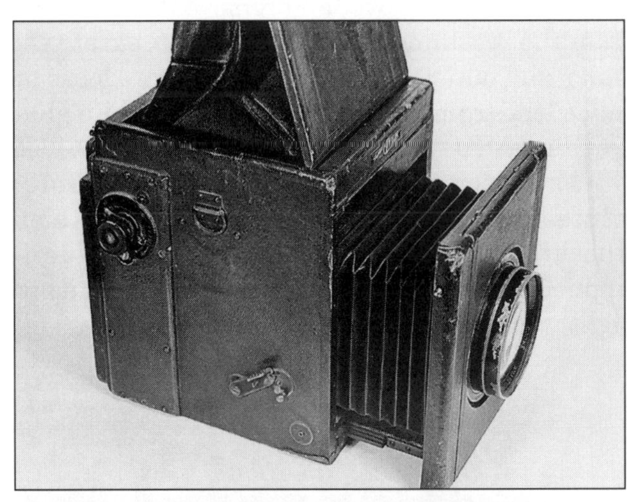

*7.1: Thornton-Pickard Duplex Ruby Reflex.*

### The Back and the Film Holder

In order to remove the film holder, release the brass locking lever at the lower left, and push the holder unit up.

Removing the complete rear frame assembly allows you to access the shutter curtains and restore the rear frame which, in the example, is falling apart.

The frame is held on by four screws on top, one through the right side, three through the bottom plate, and two at the left-hand side. To find the last two screws, rotate the outer frame 45°.

Release the frame by pressing the brass knob at the upper right. Two screws are uncovered at the left side of the rear frame (photo 7.2).

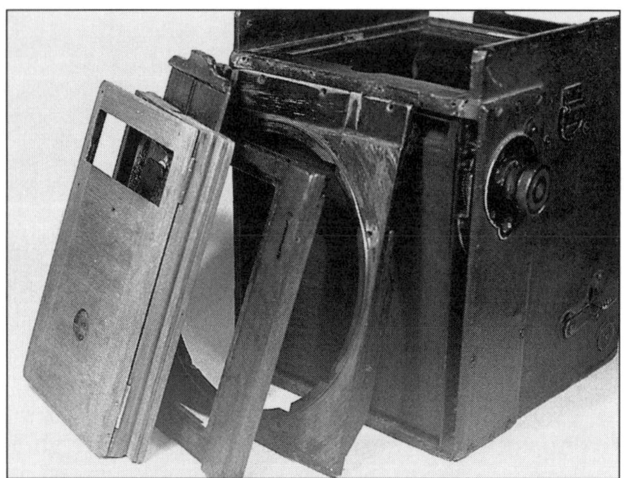

*7.2: The back frame removed.*

Turn the frame over and remove the 10 screws from the retaining plates. This will separate the inner and outer frames. If the joints are loose on any of the frames, reglue them using white glue.

Glue can be applied more easily if you pull off the loose element, or you can introduce diluted white glue into cracks and loose joints without knocking the frames apart. After the glue is applied, either clamp the parts or tie them down tight with string (photo 7.3).

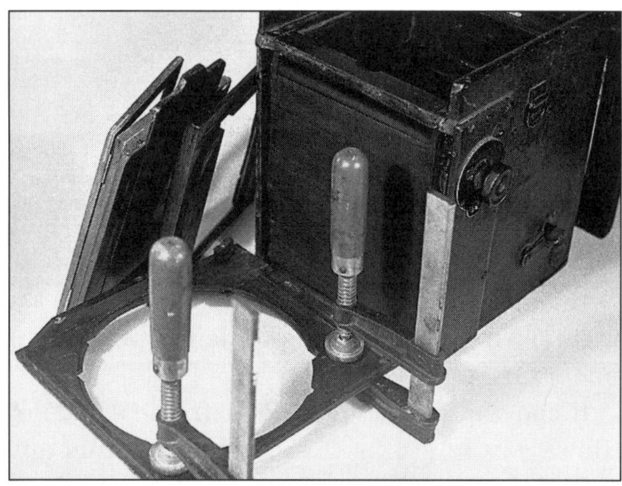

*7.3: Regluing the frame.*

Let the glue set for at least six hours. (See Chapter Six for more information on how to fix wooden body parts.)

If the black paint is peeling and chipped, you can remove the paint from all areas not covered in leather. The wood under the paint is a very nice teak that lends itself to a natural wood-grain finish. Put the wood pieces through the full treatment as described in Chapter Six. Remove the brass fittings before stripping the wood.

## The Film Holder

Strip the black paint from the film holder as well. You may find a round hole 20mm in diameter at the lower center of the film holder door. This is for a metal or plastic emblem that often falls off. You can substitute a wooden insert and a homemade emblem. Cut out a 20mm circle from an 1/8" rotary mahogany plywood (door skin). Clean out the hole and glue in the insert. Pound it in level with the door. Smooth it down with #220 emery paper on plywood backing.

If you want to fancy up the insert, burn a stylized T-P logo into it. See the logo at the top of the camera stamped into the leather. However, there is no need to strive for an exact duplicate, using straight lines to form the letters is permissible. Cut off a small piece of steel or brass plate with one 11mm side.

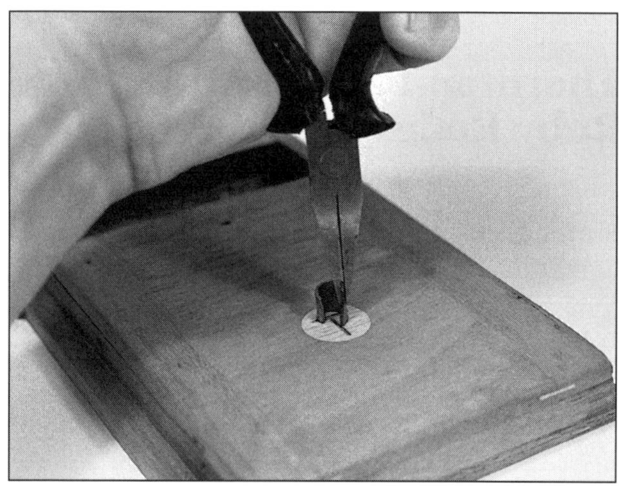

*7.4: Burn the "T-P" logo.*

Hold this plate with a pair of pliers and heat it up to the point when it just starts to glow. Press the 11mm side into the wood horizontally to form the hat of the T. Do the same vertically to form the stem of the T. Bend the same plate to form the head of the P. Heat it again and press it into the wood (photo 7.4). You'd better practice on scrap wood before attempting to do the job on the door. You can also try burning several logos into a plywood sheet. Cut out and insert the one that turned out best.

The film in its holder is covered with a stiff impregnated cloth curtain which is composed of two layers. Before the film is exposed, this cover curtain is pulled up by the wooden slide in the back assembly. The curtain curls up behind the door and is visible through an orange window provided for this purpose. This stiff curtain may buckle and bunch up instead of curling. To fix it, tease the layers of the curtain apart, and glue a thin plastic sheet between the two layers (photo 7.5).

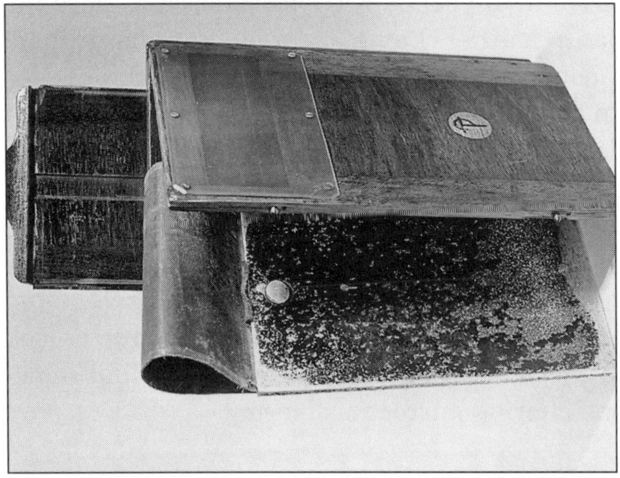

***7.5:** The film shade.*

## The Viewer Assembly

To remove the viewer assembly, press the brass knobs on both sides inward and lift up the unit. Remove the screws from the hinges. If the viewing hood is dried out and badly torn, or the stiffening boards in the hood material are warped, you will have to separate the hood material from the frame in order to restore it.

Lay several sheets of soaking wet paper towels on a non-porous surface. Place the viewing assembly with lid side up on the towels.

Leave the frame soaking for 2-3 hours. Once the glue has softened, peel off the cover strips from the bottom of the frame, pull out the nails, and separate the hood material from the wooden frame.

Dunk the hood in warm water long enough for the original glue to soften. Peel open the seam so the hood can be spread out flat. Arrange the material on several layers of newspaper. Place more sheets on top, then place some heavy books on top of this sandwich. Replace the newspaper with dry ones twice each day. Let the drying and pressing process continue for at least one week.

While the hood is drying, remove the brass fittings from the frame and lid (photo 7.6). Strip and polish the brass fittings as described below. Strip the wooden parts of black paint. If the lid or frame are cracked or the joints are loose, glue them up as described in Chapter Six.

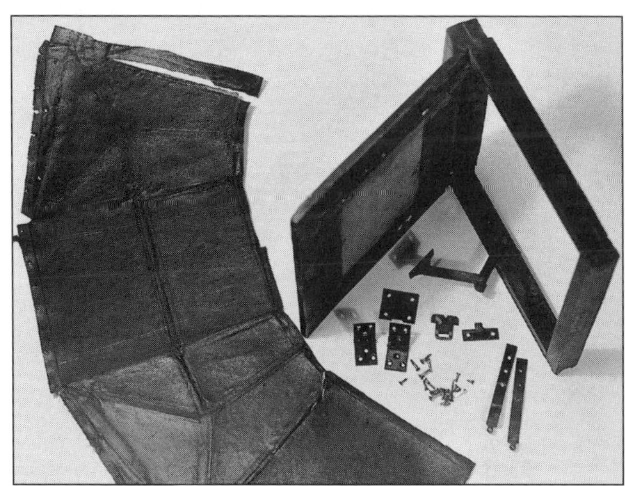

***7.6:** The viewer disassembled.*

Cut off the damaged topmost section of the hood to make it simpler and neater looking (photo 7.7). Make the cut a quarter inch higher than the edge of the cardboard stiffener to leave material for tucking inside. Use contact cement for gluing up the original seam. Torn corners can be reinforced with strips cut from the curtain material (see below). Use contact cement sparingly for gluing on the reinforcing strips and for gluing the hood back onto the frame. The glue is strong enough.

It's not necessary to nail down the edges (photo 7.8), but you can stick black cloth adhesive tape over the glued flaps the way it was done originally.

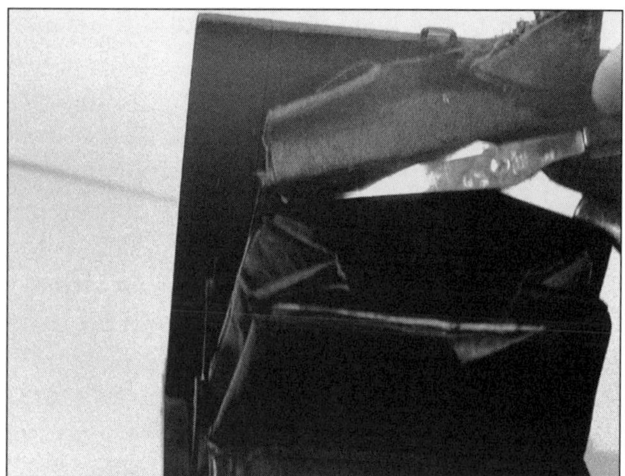

*7.7: Cut off the topmost section.*

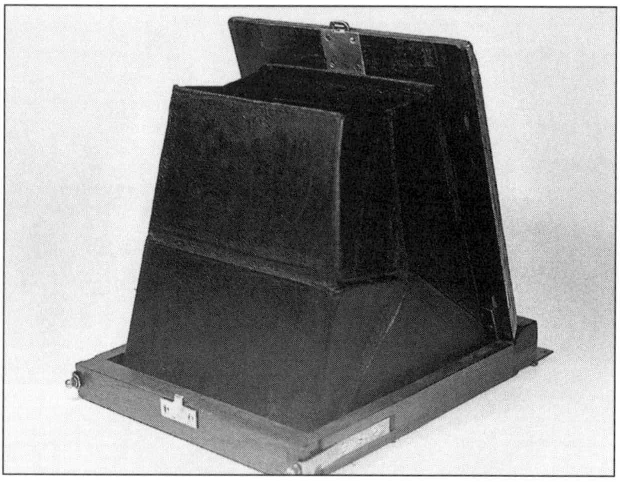

*7.8: The restored viewer.*

## The Body

The fittings must be removed from the body and cleaned up. The factory black paint is much tougher than any new paint. The paint remover is not as effective. You will have to rub hard with steel wool to remove most of the paint. Some remaining black paint in the crevices and deeper areas lends a handsome antique look to the piece. If you ever use sandpaper on brass for removing stubborn corrosion or paint, follow up with steel wool. Steel wool provides the best finish on brass.

The leather on the body may be peeling, especially at the corners and edges. Dampen the dog-eared sections, then glue them down with white glue. Hold the flaps with your finger for several minutes to allow the glue to set. If the corners are abraded, after the leather is glued down, sand the wood smooth. Rub on wood stain to match the leather's color. (Don't paint the exposed wood black.) Apply clear shoe polish to the complete body. Buff it all up with a soft brush.

If larger sections of leather are missing, try to find a similar pattern and color of leather. Cut out the damaged sections from the body leather and the exact same shape from the new material. Use white glue to glue on the patch. Don't overlap the patch with the old leather; butt the new to the old instead. Dampen the leather and press the edges together. Make sure the patch is compressed somewhat so the gap won't open up when the leather dries. Press a matching graining paper (from a vinyl repair kit, see Glossary) onto the damp leather. Lay a sheet of firm plastic foam (neoprene) onto the paper, then a plastic or wooden board on top of the neoprene, and clamp or tie down the sandwich. Let it dry overnight.

## The Mirror

The mirror coating in my example is badly rubbed off by too much and improper cleaning. You may try to find a front surface mirror, or look in the yellow pages under "glass", to find someone offering mirror re-silvering.

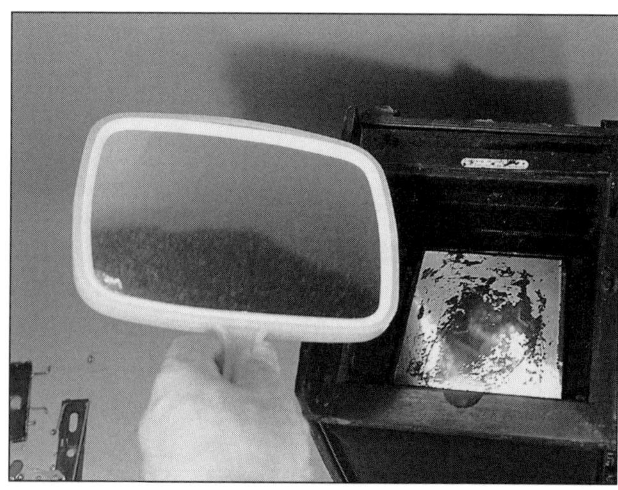

*7.9: Replacement mirror.*

If you don't want to go to that much trouble and expense, use an ordinary hand mirror, available for less than a dollar (photo 7.9). Remove the viewing hood and the ground glass. Fold up the mirror and remove the retaining brackets. The mirror is slightly glued onto the backing. Separate the new hand mirror from its plastic frame. Cut the original shape out of the hand mirror.

To cut glass, use a glass cutter on the face of the mirror alongside a metal straightedge. Press the cutter sufficiently to score the glass, but go over the line only once. The mistake most often made by amateurs is that they go back and forth several times along the line to deepen the score. A good cut is the beginning of a crack, it makes no difference how deep it is, but a back and forth motion will round the bottom of the score and prevent a clean crack-through. A freshly cut glass is very sharp. Handle it carefully. Blunt the edges with a medium hand stone under running water.

You can mount the mirror with the glass forward. While, theoretically, you'll get a double image this way, it is not noticeable in practice. Nevertheless, you can turn most rear surface mirrors into front surface mirrors by simply removing the paint from the back. (Some mirrors have an extra copper coat on top of the aluminum.)

Apply a generous amount of varnish remover, and let it sit. Wipe off the dissolved paint with tissue soaked in lacquer thinner. Don't rub hard. Gently wipe only once; otherwise, the mirror surface will get cloudy. I recommend using the mirror with the glass forward.

The mirror rest can be bent forward if the image doesn't quite come into focus at infinity. If you open the shutter, you'll find the mirror rest at the right-hand side with the mirror resting against it. Bend it forward, or glue a piece of felt or rubber onto its forward surface.

## The Shutter

You have already removed the back cover frame and examined the shutter curtains. The shutter gears are covered with a wooden slab on the right-hand side. Remove the shutter cocking knob (one screw in its side). Then remove the eight screws from the cover piece (one was removed earlier). If the shutter curtains are sound, the shutter can often be repaired and lubricated without further disassembly (photo 7.10).

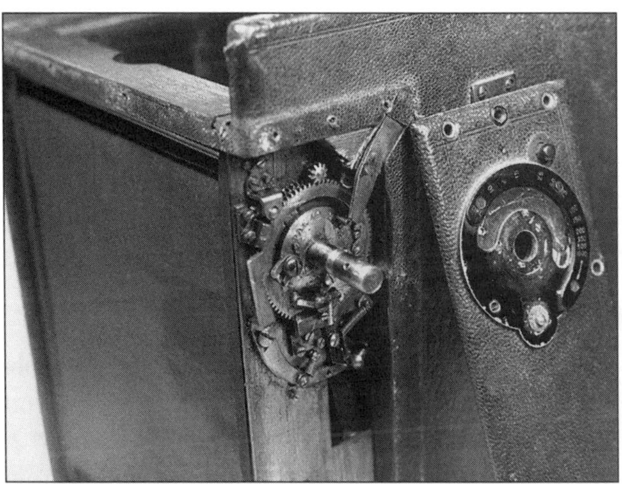

***7.10:*** *The shutter timing mechanism.*

The trigger lever is at the right-hand side of the camera. The mirror flips up when the lever is depressed and should trigger the shutter as well. If the shutter doesn't trigger, adjustment may help. See if the curtain and curtain shafts are free. Test the latch lever by pressing it backward manually. Turn the adjusting screw in its tip counterclockwise to improve the trigger action. Also note that the trigger lever must be completely depressed for the mirror to flip all the way up.

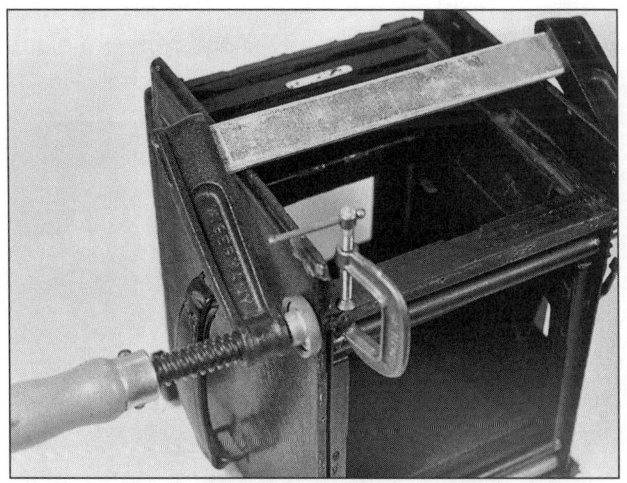

***7.11:*** *Glue and clamp the body.*

Lubricate all the bushings and shafts, including those of the curtain take-up drums and the timing gears. The curtain speed is about 1/4 of a second. It will seem quite slow. Check if the curtain shafts are sitting properly in their bearings.

If the body joints are loose, the shafts might pull out from the bearings at the left-hand side.

Glue up the body frame before proceeding with the shutter. Apply diluted white glue to the cracks and joints. Make sure the glue penetrates all the way into the cracks. Clamp the piece and let it dry for at least six hours (photo 7.11).

## Replacing the Curtains

Even though curtain replacement is possible with the shutter assembly inside the body, you might find the job easier by removing the unit. The drawback is that the shutter frame is somewhat wobbly on its own. In addition, the lower shafts tend to fall out of their bushings without the support of the body panels.

The shutter assembly is mounted in the body by only four screws: two at the right-hand side in the forward corners of the metal assembly plate and two others in the wooden frame at the left, just behind the curtain leads. The light baffle up top must be freed as well. If you want to save the baffle, dissolve the glue with warm water from the rear of the viewer frame. Otherwise, just cut it off and replace it later with new material. Pull the assembly partly out of the body, and then remove the hinge screw from the mirror arm (photo 7.12). With the shutter out, you can clean the inside of the body using a stiff brush.

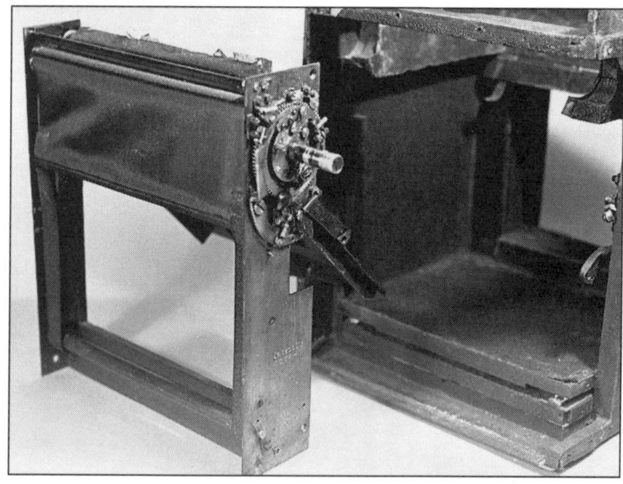

***7.12:** The shutter assembly.*

Curtain material can be obtained from specialty sources or from conventional sources. Try suppliers of industrial fabrics. Changing-bag material is also suitable.

Whatever material you use, make sure it is not thicker than .25mm, but .2mm is better for the curtain as well as for the leads. As the curtains and leads are rolled up, with thicker material, the diameter is increased proportionally and the geometry is changing accordingly.

Rubberized fabric rainware material may be used as well. In particular, the green and yellow poncho is a good source. While it's not exactly cheap, it's a good size of material that will yield many large shutter curtains. However, unless you find similar fabric in black, this will have to be dyed.

Cut out the material first: 155x210mm for the second curtain and 155x220mm for the first curtain. Use black fabric dye such as Kiwi Colors™ to dye the fabric. Pour about two inches of water into a large pot or pan. Dissolve one quarter of the dye crystals from the box (15g). Warm the liquid just below boiling temperature. Wash the fabric first, then lower it loosely into the pot. Let the dye simmer with the fabric in it for about an hour.

Using large tweezers or tongues, occasionally turn the fabric over in the liquid. The fabric side will turn a rich black, while the rubber side will turn dark green. The rubber side is turned inward in the camera, and is not visible.

Spread the fabric on a smooth counter top and brush both sides down thoroughly with a nail brush and clean water.

Once clean, spread it with the rubber-side down. Blot off the fabric side with paper towels. Let is dry for at least two hours before peeling it off the counter. Wash the pot well before using it for cooking.

Transfer the metal brace from the old curtain to the new one. Using a right angle, draw a line on the rubberized side of the fabric 9mm from the edge, perpendicular to the sides of the curtain. Smear contact cement onto the rubber 18mm wide. (The line will be at the center of the glue strip.) Place the stiffener one side against the line. Fold the overhanging strip over the stiffener. Press down the material. Do the same to the other curtain.

Use 5/16" (8mm) wide twill tape for the lead ribbons. If you can't find suitable tape you can cut out the ribbons from the material the curtains are made of. When cutting long, narrow strips, use adhesive tape to stick the ends of the strip to the table surface while cutting it. The lead ribbons for the second curtain are 420mm long, and for the first curtain they are 245mm. Make sure the lead ribbons are exactly the same length on either side. Glue the leads onto the back side of the second curtain (i.e. the side facing toward the back of the camera). There is no need to stitch; use contact cement by itself.

The original curtains are fed into slots in the active shafts, but don't worry about that, just cut off the old curtains and glue on the new ones ignoring the slots. Otherwise, you would have to remove the shafts. (With the shutter assembly still in the body, the first curtain active shaft is accessible through the top of the camera under the focusing glass.)

Install the second curtain first (diagram 7.13). Let off the shutter gears. Using contact cement, glue the upper edge of the curtain onto the active shaft drum such that the curtain's edge hangs down just 5mm from the bottom plate of the camera.

Make sure the curtain sits straight. Now cock the shutter all the way to "time." (This is called "B" today.) Don't overwind it. The winding stop is in the side cover we removed earlier (see below).

With the shutter cocked all the way to "time," the lead ribbons should touch the table surface; that is, they should be level with the bottom of the camera. Glue the excess length of the leads onto the upper take-up drum (photo 7.14).

Now release the shutter again and wind up the spring inside the take-up drum. To do so, remove the retaining pin from the end of the shaft. Bend a piano wire to an L-shape. Hold the longer stem of the L in a pin vise to be able to wind the spring with. Insert the short end of the L-wire into the hole in the shaft (photo 7.15).

Wind up the spring 15 turns counter-clockwise, and insert the retaining pin. Now cock the shutter all the way to "time" and release it. See

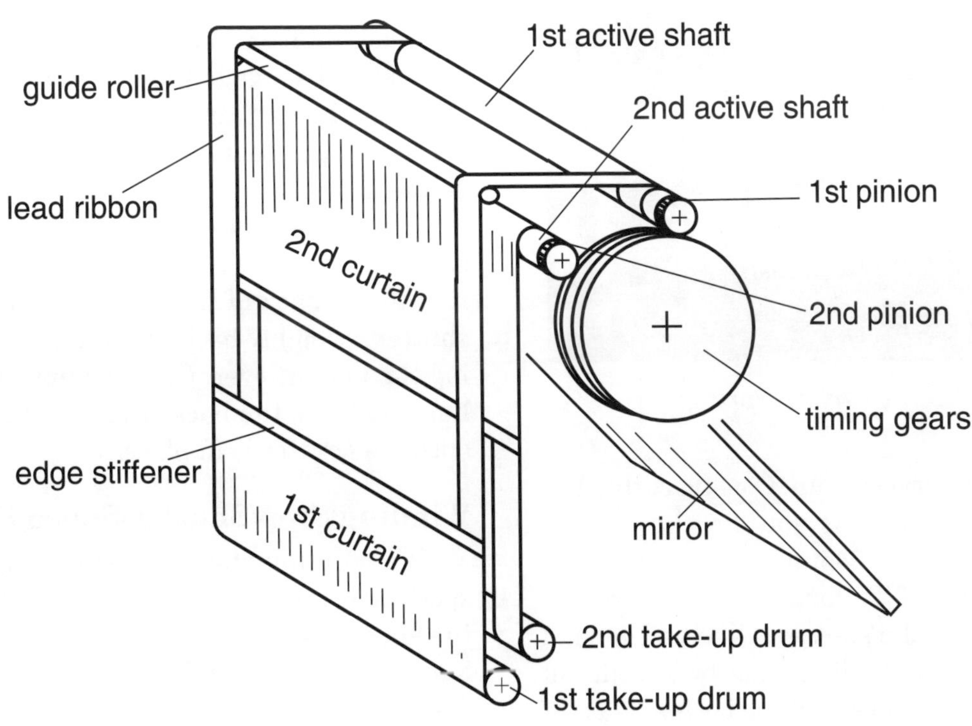


***7.13:** T-P shutter curtains.*

if the second curtain runs off smoothly and that the "B" action is operating.

Study the mechanism to see how the parts behave. Moderate play in the bushings caused by wear may be ignored.

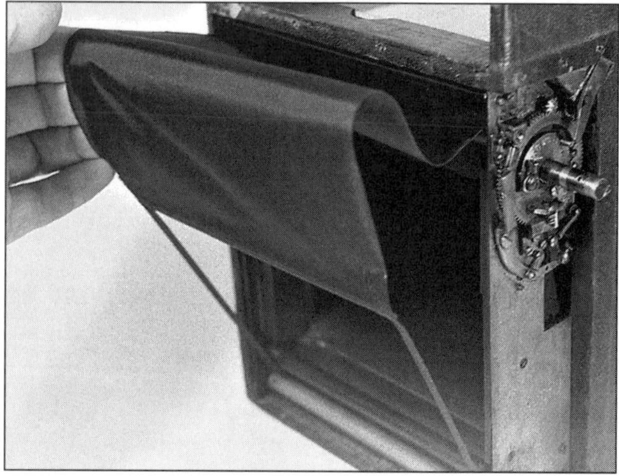

*7.14: The second curtain installed.*

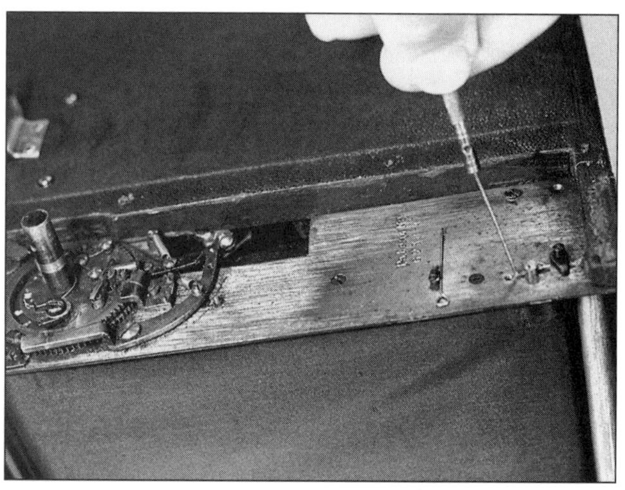

*7.15: Winding up the curtain spring.*

Installing the first curtain: Construct the first curtain the same way as you did the second. However, the leads are 245mm long and they are glued to the inside of the curtain (the forward facing side). Release the shutter. Glue on the lead ribbons to the active shaft so that the top edge of the curtain falls 14mm shy of the bottom plate of the camera.

While the shutter is being cocked, the overlap between the shutter curtains should be about 6mm. With the shutter fully cocked, the first curtain must not curl over the guide roller at the top.

Now cock the shutter and glue the lower edge of the first curtain onto the lower take-up drum. With the shutter released and using the L-wire as above, wind up the take-up spring 12 turns counter-clockwise. Insert the retaining pin all the way and clamp it down.

Expose the shutter at 1/1000 second while looking through the shutter. (See Abstract for checking shutter speeds.) If capping occurs, give the latter shaft a few more turns. If the shutter is still in the camera, winding up the first curtain tension is more difficult.

If the dimensions don't come out as described, you can either peel off and reglue the curtain on the active shafts, or you can reposition the shutter gears. Release the curtains first. To reposition the first curtain, remove the upper two retaining brackets from over the timing gears. Force the top timing gear away from the body to disengage the pinion at the end of the active shaft. Turn the active shafts to yield the position described above, then mesh the timing gear with the pinion.

For the second curtain position, just remove the bushing from the end of the active shaft to be able to disengage the pinion gear. (Warning: If either the curtain or the lead material is too thick, it might be impossible to achieve the proper geometry.)

Cut out the shape of the light baffle from the same material you used for the curtains, and glue it onto the back of the mirror. Start fitting the shutter assembly back into the body by connecting the mirror lever. Glue the upper edge of the light baffle to the back frame of the viewfinder once the shutter is in place.

### Winding Stop/Shutter-Speed Selector

The winding stop is located in the shutter-speed selector. It is adjustable in order to preset the shutter speeds. Release the lock at the bottom of the selector, and turn the stop just past the desired shutter speed. If this part doesn't work, disassemble the dial (5 screws). Clean up and straighten the dials and the locking stud. The locking stud may be corroded and frozen solid.

Flood it with lighter fluid, and slide it up and down repeatedly. Blow it out then repeat the procedure until the locking stud is free to move. Then lubricate it with moly grease (photo 7.16).

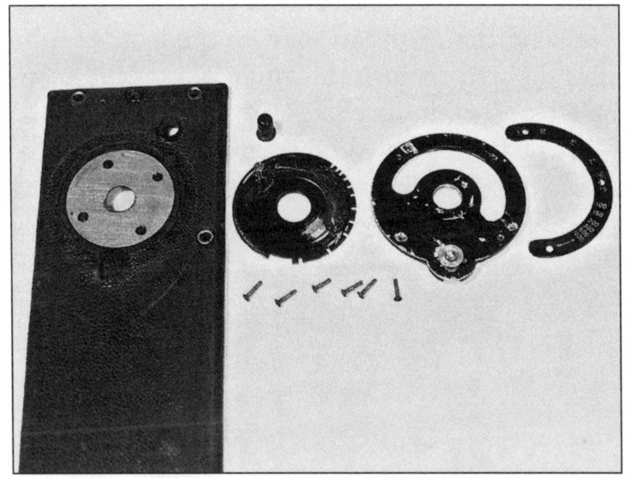

***7.16:*** *Parts of the shutter-speed selector.*

Substituting the vertical movement knob: The knob fits over the square end of the pinion shaft and is secured by a special nut. Diagram 7.17 depicts the original arrangement. Since some of

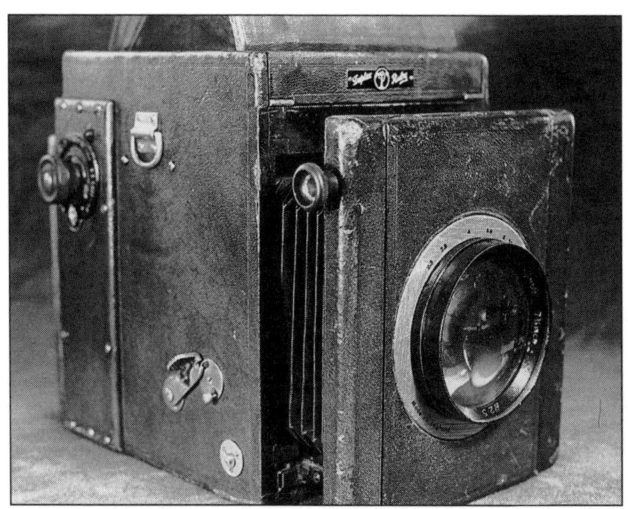

***7.18:*** *Finished knob.*

the knobs on this camera are made of brown plastic, a plastic radio knob will make a suitable substitute. The old-fashioned types are better as they usually have a neck but no pointer. The modern conical shape would be out of place on the Ruby Reflex. If you can't find such a knob in your junk box, your local radio/TV shop or antique radio club is sure to help. Find a knob that fits over a 1/4"

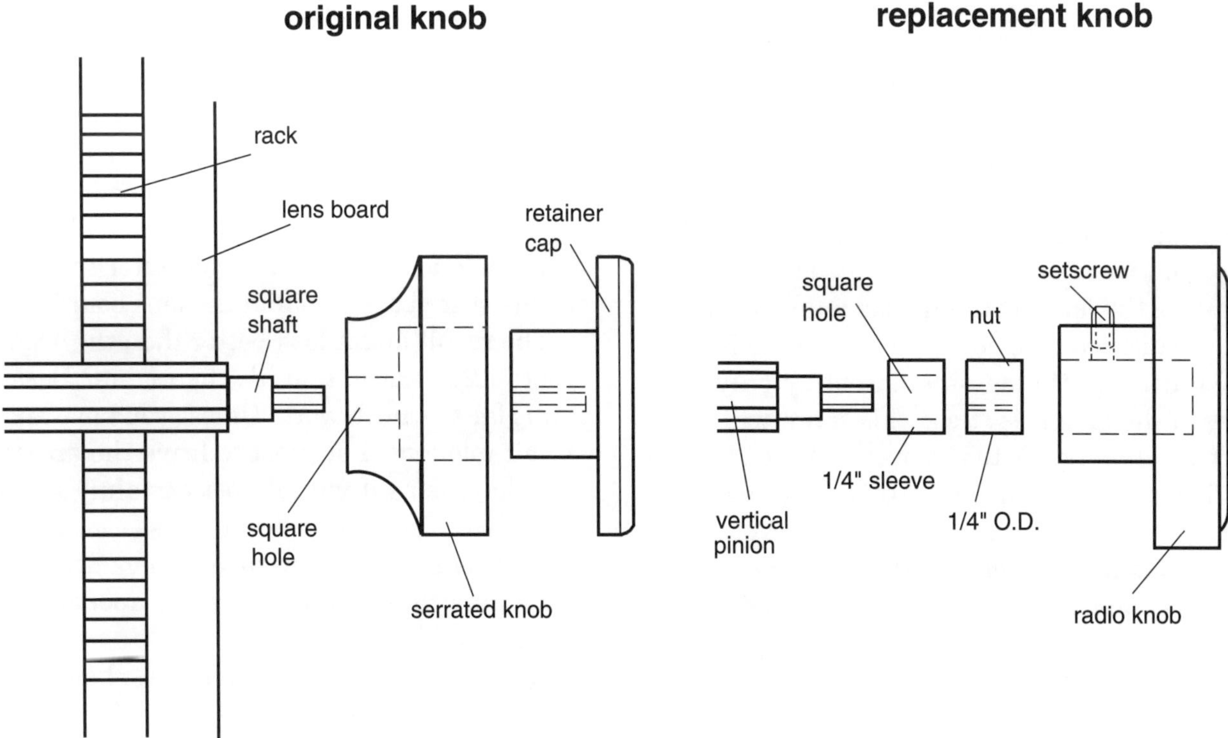


***7.17*** *Table construction.*

shaft and is secured with a setscrew. Diagram 7.17 also depicts the way the radio knob can be fitted over the square end of the pinion shaft. Fit the adapter stump and the nut onto the shaft first; leave the knob for last (photo 7.18). Chapter Six has further suggestions.

## Taylor-Hobson Cooke Anastigmat 7 3/4", f/2.5

The lens should normally unscrew from its mount. The problem is both the lens-mounting ring and the lens barrel are made of cast aluminum. In addition, the aperture barrel which incorporates the mounting threads is a paper-thin eggshell (photo 7.19).

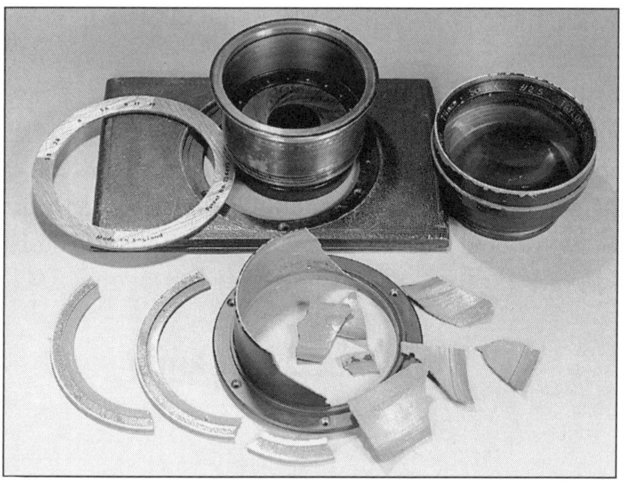

***7.19:*** *Shattered aperture barrel.*

Naked aluminum on aluminum has a tendency to cold-weld obviating any attempt at dismounting the lens. This lens has a further problem: the dismounting force exerted to the lens is transmitted to the outside barrel by only one screw. If the mount is stuck, this screw will likely break when trying to remove the lens.

When the lens is mounted, this screw is inside the camera, and it's inaccessible. However, once the screw is removed or breaks, the inside unit of the lens can be unscrewed from the outer barrel (aperture barrel).

You can overcome this dilemma by doing one of three things: 1. If the lens standard and lens are in fair condition, leave them alone. Don't attempt to remove the lens. 2. If the bellows is in poor condition, you can separate the bellows from the lens standard by soaking it in warm water. Once the bellows is off, you can get to the screw and to the lens barrel. (Chances are good that this screw is already broken.) 3. If the standard is in poor condition, you can soak off the leather from one side, and remove the guide piece that keeps the lens board in its channel.

What I did was remove the bellows to have access to the inside. I then unscrewed the lens assembly from the aperture barrel (photo 7.20).

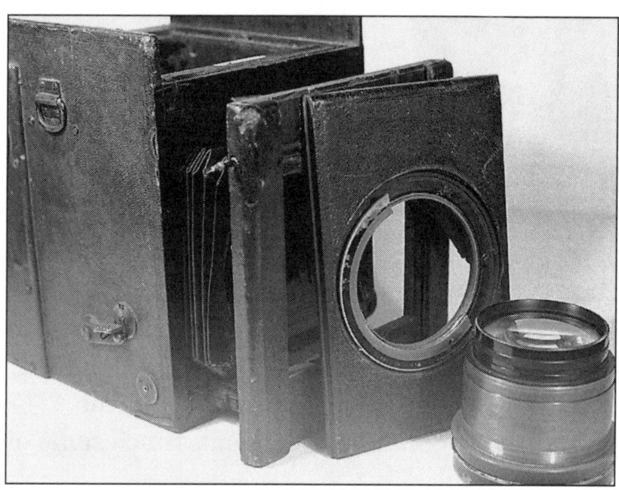

***7.20:*** *Removing a stuck lens.*

Then I broke off the aperture ring to gain access to the mounting screws. The jagged front end of the aperture ring had to be filed smooth, and a new aperture ring, out of wood, glued in place of the broken one. I also had to drill and tap a new hole for the aperture connector screw into the aperture barrel behind the lens board.

The result might look better than the original (photo 7.21), except that it's not original. Besides, it was far too much work. Unless you have another suitable lens, I suggest to leave the aperture barrel alone as it will almost certainly shatter during an attempted removal. In case you do have another lens and want to save the mounting ring, saw a longitudinal notch into the aperture barrel, and break it out of the ring.

Getting to the diaphragm blades, however, is easy. Unscrew the front lens group. Pull out the snap-ring that secures the cover plate. Shake out the plate and the blades (photo 7.22).

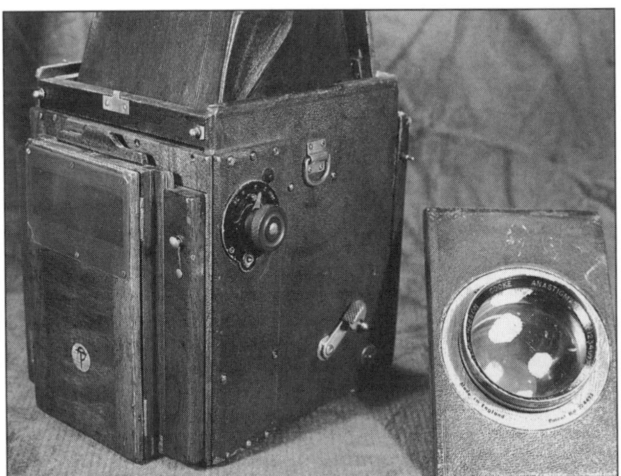

*7.21: The restored lens.*

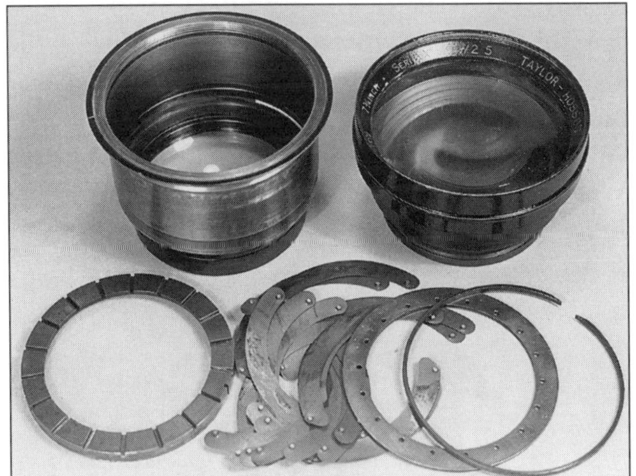

*7.22: Removing the blades.*

## Graflex Speed Graphic, Pacemaker

The Speed Graphic models are all very similar even if the formats are different. They are all equipped with the fixed-slot focal plane shutters that have been used in some of the earlier models as well. Aside from their size, early Pacemaker models are almost identical (photo 7.23). The interchangeable rangefinder cam was introduced in 1955.

The instructions below are useful for all Pacemaker models, and to a lesser extent, any other Speed Graphic model that resembles the Pacemaker.

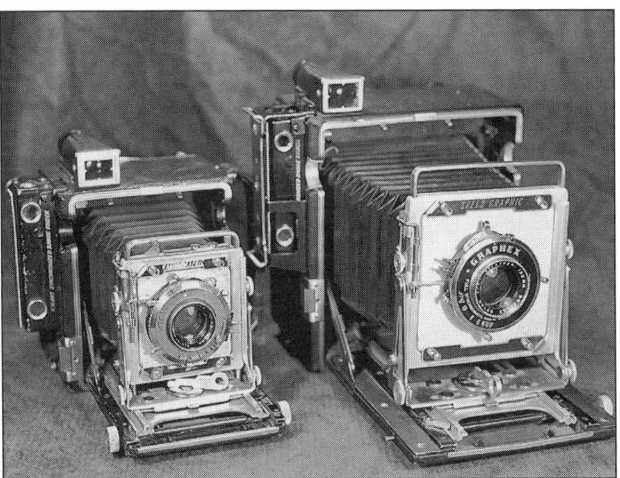


*7.23: Pacemaker format options.*

Most problems relate to the focal plane shutter, the lens shutter, or the rangefinder accuracy. The bellows is of a very good quality; it doesn't wear out or develop holes easily.

The focal-plane shutter comprises a long strip of curtain material with slots of permanent width for the various shutter speeds. Each slot is able to produce two speeds: one with the governor disengaged, and a slower speed with the governor engaged (photo 7.24).

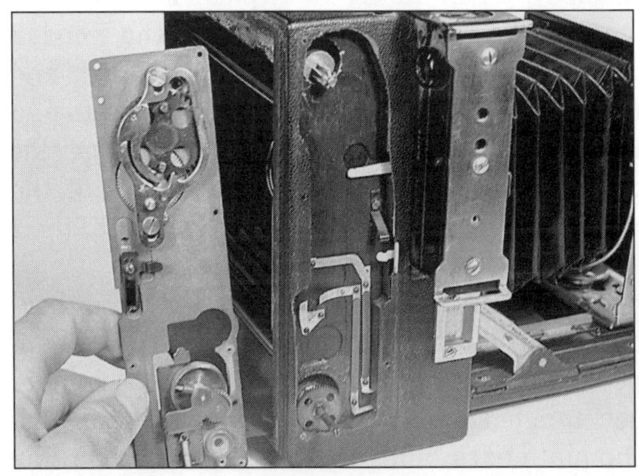

*7.24: The governor is at the lower end of the panel.*

This type of shutter never develops capping. Since the slots are permanently cut right into the fabric, they are unable to vary their width during exposure (diagram 7.25). It is possible, however, that the curtain hangs up during its run due to insufficient lubrication, lack of spring tension or

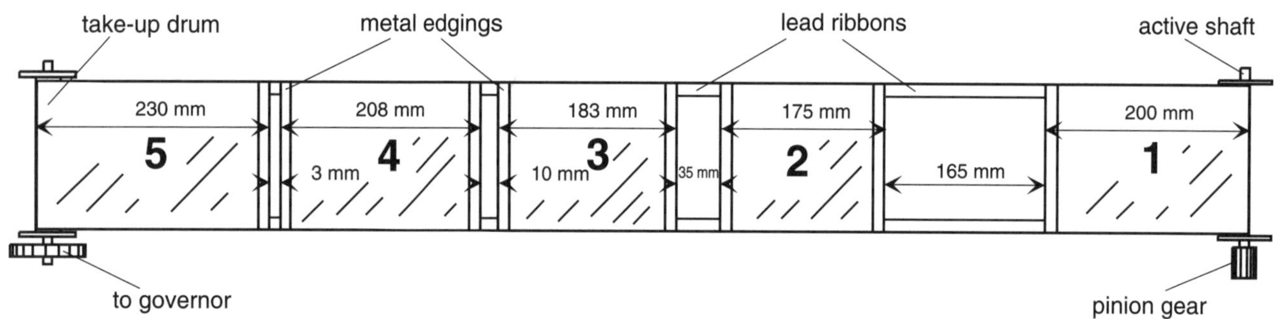


***7.25:** Graflex shutter curtain.*

obstruction in the works. Either way, proceed as follows. Remove the side panel (6 screws) and the rear frame (5 screws). See if there is sufficient tension on the take-up drums by pulling at the curtain material upward. The tension might be lost due to tampering or due to a broken or disengaged spring inside the drum.

Before removing the assembly panel, let the curtain tension down by exposing repeatedly until the shutter closes on the "T" setting. Mark the exact position of the curtain against the back of the body. When the assembly panel is removed (4 wood screws screwed directly into the wooden body), the shutter gears are disengaged, and unless the position is marked, it's difficult to find the proper mesh upon reassembly. With the side off, the shutter shafts are unsupported at the right. As a result, they tend to fall out from their bushings on the left side as well.

A brass cover plate is glued onto the body concentrically with the lower shaft. What often happens is that the glue lets go and the loose plate gets tangled up in the gears. Straighten and glue the plate back using contact cement. With this cover plate off, the lower shaft can be pulled out of the body. Pull the left-hand side of each shaft out of the bushings first. Tilt the shafts to pull the right side through the side panel. The curtain comes with the shafts (photo 7.26).

Even though the original curtain is tailored from a single piece, in order to save fabric, you can cut out the solid sections only and use twill tape to form the slots. Refer to diagram 7.25 for the measurements. If parts of the curtain are missing, the stiffening edge strip will be missing as well. Substitute the metal U-strip with a straight steel strip. Instead of the U enclosing the edge of the curtain, the curtain will be folded over and glued onto the flat steel, akin to the method we used above for the Ruby Reflex shutter. (Wooden rulers often have a steel insert in them that's suitable for this purpose.)

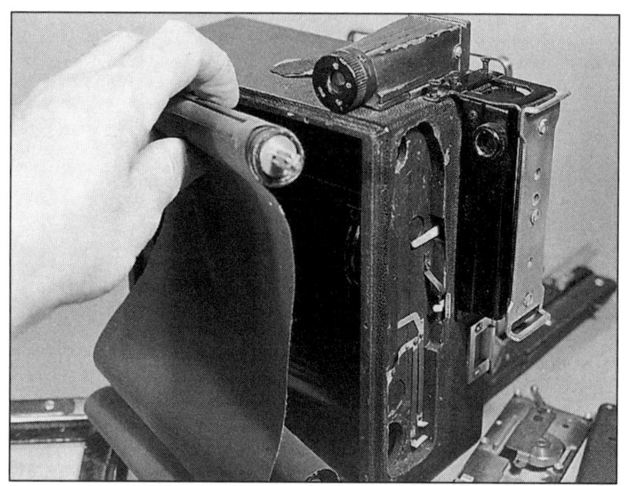

***7.26:** Removing the shafts.*

Glue the lead ribbons onto the corners of the curtain panels as well. Again, no stitching is necessary, in my experience, the contact cement itself provides a strong enough bond. The portion glued should not be longer than 10mm, as longer sections tend to retain a permanent curl and might bind up the shutter.

The original curtain is rubberized on both sides, but one-sided fabric is a suitable replacement. A changing bag provides the best curtain material, but see the Ruby Reflex above for further suggestions. Twill tape is readily available from sewing notions suppliers. If you don't find the 10mm (3/8") size that is required, cut the lead ribbon out of the shutter curtain material. Make sure, however, that neither the lead ribbon nor the curtain material is thicker than .25mm.

When ready to reassemble the focal-plane shutter, lubricate the shaft bushings with oil and the gear teeth with molybdenum or lithium paste. Lubricate the governor shaft. Clean the inside of the governor drum, but leave the drum dry.

Make sure that both the shutter speed selector and the curtain shaft are in the original position when refitting the assembly panel. If you don't know the original position, set the shutter speed selector all the way to zero. The two zeros should be centered in the window with the winding key against the upper stop.

Experiment with this while you have the side plate off. Turn the winding key around and around until the numbers come out all right. (When you're going clockwise with the winding key, you have to pull the stop away with your finger at the back of the plate.)

Let the key off one more notch to display a blank indicator window. In this position, engage the active shaft pinion, so that the lower edge of panel #1 is about 5mm shy of the lower edge of the camera frame. Check all the shutter speeds to see that the frame is fully covered when the shutter is either cocked or released.

You will have to maneuver both ends of the shafts into their bushings. Also see that the trigger mode selector falls into its proper place. Try the selector in all its three positions. ("Trip" should trip the FP shutter; "back" should route the trigger action to the FP shutter, "front" should route the same trigger action to the lens shutter.) With the curtain completely unwound, give the lower shaft fifteen full turns counterclockwise. Then secure the shaft with the setting disk and screw. The M-synch switch is at the right-hand side, behind the shutter curtain. The armature metal plate is set into the shutter curtain itself (photo 7.27).

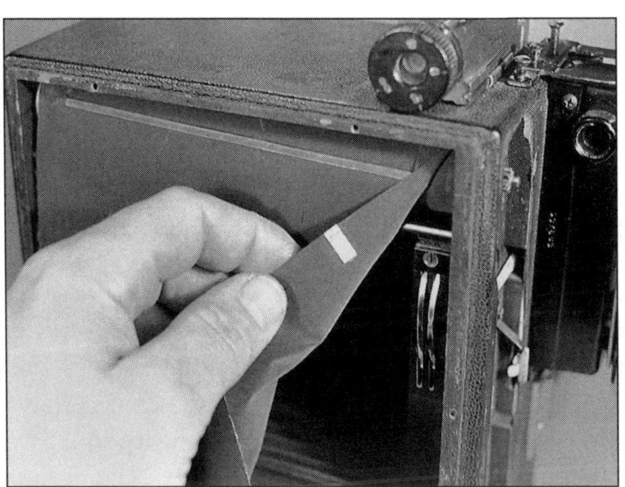

***7.27:** M-sync switch contacts.*

## The Rangefinder

Rangefinders lacking interchangeable cams are calibrated for the normal lens that comes with the camera originally. For any other focal length lenses the rangefinder is accurate at the infinity setting if the infinity stop for the particular lens has been properly calibrated. (The adjustable fold-away stops in the channel of the rail serve this purpose.) For distances other than infinity, the rangefinder will not be completely accurate.

In order to calibrate the infinity stop, roll the bed all the way back, and mount the lens in question. Move the lens standard (not the rail) until the image of a far-away object is sharp on the ground glass. Secure the stops against the base of the standard. Every lens requires its own pair of stops. It is possible to re-calibrate the rangefinder internally to any given lens, but only one lens at a time.

Models equipped with interchangeable cams come originally with one cam having three lobes for three lenses of different focal length which were initially supplied with the camera.

Be aware that each lobe on a given cam is made for one and only one lens and is stamped with the serial number of the lens. If different lenses are used, albeit the same focal length, the range finder will not necessarily be accurate along its whole range.

For additional lenses, different cams must be used that were made for the lens in question. It is also possible to make and calibrate a cam for any given lens.

You will find many old Graflexes with the stops misadjusted, the cams filed, the infinity marker out of position, new numbers and lines scratched into the distance scale, and so forth.

The rangefinder itself, while quite simple optically, is precisely and solidly made. The mechanism is sophisticated and precisely adjustable. The cover comes off easily and must be removed for any adjustment inside the unit. Just remove the flash bracket (three screws on top and two inside the camera). Two more screws secure the cover to the body (photo 7.28).

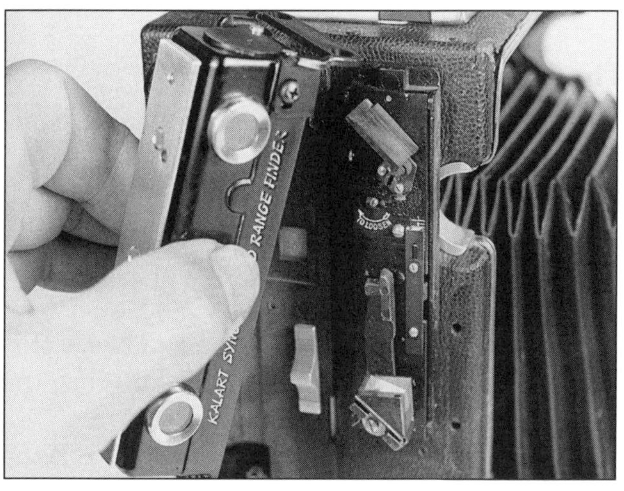


***7.28:** Removing the rangefinder cover.*

In side-mounted units, basic adjustment (photo 7.29) can be performed in the vertical direction by the screw left of the prism pivot in the prism base or by the set screw in the middle front of the unit. Horizontal adjustment is possible by the long screw next to the two-way mirror.

The sliding cams that move against numbered scales under and on top of the base plate are for linear adjustment. With those, the rangefinder can be calibrated for any lens. The rear scale is numbered from 1 to 19. The numbers are relative; they do not represent anything physical.

However, for a longer focal-length lens or to spread the distance scale, higher numbers should be used. For shorter focal length or to compress the distance scale, lower numbers should be used, i.e. the sliding cam should be loosened by the screw so labeled and the pointer brought to the desired number.

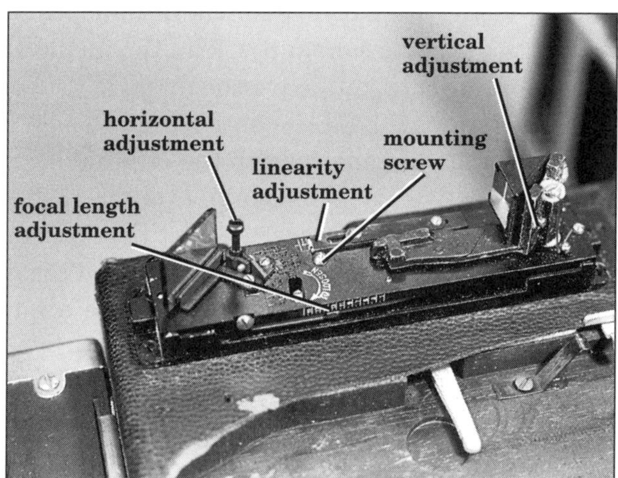


***7.29:** Adjustment points.*

The forward slider cam is adjustable against a scale numbered from 1 to 9. Larger numbers on this scale spread the distance scale at the infinity end, and at the same time, compress the scale at the close focus end. Smaller numbers on the scale have the opposite effect.

After any linear adjustment, the basic settings must be readjusted as well. In order to bring lineation into accord with a given lens, a ground glass focusing screen and an infinite amount of patience is required.

The complete optical unit is held by only one screw just behind the front slider cam.

# Chapter Eight

# Medium Format (120 and 127)

## Ensign-Cupid

Short of a pin hole, this made-in-England model is as simple as a camera can possibly get. Despite its simplicity, restoring this little toy might present a challenge (photo 8.1).

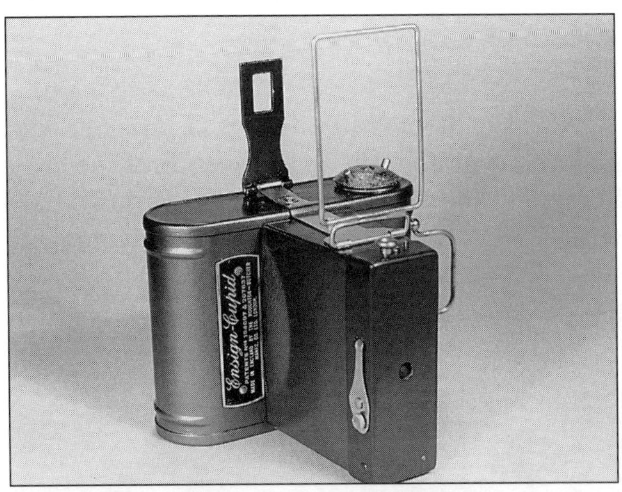


*8.1: Ensign-Cupid.*

### What You will Learn

You will learn to: remove riveted parts; restore a metal body; refinish in wrinkle-paint; make number windows and sports finder frames, and restore plaques.

### Assessment

The body is banged up, and must be straightened. The steel parts are rusty, and the camera has been "restored" with black paint applied with a paintbrush.

Even though most of the fittings are riveted on, we must remove them to be able to do the restoration properly. You can try to push out the rivets from the inside with the corner of a strong screwdriver, or reach under the plate the rivet secures with a screwdriver, and lift up the rivet head. Some will pop out easily, and some may break. Sharpen the screwdriver or the tool you're using and force it under the rivet head so it will lift the head and not only the plate that the rivet secures. Get under the rivet from as many sides as possible. You might have to hammer the end of the prying tool as well.

**Danger:** When prying with a screwdriver, sharpened or otherwise, make sure your fingers are not in front of it. Place the camera on the bench. Pry downward, toward the bench, and not toward your hand or body.

The film winding knob should unscrew from the spindle counter-clockwise. If it's rusted on, support the inside tip of the spindle on an anvil or corner of a vise, and tap the top of the knob with a medium-size hammer to loosen the rust. Penetrating oil doesn't work by itself, but it might do some good in conjunction with repeated tapping.

The shutter frame at the front of the camera is secured with three screws. Remove the screws, and pull off the frame. All the mechanism is inside this front cover. The lens board is a fairly thick aluminum plate. Mine was glued in and had to be carved out, but this piece was originally secured by screws. Once the shutter frame is removed, the lens board should fall out or can be pushed out backwards toward the film chamber.

Pull out the pivoting handle from the lugs. In order to pry out the red number windows, reach under the flare inside the back cover and push them out from the inside. If the windows are missing or cracked, you can make new ones employing the method described in Chapter Five. Since you're using the back cover for a mold, form the windows now, before painting the cover. Leave on the following parts: the film advance spindle, the leaf springs inside the film chamber, the handle lugs, and the "A" and "B" studs next to the number windows.

### Disassembling the Shutter

Pop off the pivot rivet from the "T-I" lever. The release button is riveted onto the copper latch inside and must be knocked out as well in order to separate the "T-I" lever, but leave the copper latch attached to the frame. To remove the shutter blades, unscrew the brass pivot that also supports the spring. Unscrew the shutter cocking knob from its shaft on top of the unit. Pull out the blades (photo 8.2).

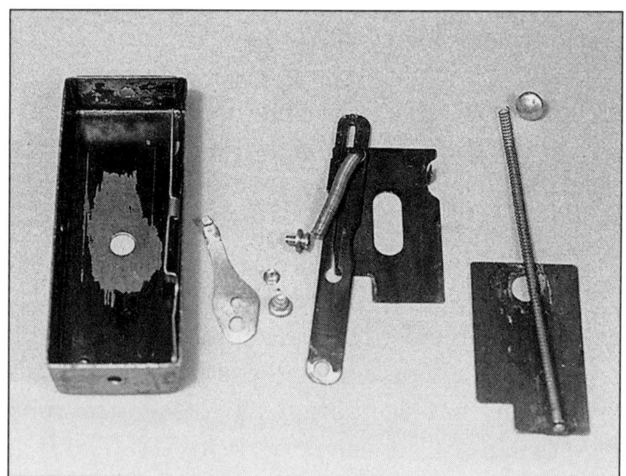

*8.2: Parts of the shutter.*

Under the parts we removed, the original color is still intact. It's a nice, dark, bluish-green wrinkle finish.

With the camera stripped of its fittings, knock out the dents in the body. Support the body from the inside with a heavy square stock. Hammer the metal around the dent from the outside (photo 8.3). The body is formed from a flimsy brass plate. Some portions of it can be straightened by hand. The back cover and the front frame are steel, much stronger than the body.

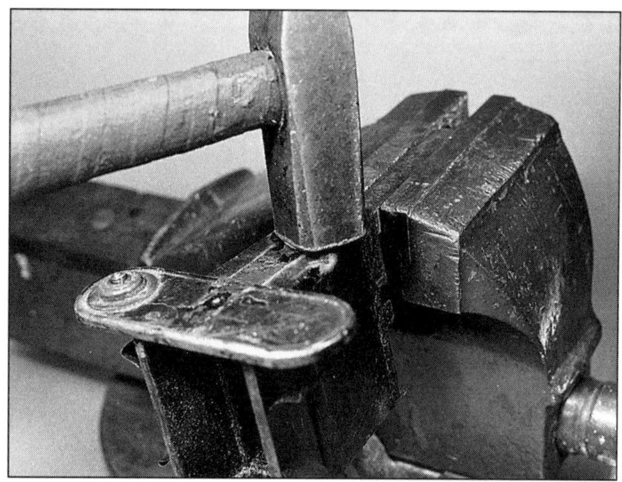

***8.3:** Knock out the dents.*

With the fittings off (photo 8.4), brush-on varnish remover liberally to the outside of the body. Scrape off the paint, and then rub it down hard with SOS™. Sand off rust from the steel parts.

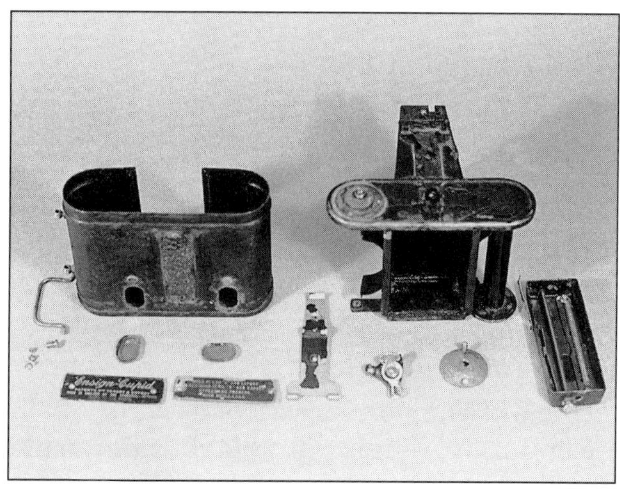

***8.4:** The fittings removed.*

The advantage of paint is that the body can be prepared with putty and primer just like the body of a damaged car. Since it doesn't shrink, two-component body filler (from automotive accessory suppliers) is most suitable for larger dents. Mix small amounts and apply it fast. Plastic body filler cures in minutes. For small imperfections and scratches, use automotive spot putty, applied with a spatula or knife. Let each application dry for a day. Cut the hardened putty back with #320 wet and dry paper.

Prepare the body, the shutter frame, and the back cover similarly. Putty must be primed as a final step; otherwise, the porous surface will show through the finish. Once all dents and imperfections are filled and sanded smooth, brush or spray primer onto the whole camera body.

Use a brush with soft natural bristles. If you opt for spraying, do it outside and use a face mask. Let the primer dry again for two days. Smooth it down with #400 wet and dry paper. The surface must be completely smooth to the touch and to the eye.

Before spraying the finishing coat, mask the handle lugs, the inside of the shutter frame, and the parts of the body that are inside the film chamber. Use masking tape, and do a precise job.

Since the Cupid came in many different colors originally, you have a choice. Use the original color if you can find it (in my case green-blue). You may, however, use any of the original optional colors (black, blue, gray, green). Note that while the body and the back cover are of the same color, the shutter frame has a glossy and darker finish. If you want to stay true to the original, you would have to use glossy dark blue, and not the wrinkle you're using on the body. If you want to "improve" on the original color scheme, you could use any paint that strikes your fancy (marble, metallic, hammer finish, etc.). Make sure, however, that the top coat is compatible with the primer. Lacquer, for instance, will lift any enamel, but enamel or acrylic are benign, as they can go over any other type of paint.

Wrinkle finish or other sprayables are available from home improvement stores or fancy paint stores. You might have to phone around, as wrinkle finish seems to be out of favour these days. Apply one thin coat only. Make sure the paint doesn't pile up or run. The resultant wrinkle is more pronounced when the paint is thicker and less so (might come out smooth) when the coat is very thin.

Experiment first on scrap metal pieces. The spray nozzle of wrinkle finishes tends to clog up more readily than normal. Buy the smallest can, and save up work for a one-time application.

Chances are good that next time you want to use it, the spray can won't work. It's good to be familiar with wrinkle finishes because this particular top coat is frequently found on other vintages and models.

## Restoring the Plaques

Straighten the plaques perfectly. Touch up the black background with black paint, or strip and spray to make it perfect. (Instead of black, you could use the same glossy color for background you're using on the front frame.)

Once the background paint is thoroughly dry (two days for lacquer or acrylic, one week for straight enamel), sand the paint off from the embossed frame and lettering with #600 paper. Glue the sandpaper onto a plastic or wood backing. Carefully sand the top of the letters without touching the background.

If the background is damaged, you can touch it up afterwards. Spray or paint clear varnish onto the face of the plaque to protect it from damage and corrosion.

## Constructing Finder Frames

One big problem, in my case, is that the sports finder is missing. The two frames comprising the viewer are just snapped under the spring retainer on top of the camera and are easily lost. Yours might also be missing. Strive for perfection when fashioning these highly visible parts. Unless these pieces look factory made, they will detract from the appearance and value of the camera, rather than add to it.

The viewing area of the front frame measures 50x32mm and is elevated from the top of the camera by 9mm. Form this frame from 1.5mm or 1/16" brass rod or galvanized wire stock. Form two rectangles: one is 50x32mm on the inside; the other is 25x4mm on the inside. Solder the two together as shown on diagram 8.5 so that the butted ends of the rectangles are adjacent to each other. The lower side of the small rectangle falls under the retaining spring.

If you're satisfied with the color of the wire, rub the frame down with SOS™ and leave it natural. Otherwise, you can paint it the same glossy color as the front cover.

The rear frame or eyepiece should be formed from a 1mm or 1/32" flat aluminum plate. The aperture is 8x12mm and the bottom edge of it is elevated from the top of the camera by 26mm. Leave longer fingers at the bottom of the plate to fold it over the hinge pin (diagram 8.5). Fold the fingers over a 1/16" round and 17mm long pin.

Again, unless you're satisfied with the natural color, paint the eyepiece a glossy dark blue or the color of the front frame (see photo 8.1). If you leave both parts natural, they must be of the same color. It is also permissible to leave the front frame a natural color, but you should paint the eyepiece.

If the original number windows are still good, clean them with tooth paste and soft tissue paper. Carefully pop them back into the oval cutouts from the inside. The ones you made have to be glued inside the back cover with the convex side facing outward.

## Putting it Together

Refitting the original rivets is quite difficult. To begin with, file off or compress the flairs on the rivet shafts. After fitting them into their holes, the rivets must be spread again.

The instruction-plaque at the back of the cover is the easiest to remount as the inside of the back is accessible. The "T-I" lever and the release knob can also be rerivetted with little difficulty. Albeit, the punch must be held at an angle.

Using a loupe helps. Substitute screws for the rivets when mounting the viewer retaining spring on the top and the cover latch parts at the bottom. If you use self-tapping screws, you save the extra step of tapping the hole.

For mounting the bottom latch, drill up the pivot hole for a 3mm screw and the other for a 2mm screw. Place a nut on both screws inside. Smear a little Locktight™ on the pivot screw and

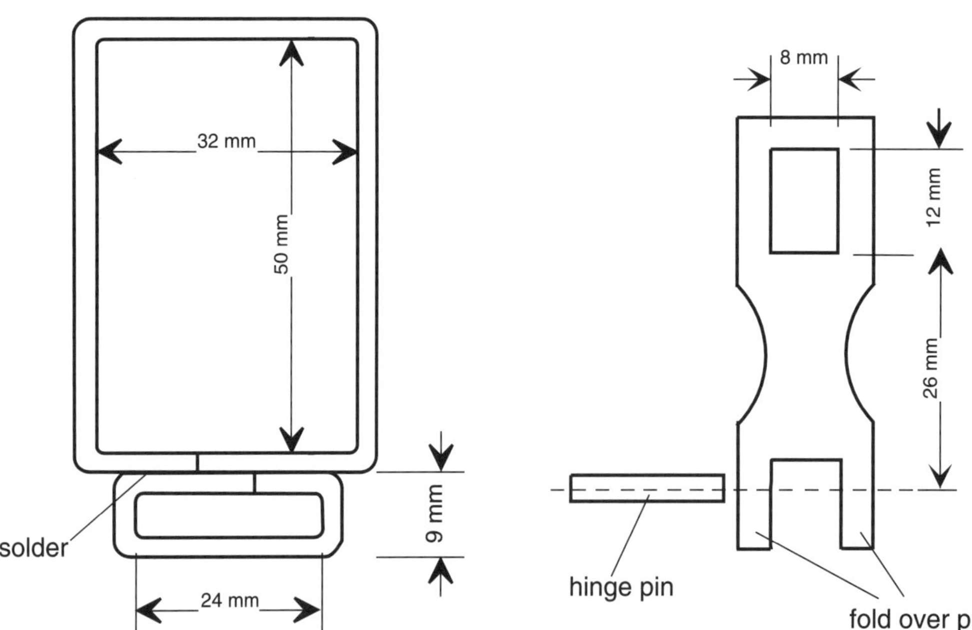


*8.5: Sports Finder frames.*

tighten the nut sufficiently to make the latch secure but still able to rotate. With the brand-name plaque you have a choice. Glue it on along with its rivets, or use screws here as well. If you must use screws with phillips slots, plug up the slots as to make them invisible.

## Kodak Premoette Jr. No. 1, 1913 U.S.A.

This is a simple little camera with a leather-covered aluminum body. Lacking supporting rails, the lens standard hangs loosely on the bellows until plugged into a slot at the front of the bed. Two slots are provided: one for close focus, and the other for far focus (photo 8.6).

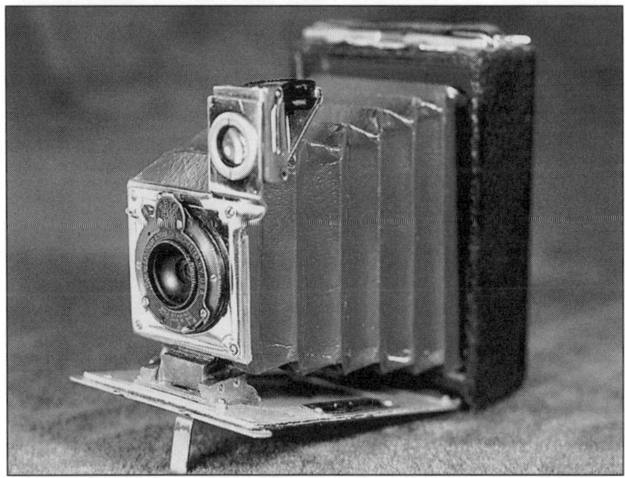

***8.6:** Kodak Premoette restored.*

### What You will Learn

You will learn: another good exercise for restoring the bellows and the leather on the body; regular cleaning and scrubbing required to bring this specimen up to showroom condition.

### Assessment

The body leather is dried-out, cracked, and flaking. The bellows is in poor shape. The aluminum body is dented. The whole camera is filthy.

The original leather is not only preferable to a replacement, but it is easier to reglue than tailoring new leather pieces. Therefore, be careful not to do more damage to the leather than already exists. Save all broken or flaking leather pieces, even the tiniest little bit.

In order to free the bellows, reach in from the rear, and remove the four screws that secure the lens. The lens assembly should fall out unless traces of glue holds it. Next, remove the four screws from the front of the lens frame.

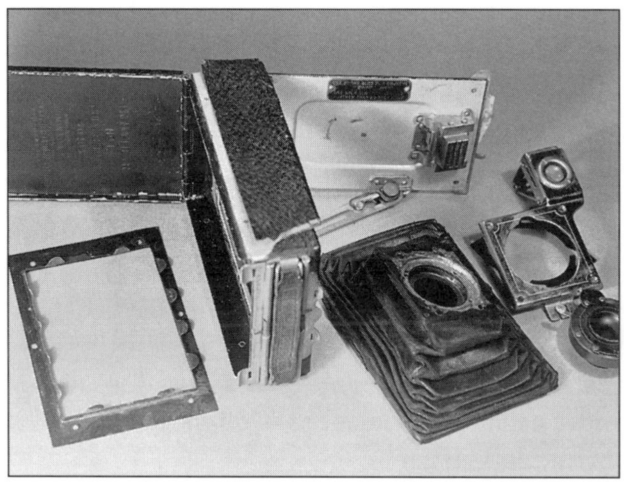

***8.7:** Pull the bellows.*

With the special pliers you made earlier (see photos 5.12 and 5.13), fold up the tabs inside the film gate to free the rear skirt of the bellows. Reaching the tabs inside the smaller film gate is trickier than with larger cameras. Once the frame is out, remove the six screws that secure the bellows. Spread the sides of the body in order to let the bellows through, otherwise the sharp edge of the body box may damage the bellows (photo 8.7).

You can straighten the sides again after the restored bellows is installed. With the lens and bellows out of the body, a thorough scrubbing can be performed without further disassembly. Use Fantastic™ and a toothbrush on the body. Use SOS™ on the fittings. Rinse everything thoroughly under running water. Do all this as fast as you can. You don't want the leather to soak up too much water.

As soon as the rinsing is done, blot off all water inside and out with paper towels. Blow the water from under the fittings. Do not use a hair drier to hasten the drying process, remember that genuine leather may shrink or crack from high temperatures.

### Restoring the Leather Cover

Feed white glue under the peeling edges and hold the leather down with your finger for at least a couple of minutes. If the leather is under tension (such as bent over the edge of the body) you will have to hold it longer before the glue sets reliably. If sections of the leather have fallen off, but you saved the pieces, soak them in cold water for a few minutes. Scrub the old glue off. Blot them dry between sheets of paper towel. Let the leather pieces dry for an hour. Glue them on using white glue before they become bone dry.

Be careful to fit the torn edges precisely. Glue on all of the pieces you saved. If sections are still missing, cut out the missing shapes from the same kind of leather and glue them on as before. White glue is preferred because, once set, it does not give the way contact cement does when under constant tension, as is often the case with shrinking leather.

If holding down the leather with your hands while the glue sets doesn't appeal to you, place a piece of urethane sponge over the glued piece. Place plywood over the sponge, and tie the whole sandwich down with string or rubber bands. Let it set overnight.

Once the glue has all set and the leather stabilized, you might find that cracks in the leather have opened wider or that small pieces are still missing. The best material to use for filling-in cracks is vinyl restoring paste (see Chapter Two). Pick or mix the right color of paste. (In this case black.) Apply it with a small spatula. (One may be included with the kit.) Do a precise job of filling in the cracks. On larger repaired areas, you can apply a suitable graining paper over the vinyl paste as per instructions in the kit (i.e. press the paper into the freshly applied vinyl paste), and let the paste dry before peeling off the paper. An assortment of graining paper sheets is supplied with the vinyl repair kit. Each sheet has a different grain pattern. Find and use the one that closely resembles the original grain.

Use black enamel or acrylic to retouch portions of the aluminum body where the paint chipped off. If the leather is frayed or the color is uneven, apply shoe polish carefully to the leather only, and buff it up with a soft brush. If polish gets onto the fittings, clean them with lighter fluid and tissue.

### Restoring the Bellows

Depending on the age and condition of the bellows, there could be several possibilities open to you for restoring it. In Chapter Two, several methods are discussed in detail to cover just about any eventuality you might encounter. The sample figures under "Tapering Bellows: Designing Your Own" (page 18) can be used for the Premoette.

## Rolleicord Vb

TLR cameras under the logo of Rolleicord were produced by the Franke & Heidecke Co. between 1933 and 1970. During all that time, the Rolleicord retained its simple, straightforward construction and lack of sophisticated features. The features were lavished on its sister model, the Rolleiflex, instead.

The Vb we are going to examine here was the last model produced under the Rolleicord name (photo 8.8). Earlier models are quite similar to this, and the instructions below are useful for tackling those as well.

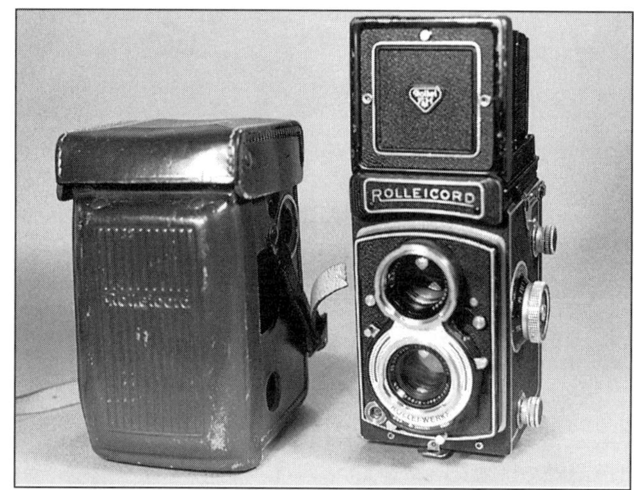


*8.8: Rolleicord Vb restored.*

The most likely malfunction you'll encounter is a sticky shutter. Other problems might occur due to impact. The aluminum cover plates are easily dented. The focusing mechanism can also wear out.

The shutter assembly is secured to the assembly plate by a retaining ring from behind. If you want to try the shutter without film in the camera, set the lever on the left front to the lower position that uncovers the red dot. This setting bypasses the double exposure prevention mechanism.

It's not necessary to pull the shutter unit in order to fix a sticky escapement. Peel off the leatherette from the front. The front cover frame has a two-piece construction on this model. Remove the PC connector locking lever first.

Be careful when unscrewing the slotted ring over the lever; the ring can be easily marred by a poorly fitting tool or unsteady hands. Remove the outer frame next. Set the shutter-speed dial to "B", the aperture to f/3.5, and the cocking lever to the release position in order for them to clear the frame. Remove the four mounting screws from the inside frame — the one comprising the filter mounts.

The control levers stay with the frame, with the exception of the shutter cocking lever at the bottom of the unit. In order to pull the shutter cocking lever through the slot in the frame: unscrew the serrated knob from the end of the lever; lift the frame over the viewing lens, and guide the cocking lever through at the bottom (photo 8.9).

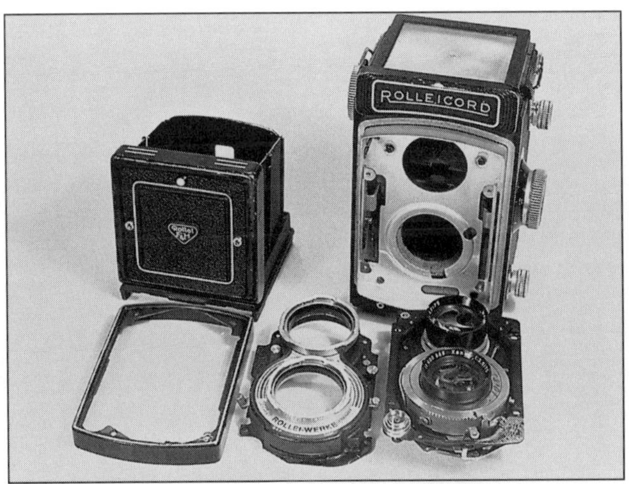


***8.9:** The front assembly removed.*

The shutter and its problems are conventional. Flood-cleaning with lighter fluid (see Abstract) is usually all that's required to bring the shutter up to like-new condition. To get inside, just unscrew the lens and the retaining ring under the lens. Lift off the rings and the shutter-speed cam (photo 8.10). If there is something wrong with the double-exposure prevention levers at the reverse side of the assembly plate, just remove the four screws in the corners of the assembly plate, plus the pivot screw at the upper right-hand corner that couples up with the parallax frame in the viewfinder. The whole front assembly comes off cleanly.

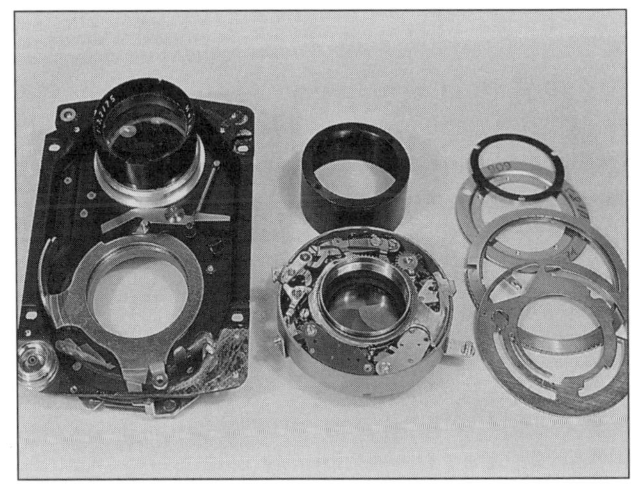

***8.10:** The shutter disassembled.*

The focusing mechanism might malfunction from wear or from frontal impact. If one or the other side is binding, before disassembling the sides, loosen up the four screws that secure the front assembly to the focusing brackets, and see if that helps. Often the binding is caused by misalignment of the brackets or misalignment of the front assembly. The oval holes in the front panel facilitate adjustment.

The film advance and the counter mechanisms are very simple. If they don't work, chances are that the side cover is dented and jams the gears or levers inside. The screws securing the panel are under the leatherette on the right hand side. The side panel is aluminum, easily dented but easy to straighten as well. The back cover is also aluminum and often needs straightening.

When refitting the inside frame over the front of the camera, position the levers properly. The shutter control levers and the self-timer lever must match up with the dials in the body.

## The Viewing Hood

The Vb has a removable soft aluminum viewing hood which can sustain dents or distortions very easily. Binding of the pop-up mechanism is usually the result of dents or distortions to the aluminum plates.

If the hood doesn't fold down or doesn't open readily, try to straighten the panels by hand. Not only the front flaps, but the side hinges as well, are spring loaded and should open automatically. Unless rusty, the hinges don't require lubrication.

If the hood doesn't open readily, it's because the panels or the hinge pins are bent, and not due to a lack of lubrication. It's easier to straighten the panels if you remove the front frame from the lid (4 screws under the leatherette) (photo 8.11).

Also pull out the horizontal hinge pin from the rear frame. Straighten the parts separately, and make sure the hinges are free to move.

If you can't straighten the panels sufficiently assembled, pull out the vertical hinge pins too, and straighten the panels by themselves before reassembly.

If it's dirty, clean the whole viewing hood inside and out with brush, liquid detergent and plenty of running water. Then blow the water off and dry the assembly with a hair drier.

With the hood off, the focusing screen is also removable. Pull the frame back, and lift it up. Now the mirror can be cleaned through this opening. The mirror is coated on its front surface. Clean it gently and only once. The mirror doesn't need periodic cleaning; it's better left alone. (See Abstract, "Optical Cleaning".)

The mirror shown in Chapter Seven is a good example of what happens to mirrors that are constantly being cleaned. You will find further instructions on how to replace mirrors in the same chapter.

A good replacement mirror for the Rolleicord can be cut out of a Polaroid mirror.

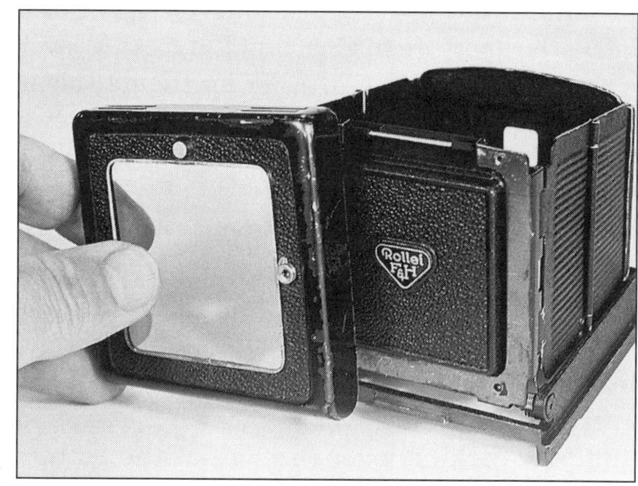


***8.11:** Removing the frame from the lid.*

Chapter Nine

# 35mm Classics

## Contax II

The instructions below apply to models II and IIa, but the Contax III models are substantially different inside. The Contax II is in a class by itself as far as the particular answer to the shutter mechanism and supporting mechanism is concerned. Partly due to the horizontal placement of the shutter shafts, this camera has one of the most complex innards among its contemporaries. Although it was built with precision, the Contax II is none too easy to work on.

Problems found in the Contax II most often relate to the shutter. You can remove the film gate from the back without having to pull the whole thing apart. This is fortunate because many shutter problems can be fixed just by removing the top and this back cover.

### Top Cover

Remove the center screw from the rewind knob. Pull the knob off, and remove the two screws from the cover under the knob. Turning to the other side, remove the three screws from the side of the winding knob. Lift off the parts. Remove the three small screws from inside of the winding knob as well as the two screws under the knob that secure the shutter-speed dial. One more screw is located in the outside front corner, under the dial.

Now lift off the chrome cover and the counter dial. Remove three more screws from the underside of the cover casting inside the film chamber (two on the rewind knob side and one on the other side). Leave the accessory shoe on. Lift off the cover casting.

If you want to get to the shutter, remove the four long screws from the corners of the film gate plate. Disengage the sprocket by pressing the rewind shaft through the hole in the bottom plate.

As you lift the back frame, the sprocket teeth must be in a favorable position for maximum clearance. It's tight. You'll have to force it a bit to get the plate off. The numerous gears at the side of the shutter belong to the slow-speed escapement (photo 9.1).

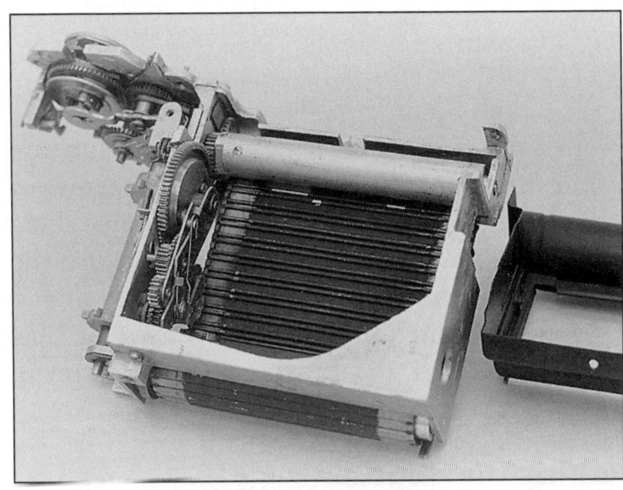

*9.1: The slow-speed escapement.*

Refit the winding knob and work the shutter. Observe the unique shutter construction. The first curtain has two spring claws at its upper margin. These claws latch onto the second curtain.

As the shutter is being cocked, the second curtain tows the first. If the latch-up between the two curtains is not complete, the shutter remains open. At the top of the frame, the spring claws ride up onto ramps on either side of the frame, releasing the second curtain.

The first curtain latches up to the top of the frame. The second curtain travels further and, according to the dial setting, opens up a wider or narrower gap between the two curtains (photo 9.2). With the back frame off, you have to help the curtains manually to couple up because, without the support of that cover plate, the first curtain swings wide, out of reach of the second.

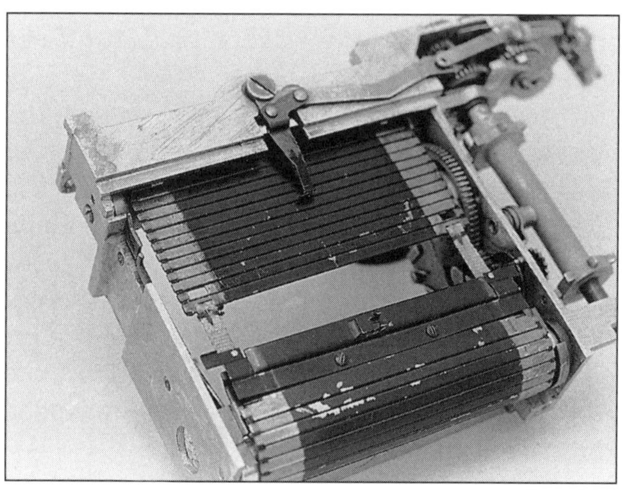

***9.2:*** *The shutter curtains.*

The latch-up function between the curtains is often faulty. The spring claws could be weak and either fail to latch up or let go prematurely. In that case, bend the springs forward to make them more secure. Even if the claws are all right, the two curtains might still fail to couple up due to a slow second curtain. The usual causes for slow curtains are dirt, dry lubricants, or low spring tension on the curtains.

## Pulling the Shutter

You can remove the complete shutter assembly from the body as follows. Remove the two screws from the steel brace on the top, just behind the rangefinder prism.

Remove one more screw up top from the front right corner and one at the bottom that secures the shutter casting. Lift the assembly a little upward and back. It comes out readily (photo 9.3).

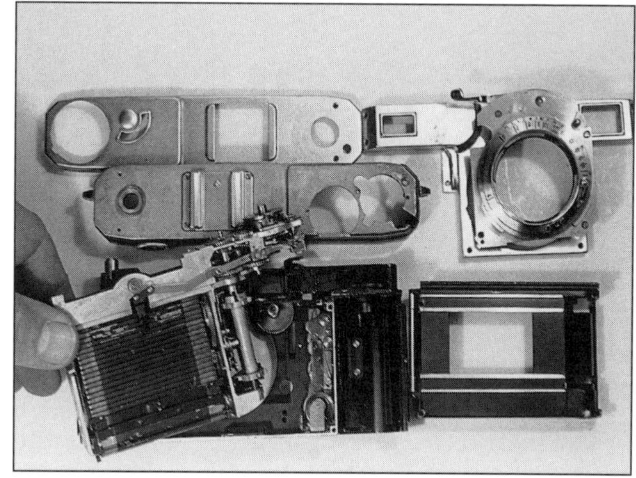

***9.3:*** *All major components removed.*

You can also remove the inside frame (light baffle) from the assembly. It's secured by two screws up top and two more at the inside bottom of the shutter casting.

With this frame removed, you can perform cleaning and lubrication more easily.

The cleaning must be done thoroughly. The original lubricant is different from what we are used to; it doesn't dissolve as readily as others. You will have to keep on flooding the gears and shafts with lighter fluid and blowing it out a number of times before all the old lubricant is gone. Only then should you flood the whole mechanism with graphite powder. (See Abstract.) In addition to the graphite, apply oil as well.

When releasing the shutter, notice which gears are rotating as the shutter runs off, and make sure to oil all of them. Cool the camera down in a fridge and try it again cold before you can call it finished.

Shutter speed adjustment is seldom required. If the mechanism works properly, and it is cleaned and lubricated, the shutter speeds should come out all right. The curtain gap is not adjustable; it's given by the mechanism.

The only thing adjustable is the curtain tension. It's located on the right-hand side of the shutter casting, just under the bottom end of the sprocket. Capping seldom occurs with this shutter because the gap is preset and the two curtains move together bound by friction through the curtain ribbons.

Before refitting the shutter assembly into the body casting, position the self-timer release lever inside. Push it toward the right and cock the self-timer to keep this lever in position. Now tilt the shutter assembly so that the right-hand side is inserted first. Lift the top up, and let the register screw fit inside its hole. If you wiggle the assembly, it will fall into place. If the assembly doesn't bottom out, but feels springy when you try to fit it in place, the self-timer lever is out of position.

## Exacta VX

While none of the models are rare or terribly expensive, being almost the first 35mm SLR (according to some experts, the Russian Sport beat the Exacta to the camera market by a few months), the Exacta is a must in any 35mm camera collection (photo 9.4).

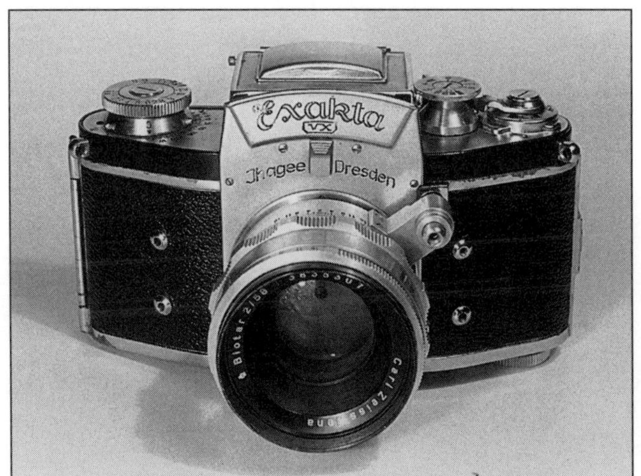


*9.4: Exacta VX*

### What You will Learn

You will learn to: replace the shutter curtain in a 35mm SLR, and perform an exterior face-lift on a metal camera.

### Assessment

Exactas are prone to dried-out and cracked shutter curtains. Many of them have been heavily used and serviced a great number of times.

The Varex (VX) models are practically identical to each other; they all have interchangeable finders, slow speeds, and a self-timer. The instructions below are applicable to all VX models, and to a lesser extent, earlier Exacta models. With the exception of the VX 1000, these models don't have an instant return mirror, but the mirror will reset during the winding stroke. The Exacta has a built-in knife for cutting the end of the film. When the film is finished, you unscrew the knob at the bottom of the camera and pull it down. The miniature sickle at the upper end of the shaft cuts the film neatly (see photo 9.5).

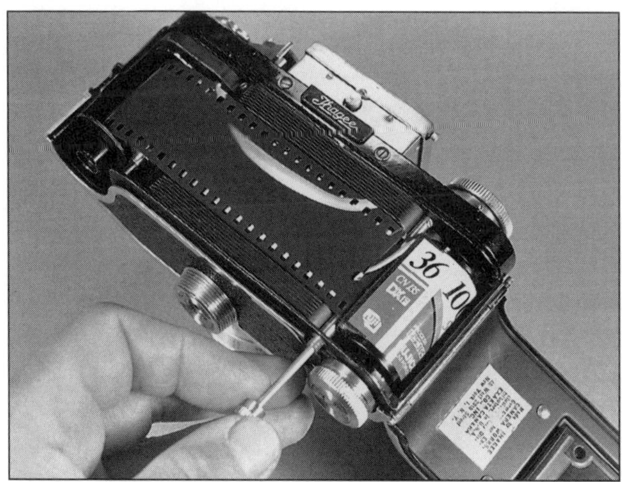

***9.5:** Cutting the end of the film.*

An exterior face lift is often required, but it's none too easy to perform. If the leather is worn, you can find a similar grain and replace the original with either leather or leatherette. You can use the original for a template, but if you're striving for perfection, you would transfer the pattern from the metal body. Cut straight lines with a sharp utility knife alongside a steel ruler (not with a scissors) to obtain the straightest possible edges.

The chrome plating tends to chip and peel from the aluminum rims. You can either find another example and combine the best parts from each into one (as we did in Chapter Five with the folding Kodaks) or restore the chrome ridges on the body. In order to do that, strip the body of leather and all the fittings, and mask the black upper rim. Go over the chrome ridges with #400 wet and dry paper dunked in oil. Follow up with #600, and finally, with crocus cloth. Buff it up with toothpaste on suede or chamois. If you do a thorough job, it will come out almost like the original chrome finish.

If the black rim must be redone, sand it smooth first with #400 paper. Mask all other areas, and spray-on fast drying acrylic enamel. Apply a fairly thick coat. Bake the piece in a stove at 325°F for at least an hour. Smooth the paint down carefully with a #600 paper. You don't want to cut right through the paint.

After rubbing it down with automotive polishing compound, apply some wax, and buff it up. While you could spray it with glossy enamel and leave it at that, the difference is noticeable. Polished paint, if properly done, looks original.

Filling in the lettering on the dials and face plate is relatively easy. Paint black or red paint over the letters. Scrape the overflow off with a cardboard spatula while the paint is still wet. Don't worry about any remaining smears. When the paint is partially dry, wipe off the smears with the flat of the cardboard spatula dampened with a drop of lighter fluid.

## Shutter

Removing the top cover plates is often sufficient to find and repair many shutter problems. Wind the crank half way to engage the ratchet; otherwise, the return spring will run off. Choose a wide blade that fits in the narrow slot. Unscrew the slotted screw and the one pin-face nut over the winding crank. Remove the shutter-speed dial and the three screws from the cover plate. (Some models have only two screws.) Lift off the plate.

The right-hand side houses the combined slow-speed/self-timer escapement. To get to it, remove the screw and the pin-face retainer, then pull off the knob. Remove the three screws from the cover plate; two in some models (photo 9.6).

Remove the bayonet mount (4 screws) and the name plate (6 screws). Remove the cover plate inside the film chamber on the upper left-hand side (2 screws). In the IIA models, the rewind button on top is loose and can be lifted off. In the VX model, knock out the hinge pin from the rewind lever, and lift off the activator metal bar. Using two screwdrivers, one from the top, one from underneath, remove the pinion gear situated between the sprocket and the winding gear. Pull out the pinion shaft; don't lose the spring. Remove the two screws that secure the assembly plate from underneath and one screw from the rewind knob side also from underneath. Two more screws secure the assembly in the upper rim, on either side of the eyepiece. Cock the shutter fully, then pull out the complete assembly (photo 9.7).

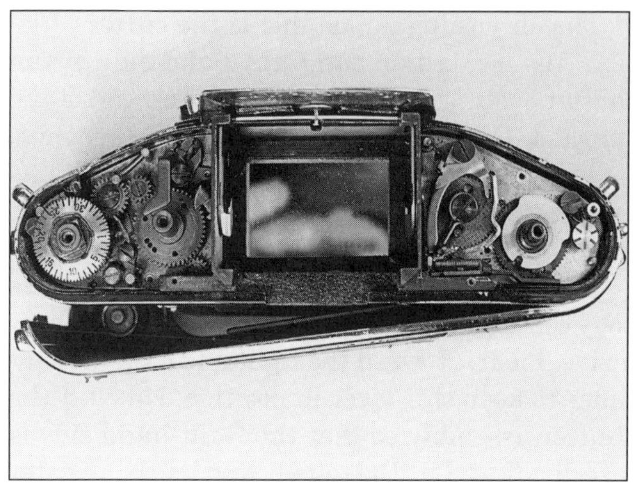

***9.6:*** *The cover plates removed.*

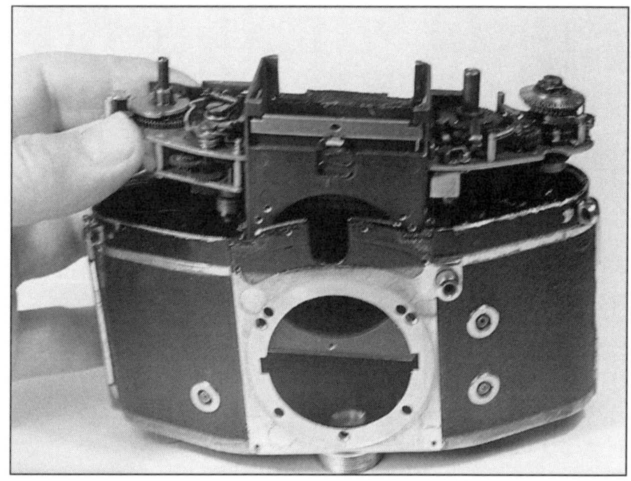

***9.7:*** *Pulling out the shutter assembly.*

The plastic base for the sync contacts tends to deteriorate and crack. Don't try to glue it together in place. Remove it first, then you can glue it together using cyanoacrylate. Since the plastic is crumbling, this repair won't be very strong, but it might last for awhile. If you want perfection, you would have to make a completely new base from fresh material.

## Replacing the Curtains

Before replacing the curtains, clean and lubricate the shutter mechanism. (See Abstract.) If you happen to have original curtain assemblies, you can replace the shafts together with the curtains. If you make the curtains yourself, leave the shafts in place and pull off only the curtains.

To unwind the active shafts, the pinion gear from the upper end of the shafts must be pulled off. Just remove the screw, then lift the gear simultaneously from two sides with curved tweezers. With the gears removed, pull off the curtains and the lead ribbons from the active shafts and take-up drum (photo 9.8). Scrape off the old glue from the drums.

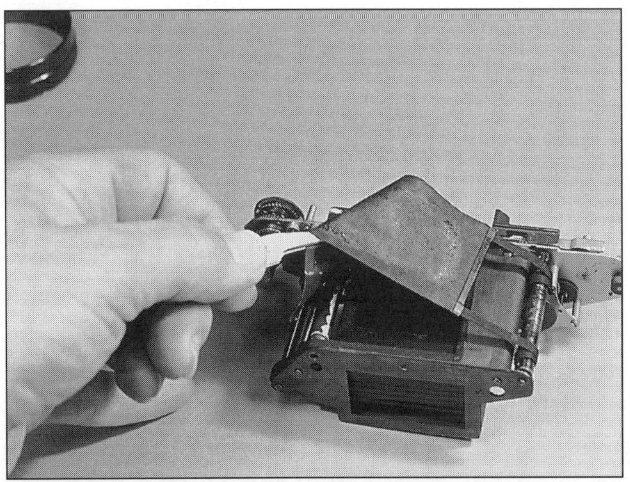

***9.8:** Pull off the old curtains.*

You can use a Pentax SP second curtain, but the first curtain needed here is much wider than the Pentax's. The best curtain material comes from a changing bag.

For the second curtain, cut out an 85x36mm rectangle from the changing bag and two 85x3.5mm strips for the lead ribbons.

Using contact cement, glue the ribbons to the corners of the rectangle overlapping not more than 7mm. There is no need to stitch or rivet the leads on as you may have seen on some curtains; the contact cement is strong enough. With the tip of a sharp knife, open up the edging metal from the original curtain to a shallow "V". Apply some contact cement into the metal "V," then transfer it to the new curtain. Thread the lead ribbons through the slots at the end of the edging strip. Tap the metal close over the new curtain with a small hammer.

Construct the first curtain the same way except that the dimensions are 47x80mm for the curtain and 3.5x115mm for the lead strips. Pull out the retaining pins from the top of the take-up shafts. With the pins out, pull both take-up drums out of the camera (photo 9.9).

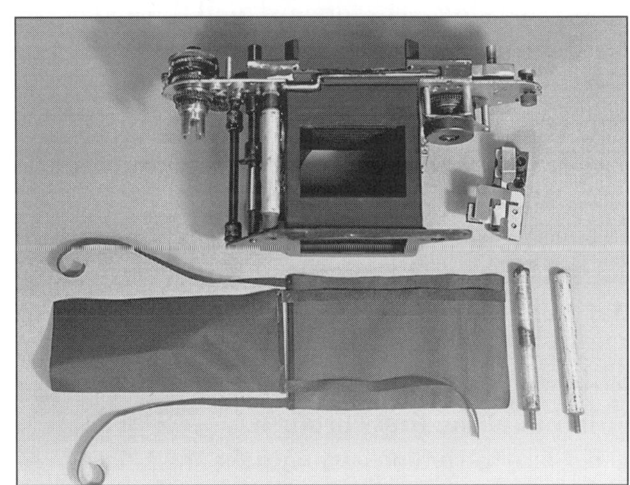

***9.9:** The take-up drums are removed.*

Install the first curtain first. The first curtain is the wider one. Use contact cement to glue about 10mm of the first curtain's edge onto the take-up drum. (The rubberized side faces forward, and the end of the shaft with the hole goes on top.) Replace the take-up shaft into the camera in the position closer to the body casting. Insert the pin into the hole in the shaft to keep it temporarily in place. Now glue the lead strips onto the active shaft (the one closer to the front of the camera).

Disconnect the winding ratchet by removing the pinion gear (the one with the ratchet pawl above it, at 2 o'clock from the winding shaft). Wind up the active shaft to the point where the curtain's edge just covers the gap between the take-up drum and the camera body (about 6mm shy of the film gate). Make sure the timing gears are in the released position, then place the pinion gear onto the top of the active shaft.

Pull out the retaining pin again and wind up the take-up spring by six full turns on the shaft. Place the pin back across the shaft. Replace the shutter-speed dial temporarily and set it to 1/25 second. Wind up the curtain by turning the dial counter-clockwise.

Double check that the curtain's edge is parallel with the short side of the film gate. With this, the first curtain is done.

Install the second curtain in a similar manner:

1. Use contact cement to glue about 10mm of the lead strips onto the other take-up drum. (The rubberized side faces forward, and the end of the shaft with the hole goes on top.)

2. Install and wind up the take-up drum: only two turns this time.

3. Glue the other end of the curtain onto the active shaft.

4. Reach under the shutter-speed dial and turn the second curtain timing gear clockwise (looking at it from the top) all the way to its stop.

5. Wind up the second curtain by rotating the active shaft, so that the metal edge strip overlaps with that of the first curtain's.

6. Place the pinion gear onto the shaft. Try it out by cocking the shutter with the shutter-speed dial.

In order to adjust the shutter speeds, the winding ratchet must be connected and the shutter-speed dial must be on. This is important since both add dynamic mass and extra friction to the first curtain system.

Pull off the ratchet wheel together with the return spring. Notice the stop stud riveted onto the top of the winding gear. With the shutter released, rotate the winding gear counter-clockwise until this stop stud is just behind the pinion gear, the one you removed earlier. Now install the winding pinion (photo 9.10).

Pull the counter claws aside while installing the winding ratchet over the winding gear. Manually wind the return spring around the ratchet hub — mind the counter claws. Now wind up the ratchet just enough to engage the ratchet claw.

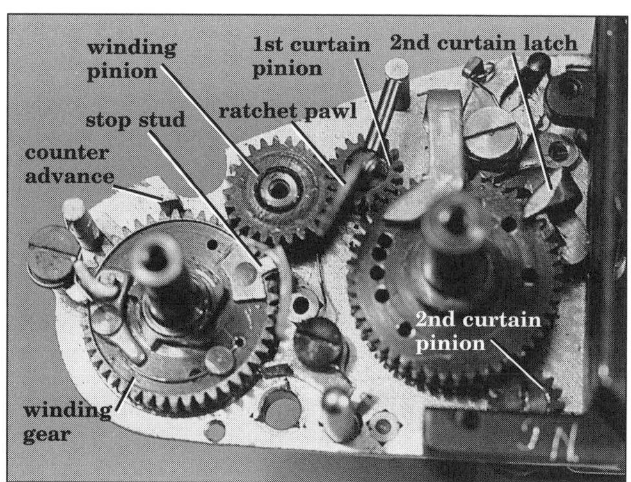


***9.10:** Install the pinion gear.*

Place the counter dial on top. If there is nothing else to fix, you can put the camera back into its housing shell. Put everything else together except the cover plate on the escapement side.

Check the shutter speeds again. However, since the curtain tension is variable in 180° steps, and other adjustment possibilities are lacking, insisting on high accuracy would be in vain.

In fact, if the shutter does not cap at 1/1000 second and all the other stops check out visually, call it good enough. If it does cap, wind the first curtain (the inside shaft) another half a turn or as many turns as required to eliminate the capping.

This is a touchy job with the retaining pin having to be pulled out for the adjustment. Insert a screwdriver into the slot in the shaft, pull out the pin, turn the shaft, then reinsert the pin.

With the unit out of its housing, the shafts tend to fall out of their bushings when the retaining pin is pulled. That's why the camera better be assembled before this adjustment is attempted. The adjustment is made easier by unhooking the coil spring over the curtain shafts.

When ready to refit the slow-speed knob, cock the shutter first, then wind up the register gear at least half a turn.

Place the self-timer cam on with the slot to the left. When placing on the knob, let the pin at the underside of it fit inside the slot in the self-timer cam as well as through one of the holes in the register gear (photo 9.11).

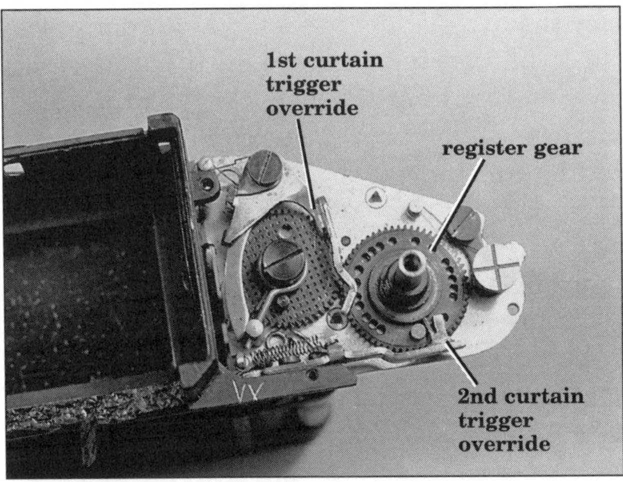


*9.11: Self-timer / slow-speed escapement.*

## Leica II

The Leica I, II and III models all have similar basic construction and shutters. Several varieties exist in each category.

Models I have a small viewfinder on the top of the camera but no coupled rangefinder or slow speeds. The lens is permanently attached.

Models II are equipped with interchangeable lens, and a coupled rangefinder, but no slow speeds (photo 9.12).

The Leica III models are equipped with slow speeds down to one second. Models III can be identified easily by the slow-speed dial at the front of the camera.

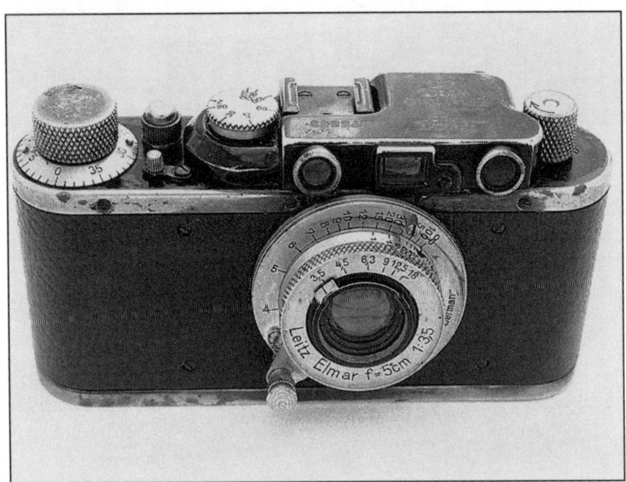


*9.12: Leica II*

In the models having slow speeds, the escapement unit is located at the inside bottom of the camera (photo 9.13). The instructions below are directly applicable to the Leica II models but will be useful for the I and III models as well.

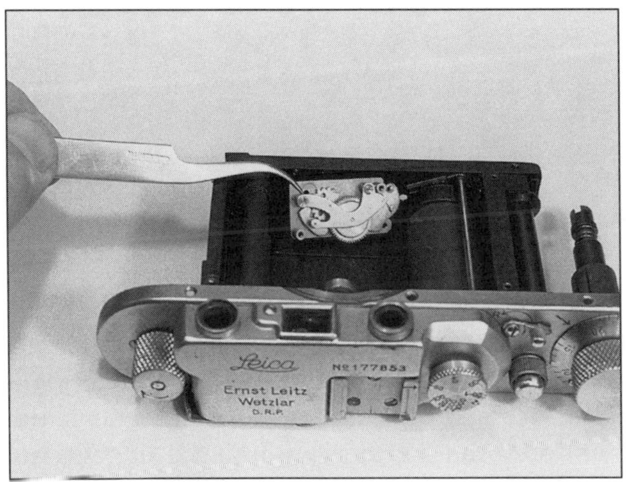


*9.13: Escapement removed.*

The shutter curtains and bearings can be accessed just by removing the body cover sleeve without removing anything from the top. The lens mounting ring must come off first. The top of the ring is marked by an "O" on the outside and must be refitted in the same orientation.

Note the positions of the shims under the ring as well. The screws are threaded into separate anchor plates inside the body casting, not into the body itself. Remove the four screws from the front of the body.

Some models have an extra screw in the bottom rim of the body sleeve. Remove the seven screws from the rim of the top cover. Push the inside mechanism out from the bottom rather than trying to pull it out by tugging at the top. Push the rangefinder coupling lever out of the way (photo 9.14).

Catch the pressure plate and the two flat springs under it. Before reassembling, don't forget to insert these parts into the body sleeve.

The shutter is straightforward. It can be worked and studied outside the cover sleeve. This Leica shutter design has become the standard of the time. As such, it should be studied in detail because you will encounter similar shutter

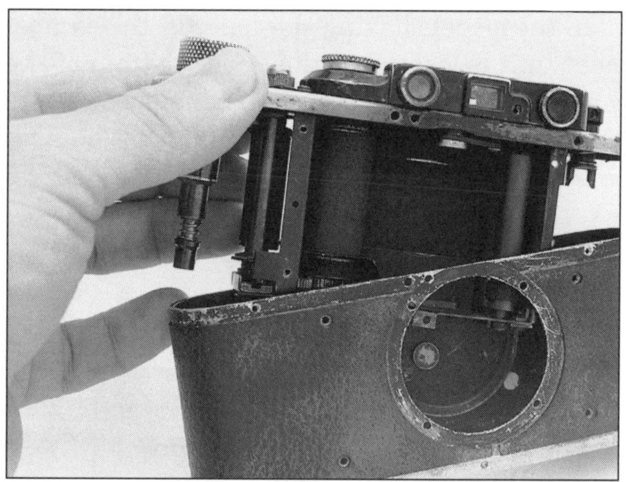

*9.14: Pull off the cover sleeve.*

mechanisms in other brands as well. When cleaning and lubricating the shutter shafts and gears, make sure that neither graphite nor oil gets onto the shutter curtains. Use a thin wire to get oil onto the bearings of the inner drum — the one the second curtain is attached to.

The spring drums and guide pulleys on the other side should be similarly lubricated. The cocking gear on the sprocket shaft and the pinion meshing with it also need a drop of oil. Curtain tension can be adjusted at the bottom, at the usual location (photo 9.15).

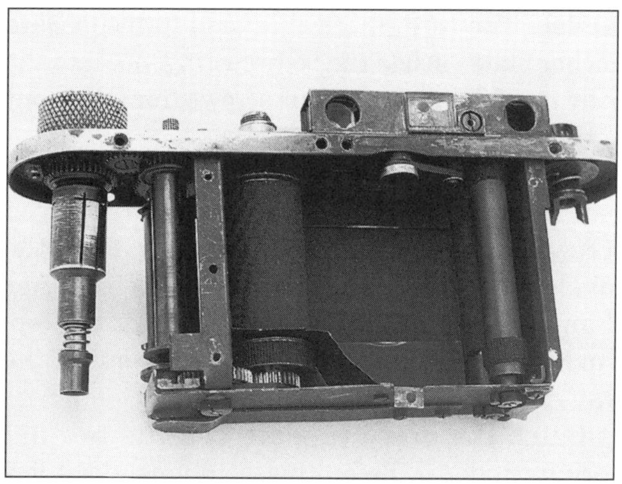

*9.15: Curtain tension adjustment.*

If the shutter doesn't time, the second curtain latch under the top cover could be faulty. To remedy problems with the latch or any problem with the rangefinder, you must remove the cover from over the rangefinder assembly. In order to free the cover, the shutter-speed knob, the accessory shoe, and the knurled rings over the rangefinder windows must be removed. Unscrewing the knurled rings could be difficult if they are tight. Be careful, as Leicas are valuable, especially when they are in mint condition. You don't want to disfigure an expensive collector's item. Rubber comes to the rescue.

First, remove the lens mounting ring in order to make room for the tool. Take a square inch of bicycle inner tube and a 3/8 socket wrench. Lay the rubber sheet over the knurled ring and press the socket wrench on top of it.

If the ring is not rusted-in, it will unscrew readily. This method can be applied for undoing other rings of similar type. The socket wrench must be large enough to allow the rubber sheet to fold over the side of the ring tightly. Unscrew all four of the knurled rings in this fashion and the two screws from the front and back of the cover. Removing the lens from the center window is easy because there are notches in its mount for a metal tool.

Remove the setscrew from the side of the shutter-speed dial, and unscrew the dial counterclockwise. (There might be one or more shim washers under the dial.) The accessory shoe must also come off (3 screws). Now pull off the cover (photo 9.16).

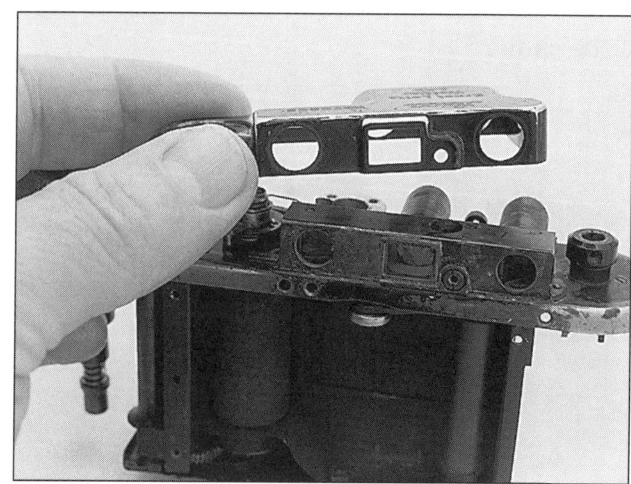

*9.16: Removing the viewfinder cover.*

The Leica shutter is very simple. Nothing is hidden. What you see is all there is. If problems

with shutter timing are encountered, the second-curtain latch may be binding, or the spring on it may be broken, loose, or too weak. The second curtain latches up when the release button is pressed. The spring over the latch must exert pressure in two directions, down and inward towards the hub.

If the latch shaft is binding, or the spring on it is broken or has been tampered with, the second curtain will not hook up reliably (photo 9.17). Notice how the adjustable prong kicks out the latch earlier or later according to the shutter-speed selected.

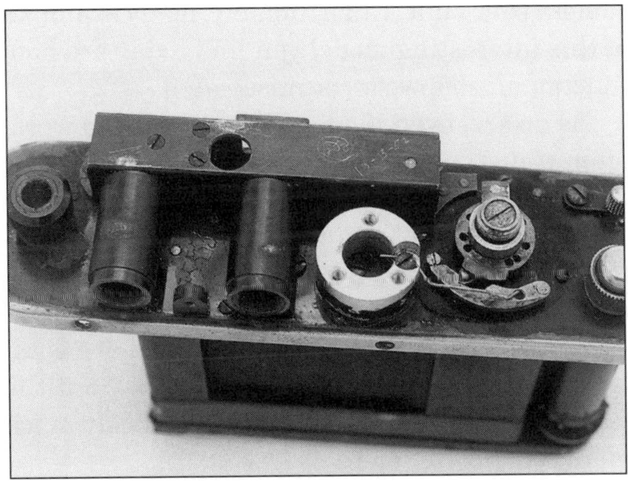

***9.17:** Top of the camera.*

The rangefinder also may cause problems. Notice that the optical elements are built inside a brass sleeve and can be removed only through one or the other end. Normally, however, the elements can be cleaned in place.

For cleaning, remove the complete RF unit. It is secured to the assembly plate by five screws from the bottom up (photo 9.18).

Unscrew the viewer tubes from the rear of the sleeve. Now it's possible to reach inside with a tissue and clean the prism and the two-way mirror. Be extremely careful, the mirror coating on the two-way mirror is soft and can be rubbed off easily. Fold a tissue to a point and hold it with fine curved tweezers. Squirt Windex™ onto the tissue and squeeze it out. Wipe both sides of the two-way mirror with the damp tissue. Do it gently and only once. Don't wipe with dry tissue.

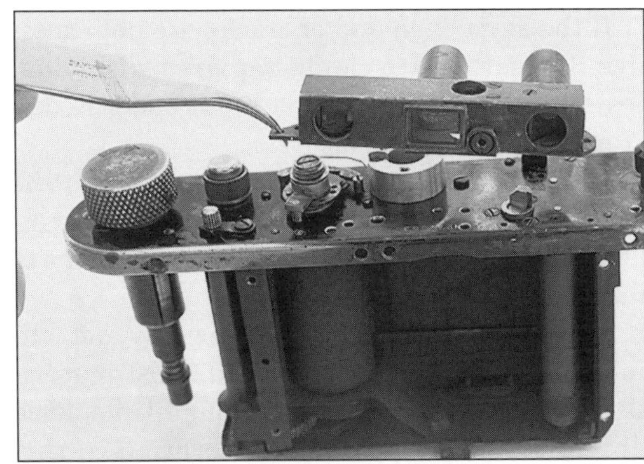

***9.18:** Removing the RF assembly.*

Adjustment of the rangefinder is easier than cleaning. For horizontal adjustment, just remove the screw from the front next to the viewer window. The adjusting worm screw can be reached through this hole. Vertical adjustment of the two images is done by rotating the small window we removed earlier — just over the lens mount. This window is actually a shallow prism. You will notice that as you rotate the window 360 degrees, the center image in the rangefinder describes a circle. Once the vertical position is fine, the horizontal worm screw must be corrected again.

Ordinary Leica models have a hard leatherette cover on the body sleeve. This material tends to shrink and often cracks. With age it becomes brittle. When removal is attempted, it often falls apart (photo 9.19).

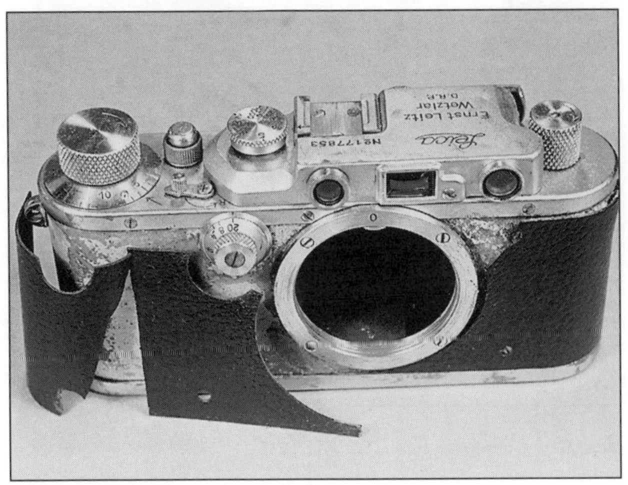

***9.19:** Shrunk and cracked leatherette.*

If the shrinkage and/or cracks are not excessive the leatherette can be repaired with vinyl paste as described in Chapter Eight under Kodak Premoette Jr. No.1 (page 84).

If the leatherette is too far gone, it must be replaced. After removing the old plastic cover, clean the body sleeve thoroughly of all traces of old glue.

Make sure the new piece fits exactly and will not need stretching. If stretched, most materials will shrink again given enough time. (See Universal Mercury, Body Restoration in this chapter for instructions on how to find and replace a leatherette.)

### The Lens

The lens might also need attention. If the camera has never been serviced before, the grease in the helical threads is probably all thickened and dried out. The diaphragm blades might also be sticking together.

For replacing the grease in the focusing mechanism, remove the stop screw from the rim of the base ring. Unlock the focusing cam, and separate the threads.

Using lighter fluid and toothbrush, wash the old grease out thoroughly. Once the parts are clean, smear bearing grease onto both sides of the threads.

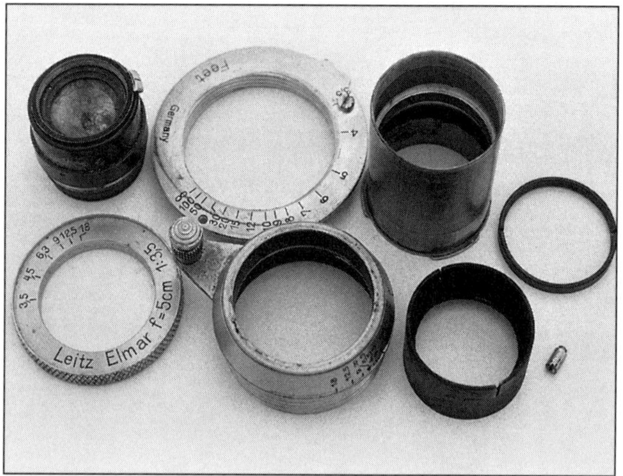


***9.20:** The lens disassembled.*

It is possible to flood-clean (see Abstract) the diaphragm blades after unscrewing the front and the rear lens groups. If, however, disassembly of the lens unit is required, proceed as follows: Pull out the baffle ring from the rear. Remove both setscrews from the side of the barrel. (One is accessible through a hole in the serrated front flange.) Unscrew the retaining ring from behind, inside the barrel. Unscrew the serrated flange from the front and pull out the complete lens assembly (photo 9.20).

## Nikkorex Zoom 35

The Nikkorex Zoom 35 may be the first ZLR camera ever built. Unfortunately, many examples of this interesting model you find today are nonfunctional, shopworn, or mistreated.

Be aware, even if one of these seems to work, often it just makes the appropriate noises while the sequence of functions might be incorrect. The shutter might not open, might not close, or the mirror might not flip up all the way. (See Abstract, SLR with lens shutter.)

The body and shutter in this model are similar to those in the Nikkorex 35 (below), but the lens and the shutter interface are obviously much more complicated here.

Due to the moving lens assembly, the shutter cocking and release mechanisms are difficult to reassemble and are sensitive to proper alignment and adjustments.

### Disassembly

Remove the three setscrews from the forward side of the focusing ring. Pull off the ring, and remove the three screws from the cover sleeve. Pull off the sleeve. Remove the three zoom rollers. Mark its position, before you pull out the front assembly. Remove the three screws from the side of the zoom ring; slide the ring off forward. Set the zoom to 43mm, and unscrew the three screws through the holes in the brass barrel.

Extricate the zoom group from inside. Set the zoom to 86mm, and unscrew the two positioning studs through slots in the side of the brass barrel. Shake out the complete shutter unit together with the inside zoom barrel (photo 9.21).

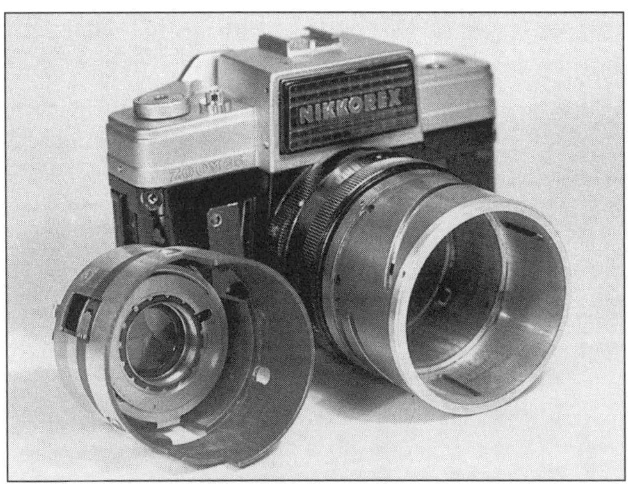


*9.21: The lens assembly removed.*

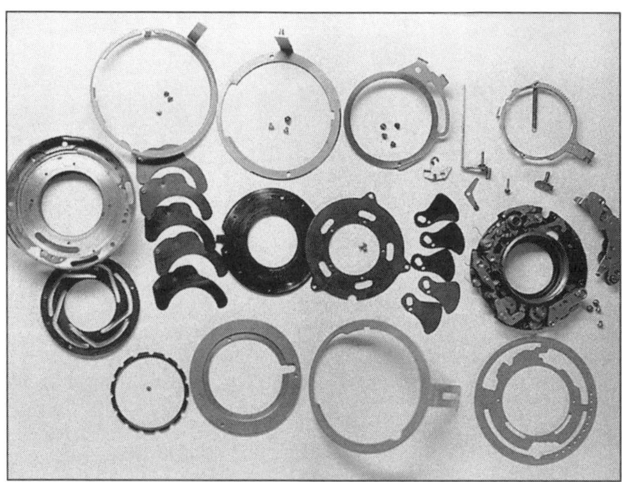

*9.22: Parts of the shutter.*

## The Shutter

Unscrew the rear and front lens groups from the shutter unit. Remove the retaining ring from the rear and carefully pull out the shutter unit from the barrel.

After removing the front cover plate and the shutter-speed cam, you can flood-clean the shutter assembly. If you must get inside the shutter, remove the rings from the rear one after the other.

The release lever is secured by an E-clip. Remove the four screws from the shutter base and pull the two halves apart. The shutter blades fall out, and can now be cleaned with tissue and lighter fluid.

The diaphragm blades stay put in the bottom cup. If you must disassemble the diaphragm unit, mark the exact position of the plates and blades. Draw a diagram of the parts. It's fairly tricky to put the diaphragm blades back together (photo 9.22).

Before inserting the shutter into the barrel, examine and straighten all levers with special attention to the shutter cocking links. These parts are often bent out of shape. The cocking train is critical for alignment. If the cover flap doesn't flip all the way up, the shutter won't release.

If, on the other hand, the cocking links are adjusted for the flap to release the shutter, then the shutter may not latch up when cocked. There is an adjustable link at the bottom of the camera (photo 9.23), but its range is limited. If

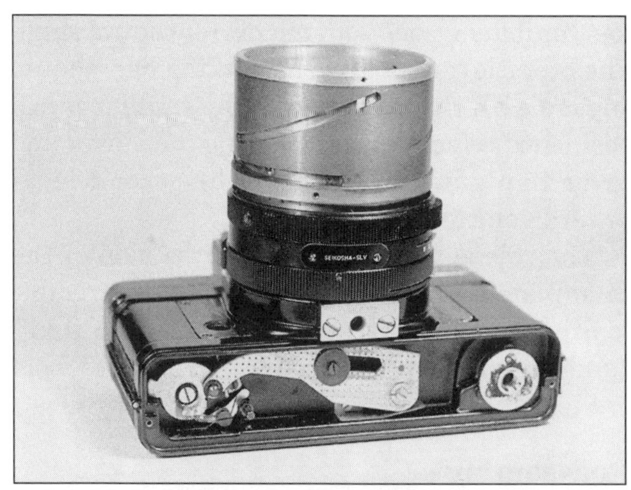

*9.23: The adjustable cocking link.*

the other parts are bent or out of alignment, an adjustment will produce the above effects.

## The Mirror Mechanism

If the camera doesn't work and it has been previously worked on (very likely), the cocking or mirror mechanism may be out of position. Peel off the leatherette from the front of the camera, remove the four screws and just lift off the complete front assembly ( photo 9.24). No need to worry about the sync wires. With the lens assembly out, the mirror and cover flap flip up.

Look inside the bottom of the mirror cage and notice the two levers there. These two are linked to the mirror and must be repositioned before refitting the front assembly. Turn the smaller

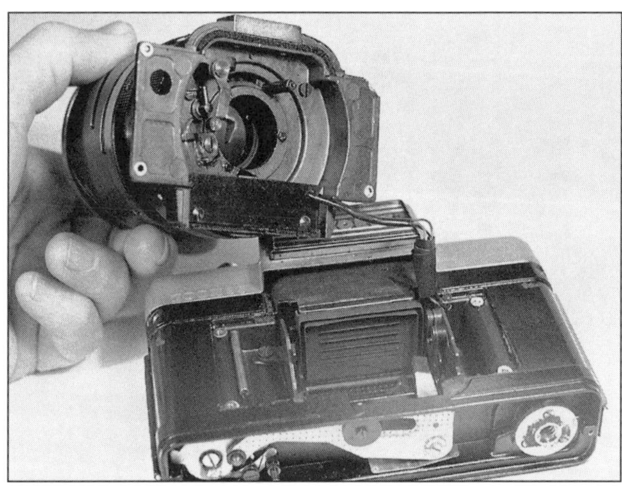

***9.24:*** *Removing the front assembly.*

lever counter-clockwise (looking at it from the top) until it engages with the mirror control shaft. The other lever, next to the cocking bar, should engage with the other end of the small lever. If positioned correctly, you can bring the mirror and cover flap down by pushing the second lever toward your left.

The release lever at the reverse side of the front plate and the mirror release lever are able to flip over as well. Turn the lever at the right-hand side of the mirror cage up to engage the pin in the side of the cover flap.

## Reassembly

Fit the front assembly (minus shutter) into the body before inserting the shutter. Position the levers in the body as described above. In addition, wedge the release lever through the adjusting hole in the front cover plate to prevent it from flopping around. Make sure the wires are tucked away at the side of the mirror cage.

Insert the top ridge of the front assembly under the top cover, but leave a gap at the bottom between the body of the camera and the front assembly. Hold the camera up-side-down to let the mirror release lever fall back (upward). Reach in through the bottom with a long screwdriver and press the mirror cocking lever to the right of the camera (your left) to bring the mirror down. Lower the front assembly onto the body making sure that the shutter cocking post at the back of the front unit falls between the cocking bar and the mirror control lever in the body (photo 9.25). It might require several tries before you get it right.

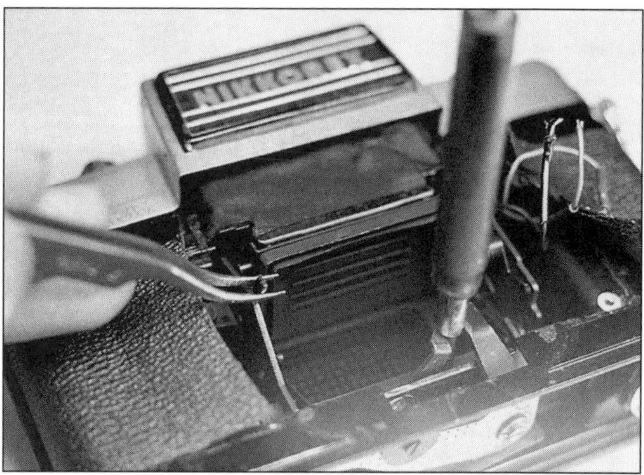

***9.25:*** *Fit the shutter cocking post between the two levers.*

## Testing

With the shutter out of the way, you can look inside the barrel and see the mirror coming down as you operate the winding crank. The mirror, however, doesn't latch up without the shutter in place.

Test the release by reaching inside the barrel and pushing the release lever toward the side of the barrel. If the connection is correct the lever should move when the release button is pressed.

Refitting the lens assembly requires patient attention to all the parts that must connect inside the barrel. First, study the levers on the shutter and their counterparts inside the barrel. Be certain you know what should connect with what. Make sure the sync contact plates are straight.

Next, position the shutter-speed fork, the diaphragm stud, the sync mode switch lever, as well as the shutter cocking and release levers.

As you insert the shutter assembly, you can peer in at the side of the assembly and guide the levers into their respective position by a long-bladed screwdriver. This too may require several tries before you get it right.

## Other Problems

The special screws for the zoom rollers are often bent or broken. If you don't have the original replacement, substitute 1.4x7mm screws. If the rollers will not roll any more, there is no cause for concern. The zoom works just as well whether the rollers roll or just slide.

The "pentaprism" is actually a mirror arrangement, not a prism. In order to clean this system, the intricate mirror arrangement must be pulled apart, cleaned, and reassembled again. It can be done, but it's a lot of work.

The simple light meter system is Selenium-based and is independent from the camera dials. If it doesn't work, most likely the selenium cell is dead. Chances are good that the meter movement itself is fine.

## Nikkorex 35

The Nikkorex 35 (non-zoom model) has an identical body and shutter to the zoom model above, but the shutter mounting and shutter control parts are much simpler.

Unscrew the front lens group with a rubber tool. Remove the three screws from the "SEIKOSHA-SLV" ring. Another three screws that secure the pressure ring are uncovered. With the pressure ring off, the flat spring washer and the ASA dials are free. The variable resistor is glued into the under side of the ASA ring.

Pry off the plastic insulating ring from the black inside ring. (If it breaks, you can either glue the pieces back on, or just forget about the insulating ring; it's not needed.) Remove the three uncovered screws and pop the black ring. Remove the retaining ring from the center of the shutter to free the cover plate and the shutter speed dial. Maneuver the dial carefully over the brushes without damaging them: lift the dial, push it up a bit, then pull it through (photo 9.26).

Remove the shutter-speed cam, but be careful not to lose the click-stop stud and the spring (photo 9.27). The shutter now is accessible and most problems can be corrected. Even flood-cleaning the blades is possible (see Abstract).

If the light meter is intermittent, especially when the dials are rotated, the resistor and the brushes probably need cleaning. Gently wipe them off with tissue and lighter fluid. If lighter fluid doesn't help, try toothpaste. Be gentle with the resistor; the resistance compound is not as hard as modern compounds. For other problems see the Zoom model above.

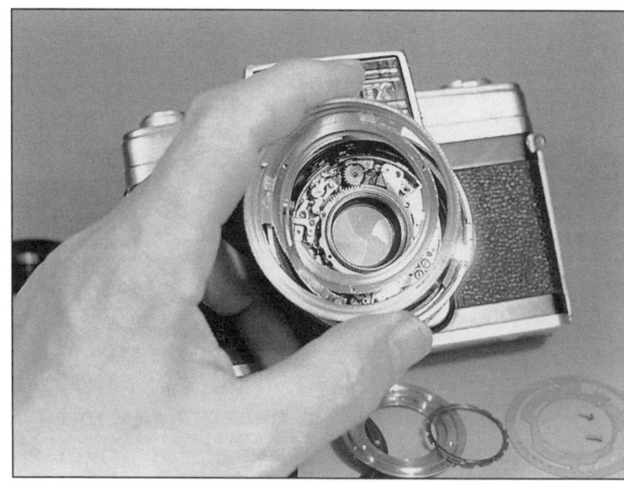

***9.26:*** *Removing the shutter-speed dial.*

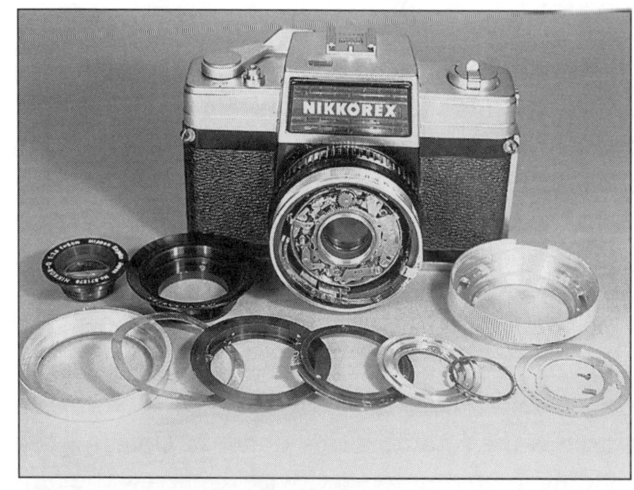


***9.27:*** *The font rings removed.*

## Universal Mercury II

The Mercury is a half-frame 35mm model with a rotary shutter (photo 9.28). This is an unusual looking camera due to the rotary blades sticking out over the top in a crescent shaped extension of the body. Depending on what you have to do, fixing this camera could be an easy job or a difficult one, especially when it comes to cosmetic restoration.

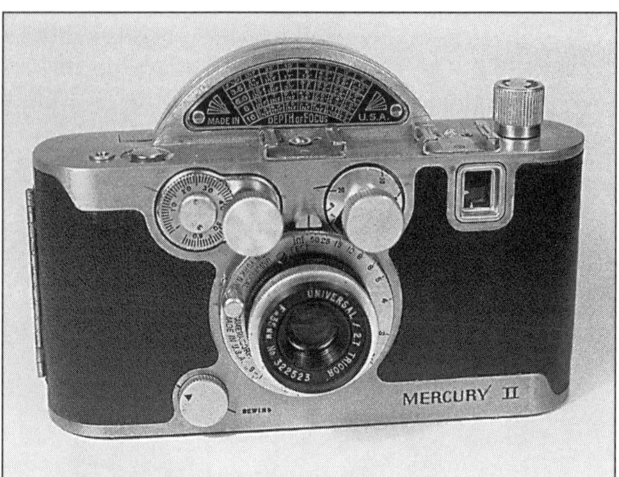


*9.28: Mercury II*

To take a peek at the mechanism, just remove the two screws inside the top of the film chamber. Push the cover plate up and out. With this cover off, you can observe the shutter mechanism, and lubricate it partially as well. If the shutter is slow, all that may be required is a drop of oil at the shaft of the rotary shutter blades. If it's still not good enough, you can try to flood-clean the mechanism without further disassembly. If, on the other hand, you want to fully restore the body, or the shutter doesn't work at all, you will have to strip the body quite thoroughly.

Don't peel off the leatherettes for disassembly; there are no screws under them. In order to separate the inside mechanism from the cover housing, unscrew the lens, then remove the focusing ring from the front of the camera (3 screws). Unscrew the retaining ring under it. Unscrew the winding knob counter-clockwise. Unscrew the pin-face screw over the counter dial counter-clockwise. Pull off the dial, remove the three screws under the dial, lift off the small cover plate, and unscrew the winding gear from the winding shaft, also counter-clockwise.

This last operation, you can perform with a small pointed pair of pliers engaged with the gear cogs. One more thing: using a small hex key, remove the setscrew from the side of the shutter-speed selector knob. In addition to the setscrew, a cross pin across the shaft and knob secures the knob as well. The pin is tight; don't try to punch it out without supporting the knob. Let the knob lay over a sturdy support such as a vise or anvil. Using a good quality punch and a fairly heavy hammer, punch out the pin. Now the complete shutter assembly can be pulled out of the housing (photo 9.29).

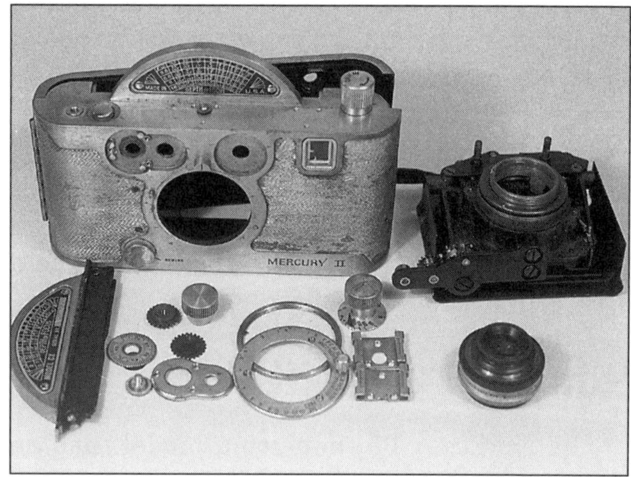


*9.29: The shutter unit removed.*

The shutter works and can be tested outside of the housing. It's an extremely sturdy mechanism, chances are that all it needs is a good cleaning and some lubrication to put it back into working order.

## Body Restoration

The Mercury has got a sturdy cast aluminum body. Unfortunately, the shiny aluminum finish tends to darken and take on a mottled, oxidized look over the years. It's none too easy to restore the finish. Disassemble the camera as above, plus remove the accessory shoes from the top, and peel off the leatherette pieces. Ideally, you would knock out the rivets in order to strip the body completely of all plates knobs and buttons. That, however, would be too much work and would probably cause some inevitable cosmetic damage.

Since the plates are recessed anyway, I'd recommend that you mask them. Lay masking tape over the plates, then cut around them with a sharp utility blade. Work carefully so as not to damage the plates or the body. Press the tape down thoroughly, especially around the edges. Do the same with the viewfinder frame on the front of the camera. The rewind knob should unscrew counterclockwise, but if it's too tight or glued on, you can leave it on rather than risk damage to the knob or the shaft.

Once the body is stripped and masked, try SOS™ and water for polishing the aluminum. Depending on the condition of the aluminum, Twinkle™ polishing paste or other brass cleaner might work better to clean and polish the aluminum. You can also use a toothbrush dunked into the polishing compound to brighten up the hard-to-reach places.

Clean heavier corrosion with #600 wet and dry paper. If #600 doesn't cut it, try #400 until the metal is clean, but then you must go back to #600 again. Apply horizontal strokes only; do not crisscross.

After the sanding, go back to SOS™ and water. All this takes a while. The more patient you are, and the longer you keep at it, the better the finished job will look.

Once the polishing is done, wash off the whole body with a toothbrush dunked into Fantastic™. Rinse the camera in running water. Mop it dry with paper towels, then blow it off inside and out. Dry it gently with a hair drier. Avoid touching the polished sections with your fingers.

If water got into the viewfinder, you can clean it out through the eyepiece hole. Pry off the little cover ring (just pressed on). Do not pry at the lens! To remove the lens, try to shake it out first. If it's stubborn, press a length of aggressive adhesive tape onto the face of the lens for a handle.

Glue a piece of paper tissue to the end of bamboo stick. With this tool you can wipe off the inside surface of the objective lens through the eyepiece hole. Do not use Q-tips or any fabric or cotton, whether natural or synthetic — the strands from any fabric can get caught at the rough edges and won't ever come out.

Fluff from tissue, on the other hand, can be blown out readily. Besides a synthetic cotton swab has no absorbance to speak of. Don't risk damaging the body or the frame by prying at the viewfinder frame.

You can polish the face of the knobs with #600 paper and polish the serrations with a toothbrush. The shutter-speed dial, however, is made of anodized aluminum and should not require polishing.

You must varnish the body immediately or the aluminum will turn dark again (especially if touched with fingers). Using a sprayable varnish, spray all polished areas until you get full coverage. One coat only. Don't be too generous with the varnish, or it will show. Spray the knobs and the separate crescent cover as well.

Let the varnish dry for at least one full week without touching. Peel off the masking tape only when the varnish is thoroughly dry. With a slightly moistened toothbrush and a paper towel, clean up the plates of polish residue.

See page 90 in this chapter if the engraved legends and marks are in need of rejuvenating. The "Film" at the back, "Rewind" at the front, the register marks for the counter and the shutter-speed dials, and the letters on top of the rewind knob should be blackened.

Wash the leatherette pieces with toothbrush and Fantastic™. Rinse them in running water. Use contact cement sparingly to reglue the pieces. Make sure you don't smear the glue anywhere it doesn't belong.

If the leatherettes are missing or beyond hope, you can cut out new ones from a sheet of leatherette. Suitable material can be found in foam and plastic shops. Solid vinyl leatherette can be salvaged from a variety of fashion accessory and clothing items such as handbags, hats, gloves, and luggage items. Another good source is looseleaf binders and many other stationery products.

You should collect any and all leather or leatherette pieces you find to have a selection of grain pattern, thickness, and color at hand. It is very difficult to match an existing piece. If you must replace one, you pretty well have to replace all the pieces for an acceptable result.

Take the pattern off the original piece. If it's missing, take the pattern off the camera body itself. You can use a paper sheet for this. Press it into the recess on the body, then transfer the pattern onto the leatherette. The match must be perfect.

Count on a number of tries before you get it right. If the match is not perfect, if gaps are showing between the leatherette and the body, if the corners turn out square instead of round, the result will look like a bad patch-up job. Fabric-backed material can be glued on using contact cement. If solid vinyl sheet is used, rough up the back of it with #80 sandpaper before gluing it on.

If the camera body is curving, such as in the case of the Mercury II, apply contact cement to the body as well as to the back of the vinyl sheet. Let the glue dry for 15 minutes, then press the sheet onto the body hard. Use the handle of your tweezers to press the edges down. Gently warm it up with a hair drier to help the vinyl conform to the curve.

Reassembly is easy. Fit the mechanism into the body, and tighten the retaining ring on the front. Fit the shutter-speed dial on before you do the focusing ring because the flange on the shutter-speed dial should go under the focusing ring. Before inserting the cross pin into the hub of the shutter-speed dial, ascertain that the dial is fitted to the shaft the right way and not turned around 180°. You can press the cross-pin into its hole with a pair of long-nosed pliers. Photo 9.28 shows the restored camera.

## Universal 35mm, F2.7 Lens

When contaminated with oil it's better to clean the blades even though the diaphragm may still work. While a little oil shouldn't bother a manual diaphragm, when the oil thickens, it can glue the blades together so they may break when aperture setting is attempted. Just unscrew the front and rear lens groups. You can flood-clean the blades without further disassembly. With the front group out, the aluminum ring can be pulled off. Polish the ring the same way you did the body. (Try SOS™ first.)

## Zeiss Contaflex

The suffix "flex" in a camera name almost always stands for "reflex". You may, therefore, expect a camera with "flex" in its name to be either a twin-lens or a single-lens reflex. Indeed, a TLR Contaflex does exist, but most of the Contaflex models are 35mm SLRs equipped with lens shutters.

There are dozens of models offering different optics and other features. The early models are numbered with Roman numerals or Greek letters. They are similar in construction. The difference is in optics and built-in light meters or a lack of one. The Rapid, Prima and Super models are similar to each other but different from the earlier, numbered models.

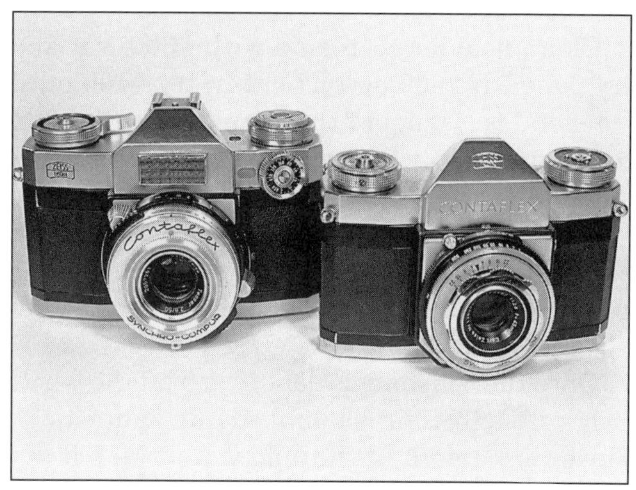


***9.30:*** *Contaflex Super and Contaflex I*

We will cover the Contaflex I in the first category and the Contaflex Super in the second. The instructions below can be used for other models in the same category.

Photo 9.30 shows the two models side by side. Notice the rapid winder, the interchangeable front group, the in-the-body focusing mechanism, and the meter knob in the larger, more sophisticated model.

## Contaflex I

The shutter cocking, timing, and blade activator mechanisms are accessible from the front. Remove the setscrews from the side of the focusing distance scale, just under the focusing grip. You must find the set screws in the focusing grip ring by feel. Reach through one of the holes in the distance scale ring with a small screwdriver, and by rotating the ring, feel for the three holes underneath.

Once a hole is found, feel for a slot inside it, then unscrew the setscrew therein by a few turns, but leave the screws in the hole. Lift off the focusing ring. Mark the infinity position of the front group.

Carefully unscrew the helical threads and, when the group comes free, mark that position as well. Notice the dimples in the side of the mount.

When reassembling the lens you want the setscrews to find their way into those dimples again and the focus to be accurate as well. If you don't start the threads in the original position, the focus can be adjusted, but the screws will not fall into the dimples. Using a plier wrench or spanner wrench, unscrew the second lens group.

Be careful not to damage the helical threads. (Some technicians find it easier to remove the two lens groups together without separating them. You need a special wrench for this that fits between the two groups and can engage with the slots in the second group.)

Once the lens is out, turn the locking eccentrics flat side toward the center, then turn the cover plate counterclockwise until it comes free. The shutter-speed cam comes with the cover plate. The shutter mechanism is now exposed (photo 9.31). You can separate the shutter speed cam from the other rings by turning the "Synchro-compur" ring until it unlocks and falls out.

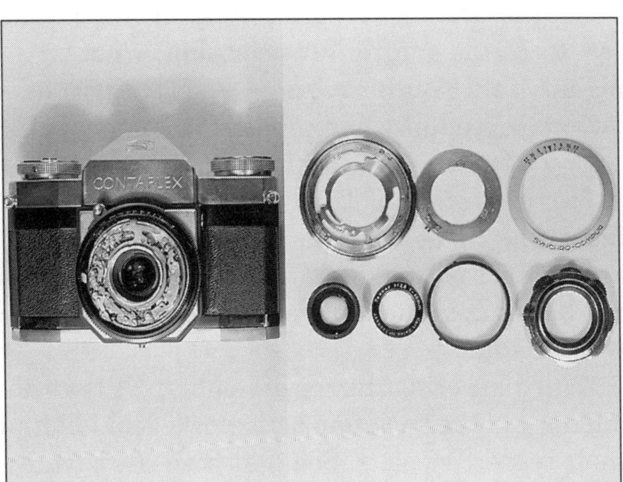


***9.31:** The shutter is open.*

Turning to the top, remove the three screws from the side of the winding knob. Pull off the knob together with the trigger and counter parts under it. Next, remove the three screws and the brass ring they retain. There is one screw in the top cover under the brass ring.

Turning to the other side, remove the screw from the center of the rewind knob. Pull off the knob, and unscrew the brass retaining ring under the knob. Using a rubber tool that fits snugly over the eyepiece ring (see Abstract), unscrew the eyepiece. Lift off the cover. Some of the mechanism is accessible from here.

If you remove the pentaprism together with its metal bed (just 3 screws), note the positions of the shim washers. Some of the mirror and rear flap mechanism can be accessed through the opening (photo 9.32).

Refitting the brass winding disk enables you to work and observe the mechanism.

Most of the cocking and advance gearing is under the top casting. Four screws at the periphery retain the casting, but a shaft bridging to the front must also be pulled out in order to separate the top from the front.

Bend a pair of straight tweezers sideways so you can grab the protruding butt of the shaft (photo 9.32). Undo the setscrew first, then pull out the shaft.

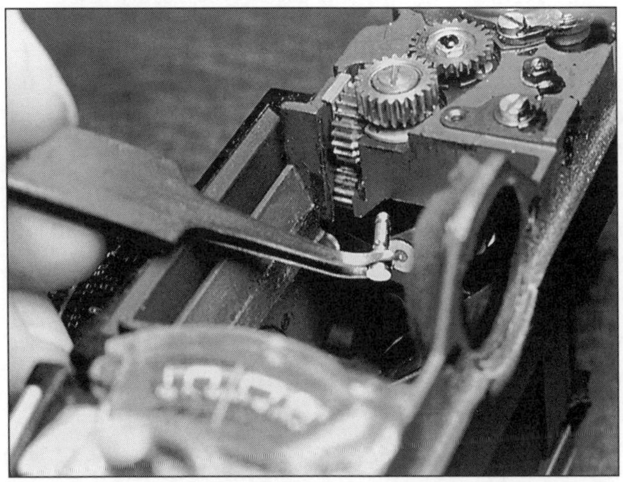

***9.32:** Pulling out the bridging shaft.*

The gears are well-made; they hardly ever need replacing. Often, cleaning and lubrication is required because of sand, corrosion, or film chips restricting the free movement of the gears. The cocking gears must spin when the mechanism is released. Restriction in these gears could prevent the shutter from firing.

If the front casting must be removed (recommended when the shutter unit is pulled), carefully peel off the leatherette from the front of the camera.

The leatherette on the Contaflex is somewhat brittle. If it's bent at a sharp angle, permanent creases or cracks may result. Remove the four screws from the corners of the front casting. With the gear housing on the top removed, the front is now free (photo 9.33).

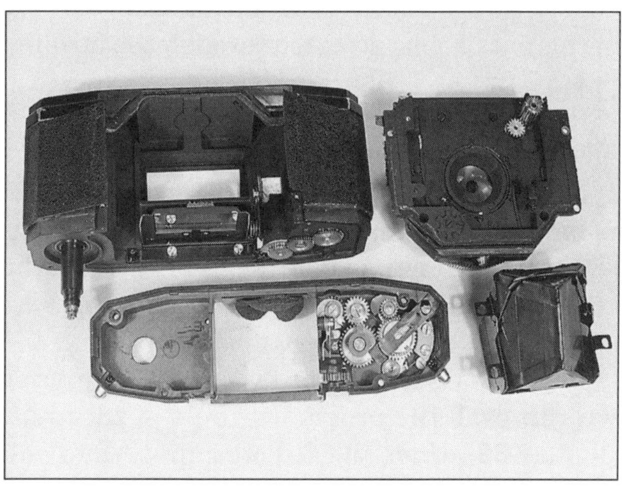

***9.33:** Removing the top and front castings.*

If the shutter unit must be disassembled for cleaning or replacement, it's possible to remove the shutter retaining ring through the mirror chamber with the front unit still in place, but reassembly is difficult. Release the camera so the mirror is up.

Reach in through the film gate with plier wrench #2 (see Abstract) or a suitable spanner wrench, and undo the retaining ring around the rear lens element.

Remove the "M-X" lever from the front of the shutter. Unclip the sync wire from the back of the unit and help it through the hole in the base plate as you're pulling the shutter assembly.

Handle the wire with care as the insulation is easily frayed. If that happens, the wire may not go back through the hole or it might short to the ground.

Notice the large ring gears at the back of the shutter. If the shutter blades or the diaphragm blades are hesitant, these gears could be binding. Flood-cleaning them with lighter fluid usually helps. The inside ring gear is the diaphragm activator, spring-loaded through the brass gear at the 5 o'clock position inside the body.

If you turn the camera around, you'll find the spring winding disk in the mirror chamber. When the shutter is pulled, the spring runs off. After reassembly, the spring must be re-tensioned by turning this disk (see below).

### Reassembly

It's easier to refit the shutter with the front unit out of the body. When inserting the shutter unit, see that the prong on the aperture activator finds the notch in the toothed ring in the body.

Once the shutter is installed, set the aperture to f/22 and wind up the stop-down spring by turning the wheel counterclockwise about a quarter of a turn (two notches) after the aperture has stopped down to f/22. (As you're turning the spring wheel, the aperture should be stopping down.)

Fit the front assembly into the body. Turn the brass shutter cocking pinion (at the back of the front unit) clockwise all the way to its stop, and come back one tooth.

This is critical. An incorrect mesh of the gears results in the shutter not releasing or not latching up. If the shutter releases when the trigger is let up instead of when pressed, then you came back too far with the cocking pinion.

Before refitting the gear housing on top, insert the tip of the bridging shaft into the hole and temporarily tighten the set screw on it. Let off the gears in the top assembly by pressing the release shaft.

When lowering the top assembly, see that the mirror and the back flap activator levers fall into their respective slots. See that both the advance gears and the cocking gears mesh properly. Help the advance gears find their way by wiggling the sprocket. Once the top assembly is on, push the bridging shaft all the way in, and tighten the set screw on it.

When reassembling the helical threads, be patient. Undamaged threads will mate easily, but only if the two halves are held parallel to each other.

Never force the helical threads! If you start the threads at the mark you made earlier, the infinity position will come out all right.

The threaded plug at the rewind-fork side inside the film chamber is for opening a hole though which dust from the viewfinder can be blown out. The smaller plug at the bottom allows access to the mirror adjusting worm screw.

## Contaflex Super

If the shutter doesn't latch up or self-triggers, try to adjust the cocking stroke at the back of the camera through the film gate.

A crescent-shaped rack is visible towards the bottom of the camera where the rack engages the cocking pinion. Loosen up the two locking screws and adjust the eccentric screw at the tip of the crescent (photo 9.34). If this doesn't help, set the crescent back where it was.

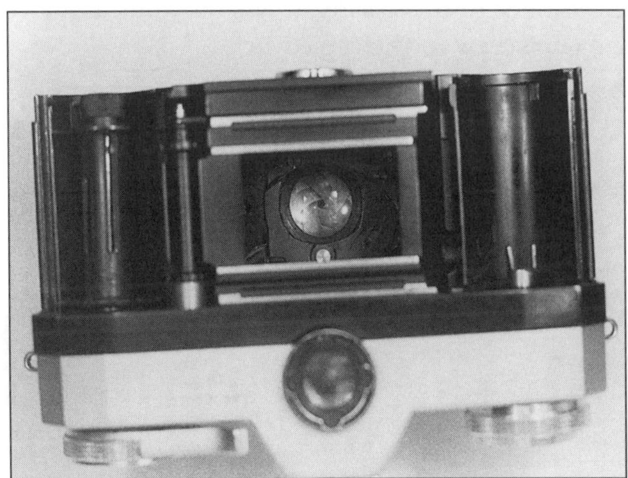

***9.34:** Adjustable rack.*

In this model, it's possible to get inside the shutter from the front. Remove the "Contaflex" plate (three screws).

Remove the four screws from the rim of the bayonet plate. A locking pin in its rim secures the lens. Turn the head of this pin 180° and then pull it out.

Using a tight-fitting rubber hose, unscrew the lens. Lift off the cover plate. Unclip the retaining ring and lift off the shutter-speed cam (photo 9.35).

It's now possible to get to the escapements and other control mechanisms inside the shutter. It's also possible to flood-clean the mechanism and the blades without further disassembly.

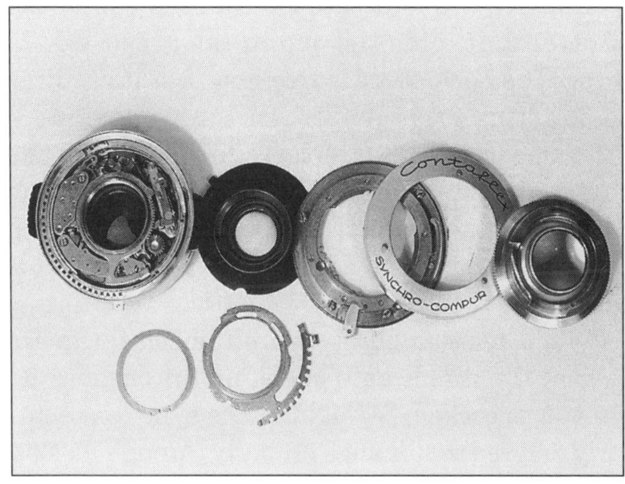


***9.35:** The shutter is accessible from the front.*

If the shutter must be disassembled for repair or replacement of the blades, you must pull the complete assembly from the body.

First, check the light meter. If it's accurate, you want to get the dials back where they were before disassembly.

Note the position of the shutter dials, and set the focus to infinity before pulling the assembly. Turn the camera over.

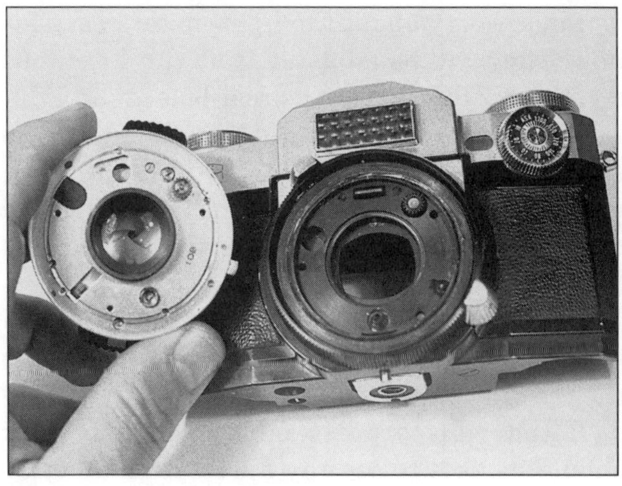

***9.36:** Removing the shutter unit.*

Notice three screws through the film gate in recessed holes. Wind the camera to the point when the crescent rack uncovers the screw at the 10 o'clock position relative to the lens.

Remove the three screws and pull the shutter unit out (photo 9.36). With the shutter out, mark the position of the inside focusing barrel.

Remove the four screws from the rim of the shutter unit, plus the one in the green V-X-M lever. The back cover is free now, but it requires some prying to get it off.

Removing the rear lens group helps. With the cover cup off, you still must remove the diaphragm activator rings and the V-X-M ring to be able to get the screws that hold the shutter halves together.

When reassembling the unit, mesh the gears so that the diaphragm opens up fully when the shutter is cocked. Straighten the sync connector strip and see that it slips properly through its slot.

In fact, using a small needle file, you can taper the slot from the entry side (inside of the cup) in order to make it easier for the insulating sleeve to get through. The tab at the end of the diaphragm cam should fit inside the slot in the aperture ring.

If you cock the shutter with the cover on, the tab might click into place. The green V-X-M lever must also be in place before refitting the cover cup. It's possible to force the lever in with the cup already on, but not without causing some cosmetic damage.

Don't worry about the light meter gears for now. They will be adjusted from the front, but don't forget to screw-in the rear lens group.

Turning to the front of the unit, fit on the shutter-speed cam at the 1/500 position. With the aperture dial at f/22, turn the brass ring (the one connecting the dials) clockwise all the way to its stop.

Place the shutter speed dial on, making sure the slot in the dial matches up with the tab on the cam.

If the dials are assembled correctly, you should be able to set any aperture number at both ends of the shutter-speed scale, up to and including "B". Setting the long-time exposures (the green numbers), however, restricts the range of the aperture.

Place on the cover plate and the bayonet ring. Set the dials and the ASA knob to the positions you noted before removing the unit. Reset the body mechanism by cocking it fully, then releasing it. Check that the position mark on the inside focusing barrel hasn't moved. Insert the shutter unit into the body. Use a magnetic screwdriver to start the screws that secure the shutter unit.

Check the focus. If the focus needs adjusting, remove the grips and the scale from the focusing dial. Loosen the four setscrews in the side of the dial. Turn the dial to the correct position, and retighten the setscrews.

### Top Cover

Unscrew the ring from the release button. Try rubber first. If the ring is stuck, use parallel serrated pliers carefully. Lift off the counter dial. Unscrew the four screws through the holes in the black plastic register disk. Lift off the complete counter assembly.

Lift off the winding crank. If you don't disturb the winder return spring, it will stay put. Remove the one screw in the top cover.

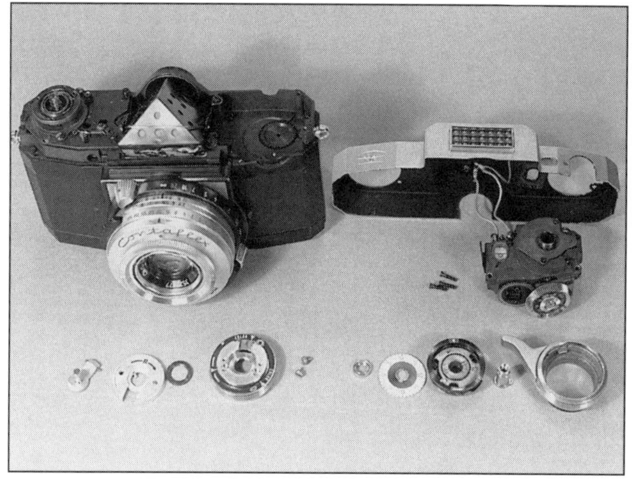

***9.37:** The light meter unit is easy to remove.*

Turning to the other side, remove the cover plate from the rewind knob, then the retaining ring under the plate. Now you can unscrew the rewind knob the regular way. (Hold the fork inside and turn the knob counter-clockwise.)

Finally, remove the two screws from the top cover on that side. The cover can be lifted off now, but it stays hanging on two wires. Except for the light meter, the mechanism up top is quite similar to that of the Contaflex I. (See above.)

The light meter is adjustable electronically by replacing the selenium cell, or changing the resistors. It is adjustable mechanically by changing the mesh of the gears.

To change the mesh, simply loosen up the three screws in the corners of the light meter unit. Lift up the unit, and turn the ASA knob or the shutter dials. The complete unit can be lifted out easily without any complications (photo 9.37).

Chapter Ten

# Miniature Format

## Minox C

Small, and cramped with a complicated mechanism, the Minox models can try the skills of any technician. All models are equipped with a before-the-lens guillotine shutter. Instead of a variable aperture, a neutral density filter can regulate the incoming light intensity. The early models (II, III, III-S) feature a mechanical shutter, timed via a mechanical escapement. Models A, B, and BL saw a coupled selenium based light meter added to the basic body, while the C is equipped with an electronically-controlled shutter.

The C is one of the earliest electronic cameras. It has two solenoids: one for each shutter curtain. A common problem with the C is sticky solenoids. If the shutter doesn't trigger or doesn't time properly, the solenoids are probably contaminated. Unfortunately, the battery is right next to the electronic parts. If the battery leaks, the acid will contaminate the solenoids and the electronic circuitry. Even if the battery is not leaking fluid, the escaping fumes can do similar damage.

Before disassembly begins, release the shutter. If the electronics do not work, the shutter will remain cocked even though the release button has been pressed. Check the shutter blade in front of the lens. A visible circle on the blade means that the shutter is still cocked. In order to release the blades manually, pull off the left sliding cover first. You can either pop it out of its channel, or make an L shaped flat tool that fits into the groove at the inside bottom of it. Looking down into the cover past the PC nipple, you'll see this groove. Force the L-shaped flat tool under the body of the camera in order to release the catch that prevents the sliding cover from sliding all the way off (photo 10.1).

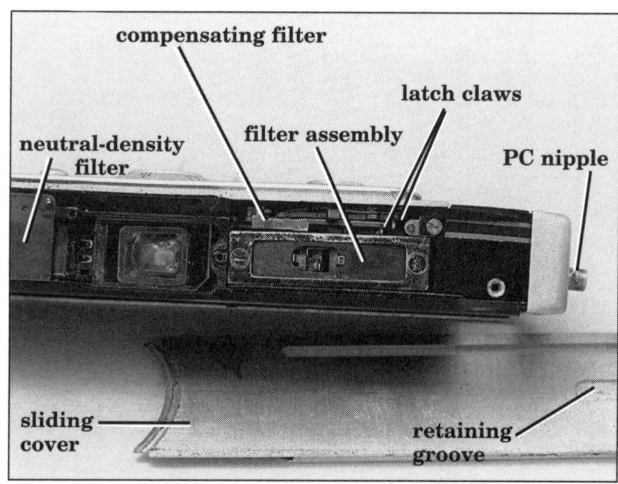


***10.1:** Pull off the sliding cover.*

Once the cover is off, remove the little side cover with the PC nipple. Remove the two small screws from the front cover, and lift it off (photo 10.2).

If you now peer into the gap between the top cover and the light sensor assembly, you will see the shutter operating arms and the latches that hold up each blade. Reach in with a small screwdriver, and push the two claws downwards; this will release the shutter blades.

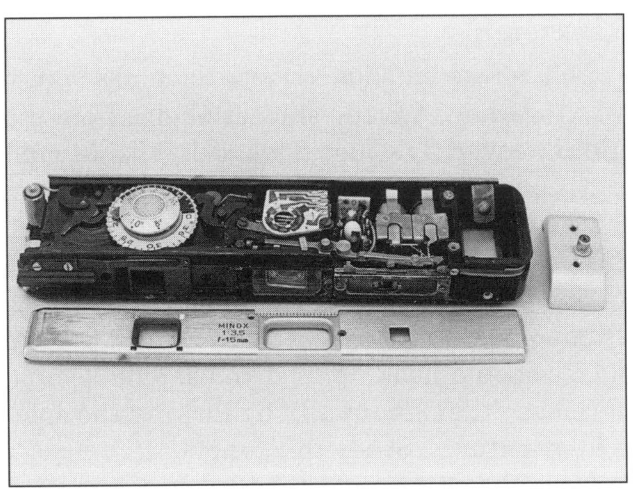


*10.2: Remove the front and side covers.*

Once you're certain that the shutter is released, turn over the camera and find the screw with the star slot in the side of the film chamber. Screw this out about three turns to release the sliding cover on that side.

As you are pulling the cover off, a little extra effort is required to get it past a click stop. The film advance rack as well as the shutter blades and springs come with the cover (photo 10.3).

(If the blades are still hooked-up when pulling the cover, the springs will permanently stretch, and damage to the the blades may occur as well.)

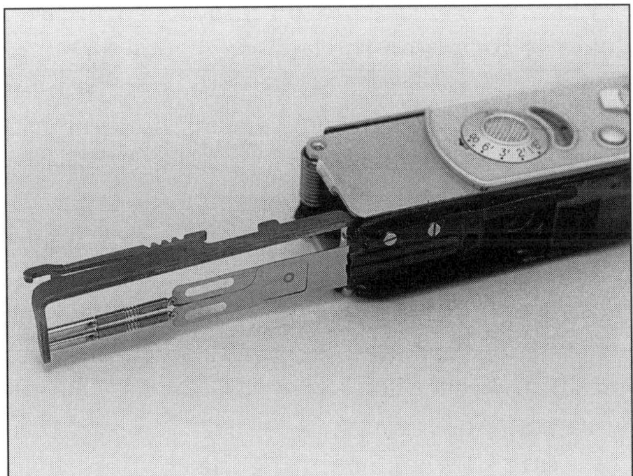

*10.3: Pull out the blade assembly.*

The top cover is held by three screws, plus the right-hand side is hooked over the body (photo 10.4).

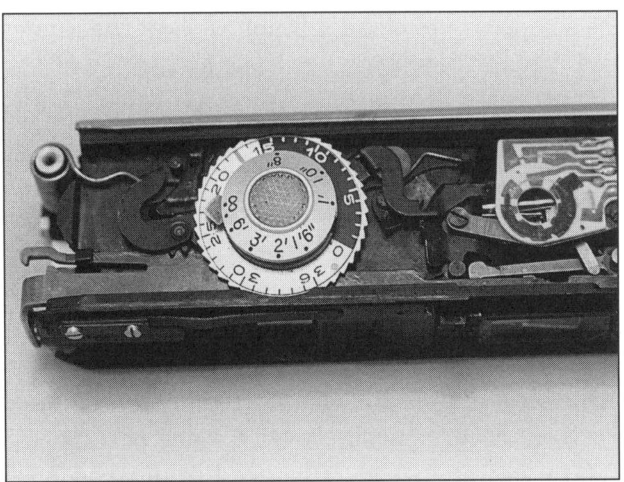

*10.4: The top cover removed.*

If the solenoids are sticky, remove them to get to the hinges where the corrosion or dirt has built up. Remove the two screws from the small ceramic board with the ASA resister. Unsolder three wires (black, blue and gray) from the edge of the board under the ceramic one.

Notice that the black wire continues on to the ceramic board, bridging the two. Turn the camera over and remove the nine mounting screws. With the bottom screws removed, the electronic components are loose (photo 10.5). Unsolder the battery contacts to be able to work freely on the solenoids.

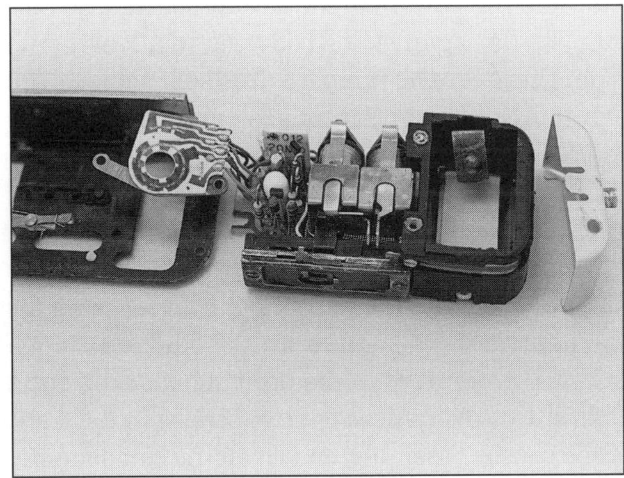

*10.5: The electronic assembly.*

Acid contamination can be dissolved in water. Corrosion must be scraped or filed off. Do a thorough job of cleaning the armature hinges. Once the solenoids are clean, a touch of oil at the hinges and a little black moly grease at the tip of the armatures will insure snappy operation. Make sure you get the spring at the end of the shutter-activating arm back into its proper place. This spring operates the little lever that closes the flash sync switch.

The front cover is retained by the small end-cover piece in addition to two small screws. Remove the two screws from the cover and the three screws from the end piece. The other side of the front cover is hooked over the end of the body.

The power switch is located under the ASA board and is operated by the winding rack and the release mechanism. It is OFF until the release button is pressed and remains ON until the sliding cover is closed again. As the circuit draws more current than today's C-MOS circuits do, you'd want to keep the sliding cover closed to preserve battery power.

The discrete-component electronics would be reliable were it not for the ever-present threat from leaking batteries. In addition to contaminating the solenoids, the battery acid can seep between the circuit board and the insulating layer and erode the printed conductors.

If the electronics don't work properly (one or the other solenoid is not energized), clean and examine the bottom of the circuit board. The bottom lies flat against the body casting, leaving no room there for the jumper wires so if some of the printed conductor strips are corroded, jumper them on the top side of the board.

The ASA filter is spring loaded. If the parts are sticking, the filter will not move even when the ASA knob is rotated (see photo 10.1). The other filter in front of the light sensor compensates for the neutral density filter and should also move freely. If the filters in the light sensor unit don't slide smoothly, remove the two screws in the front of the sensor assembly, and clean the components.

When you refit the front cover, make sure that the thumb slide bar over the viewfinder hooks up properly with the claw at the end of the compensating filter arm and with the neutral density filter at the other side. These two filters must move in tandem.

## Reassembly

Before reassembling, remove the film advance rack together with the shutter blades from the sliding cover. It's just hooked in inside, and comes out easily. Insert the shutter blades, then the copper rack, into their respective channels. Push the rack all the way in, then pull it out again to the click stop but no further. (Remember, the stop screw is still out!) The blades should hook up, and you should be able to release them manually by flicking the solenoid armatures. Study this function.

Once the shutter mechanism works, replace the top cover. Set the ASA dial to ASA 6 and push the sliding arm at the underside of the cover to the left, in contact with the eccentric. Make sure the counter dial and the focusing knob are centered properly, and the focus stop plate (looks like the tip of an arrow sticking out from under the focusing knob) is pointing straight toward the right (looking at it from the back).

This stop plate has to fit inside a notch in the underside of the top cover. The counter dial must be under the body rims on both sides (see photo 10.4).You will probably have to reposition the counter advance claw to get the dial in position. Center the dial exactly; it has to fall inside the recess in the under side of the top cover.

Place the release button into the cover first. Hold the cover and the camera upside down, or glue in the release button with a little light grease. Hook the right-hand side of the cover over the edge of the camera top.

Lift the left side of the top just enough to be able to reach under the cover with a thin blade, and push the ASA filter cam to the right. Pop the rear edge of the top plate under the lip of the back cover. If the ASA dial doesn't turn from end to end, lift the cover and try to position the ASA filter cam again.

Be careful when operating the shutter, there is still no stop! Check that the counter dial advances and that the focusing dial turns from end to end (from infinity to 8).

Once these functions are fine, you can replace the front cover. With the cover on, operate the sliding bar at the front of the camera to see that the neutral density filter and the compensating filter both move in tandem (see above).

Insert the left-side sliding cover into its channel on the bottom and push it home. It should slide all the way close with the stop claw clicking in as well. Push the right-side sliding cover on, and closed it all the way. The claw end of the copper advance rack should click in inside the cover. Lastly, screw in the stop screw inside the film chamber.

Try the different settings. Make sure the shutter actually opens and closes and not just clicks. If it works fine, you can congratulate yourself without any false modesty.

# Abstract

The following basic notes are abstracted from ***Camera Maintenance and Repair, Book One*** and ***Book Two*** by Thomas Tomosy, published by Amherst Media.

## Important Rules and Precautions (Book One)

Below is a list of blemishes beginners usually inflict on cameras and how you can avoid making the same mistakes.

1. Screw slots are rounded off: Make sure the screwdriver bit is sharp and fits into the screw slot. Press the screwdriver sufficiently into the slot, so it won't pop out and deface the screw.

2. Scratches, tool marks, especially around fasteners: Use the proper tool for the job. General purpose tools require more skill to use. Don't hesitate to regrind a tool for the specific job at hand, or to make a special tool. Whenever you have a choice, use a rubber tool rather than metal. (See Rubber Tools below.)

3. Cover plates scratched, scored, bent or missing: When removing cover plates, dials and name plates secured with contact cement, reach under them with a sharp sewing needle, lift up one corner, then with a thin blade, work them loose carefully. If the plate gets bent, straighten it perfectly before gluing it back on. If scratched, touch it up with a black felt-tip marker.

4. Leatherette torn or bumpy, smeared glue: Lift up one corner and peel it back, using strong tweezers. Work slowly and methodically; otherwise, the leatherette may rip.

Adjusting holes or screw holes are often covered with thin steel or brass plates. While peeling the leatherette, these small plates may bend. You must straighten them before sticking them back on because the glue will not hold them flat, and the leatherette will become bumpy.

5. "Crowbar marks" around the edges of covers: Never force a metal blade or bar under the skirt of a cover and try to pry it loose. Metal covers never need prying; it's always possible to wiggle them loose once all screws and retainers are removed.

6. Don't leave your fingerprints anywhere, especially where they are visible. Check and clean the viewfinder optics before replacing the top cover.

Other than diminishing the cosmetic appearance of the camera, it's easy to cause mechanical damage as well. To prevent this from happening, pay special attention to the following rules:

1. Take your time, especially when learning a new camera. Never get impatient. Try to enjoy what you're doing.

2. Keep your bench organized. Never work on a cluttered bench. The work is in front of you, the parts laid out behind it, and your tools (just the few you're actually using) should be to your preferred side.

3. Don't lose parts. The surest way to lose parts is by working on a cluttered bench or by dropping

them. Parts have a tendency to spring, to roll, or fly. If you don't watch out for this, you'll spend half of your repair time on your hands and knees searching for invisible little doodads.

4. Know how everything goes back together. Always study the mechanism before disassembly. Before removing a part, determine what it does, how it is orientated in the assembly, how it is connected to and interacts with, its neighboring parts.

If you're not sure you'll remember how it goes back, draw a diagram, and make sketches and notes. If you must remove some gears, always mark their position relative to each other by scoring the meshing teeth.

5. Don't damage anything. Don't apply excessive force. Don't try to bend hardened steel, cast-aluminum alloy, or plastic parts.

Never force a stuck part or assembly when trying to remove it. Locate the point of resistance by carefully prying one side of the assembly and then the other, noting the pivot point.

6. Don't be screwdriver happy! Try to figure out the short and easy way to get to the problem, and remove only the parts that must be removed. Correct a false start by replacing the parts that were removed unnecessarily.

7. Never put any glass parts (lenses, prisms, etc.) on a hard table surface. Always lay a paper towel down first, and place glass parts on it.

8. Never pry at glass optical parts in order to remove them from their mount. If possible, push it out from the other side or invert the assembly, and let the element fall out onto a soft cloth if the next element is retained. Otherwise, try to pull it out with adhesive tape or with a rubber suction cup.

Be careful not to touch one glass element to another during removal or refitting.

8. Do not overlubricate. Excessive oil in the mechanism does more harm than good. It may even cause permanent damage. Do not flood with oil or any oil solution.

9. Do not use strong solvents such as Acetone or lacquer thinner for general cleaning.

10. Never apply Krazy Glue™ directly from its tube. Always take a tiny drop onto the tip of a small screwdriver, and touch the drop to the part you're gluing. Capillary action will pull the liquid right into a tiny crack. Apply the tiniest amount, as the excess will run and may glue some moving parts together.

In some applications, the glue alone does the job; in others, reinforcement with steel pins or screws is required.

## Tool Alternatives (Book One)

### Compressed Air

While a compressor is the best for mechanical cleaning, it's noisy and expensive. Aerosol cans are expensive and don't last very long for air-intensive mechanical cleaning.

Rubber squeeze bulbs may be used for light optical cleaning. The most economical solution is a rubber foot pump intended for inflating air mattresses. This pump is good for either optical or mechanical cleaning.

### Round-nose Pliers

If used for pin-face screws, the tips must be fine enough to fit the holes in the screw head. Retaining rings have either square slots or round holes for the tool to fit in, and the tip of the tool may be shaped accordingly. This tool will slip easily and damage the parts or covers if used carelessly.

### General Purpose Plier-wrenches (photo 11.1)

These wrenches are homemade from good quality long-nosed pliers by heating the tips to cherry red with a propane torch and bending them to the desired shape.

When satisfied with the shape, reheat the tips again evenly to cherry red, then quench them in used crankcase oil, not in water. Then you can grind the ends to fit the slots in retaining rings.

The middle one in the photo (#2) is required frequently for removing retaining rings that hold the shutter assemblies in rangefinder or folding cameras. The same pliers may fit the front rings (name ring) inside the filter ring on many lenses.

Some of the front rings have slots in them, some holes, some nothing. If they have no holes or slots, then use a rubber tool.

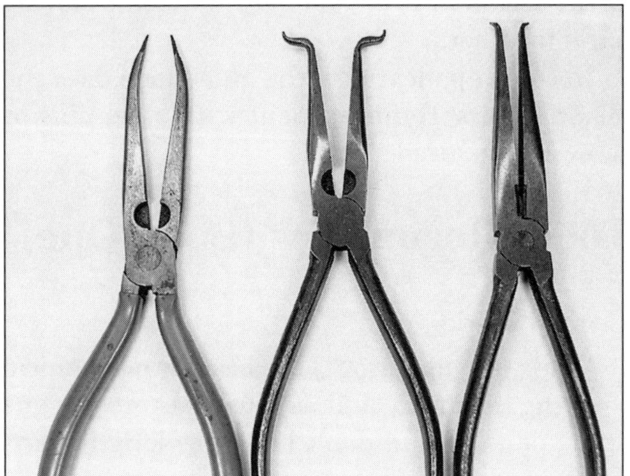

*11.1: Homemade plier wrenches, #1, #2, #3.*

## Rubber Tools (Book Two)

A ready supply of rubber items can be found in household, hardware, auto accessory, or plumbing supply stores or departments. Some of these items can be used as-is; others can be easily modified.

Useful items to look for are rubber hoses, sink stoppers, rubber gaskets, O-rings, rubber furniture leg cups, laboratory glassware stoppers, rubber grommets, and bicycle, motorcycle, and truck inner tubes, etc.

### Applications for Rubber Tools

1. In order to remove a name ring from a lens assembly, you need a rubber tool that fits inside the filter ring and lies flat against the name ring. There must be a hollow inside the tool to clear the convexity of the front lens element. Rubber furniture leg cups are ideal for the small to medium sizes. Rubber hose may do the trick for the smallest sizes.

A large size ring tool can be made from thick sheet-rubber (inner tube for trucks) by wrapping a strip of it around a round object, such as a plastic drain pipe, a metal spray can lid, or a thick drinking glass.

Another way to make a large rubber ring is by starting with a ring or cup shape again and smearing silicon rubber onto the rim of it. Let it cure for two days before use.

2. A rubber strip from a bicycle inner tube is used as a non-scratch liner inside a ring wrench. This method can also be utilized to tightly fit a loose-fitting ring wrench.

3. If the ring to be undone is sitting up front of the assembly, such as a filter stuck on the lens, use a rubber sheet flat on the table; turn the lens assembly face down with the filter butted against the rubber sheet, then use both hands to give the lens assembly a good twist to unscrew the filter. Glue, nails, or clamps can be used to secure the rubber sheet or slab to the bench.

4. A rubber hose 11mm in diameter can be used to remove the release button from many modern Yashica and Contax cameras, or a small beaker stopper can be adapted for this purpose by carving or drilling a concave into the face of it.

5. Cylindrical rings and collars are extremely difficult to undo with anything but a well-fitting rubber tool. They are usually found around release buttons (Minolta SRT series), sometimes on winding cranks, or in older cameras as decorative fittings on rangefinder optics (Leica II and III series). Find a sturdy rubber hose that fits the ring or collar tightly and you can unscrew any of these without any possibility of damaging the part. See also Leica II in Chapter Ten, this book.

7. A large smooth headed screw can be unscrewed with a beaker stopper. Even if the large head is equipped with holes for a pin-face screwdriver, it is better to try rubber before resorting to a metal tool.

If any of the rubber tools don't seem to be sticky enough, and they slip on the part instead of grabbing it fast, clean both the part and the tool with lighter fluid.

If the rubber is treated with something such as an inner tube treated with talcum, you will have to wash off all the talcum using lighter fluid or Acetone™.

Some rubbers tend to oxidize over time and develop a hard non-sticky surface layer. If the rubber is not too old, sanding off the hard top layer will help. After many years, the rubber may become hard and brittle throughout. At that point it should be discarded.

## Optical Cleaning (Book One)

### Cleaning Coated Glass

Use acid-free glass cleaner (Windex™) and facial tissue. Paper products meant for wiping will not damage the lens. It's the dirt, the grit, and dust on it that does the harm. Blow the dust off before cleaning. Ball up a small piece of tissue and apply Windex™ to it.

Don't spray onto the lens. Gently wipe the lens with the soaked tissue. Take a clean piece, ball it up, breathe on the lens, and wipe it off. Never wipe dry glass with dry tissue. Do not rub! Start at the center, wipe in one direction in a spiral working outwards. Discard the tissue. Take a new one, and repeat until satisfied.

If the lens is very dirty, especially if contaminated with oil, grime, or finger grease, start with lighter fluid the same way as described above, and follow up with Windex™. Alcohol works as well.

Most importantly, prevent dirt from contaminating the lens. Keep the lens cap on when the camera is not in use. Vacuum the inside of the camera case and/or the gadget bag frequently. The less frequently you have to clean the lens, the better.

### Cleaning The Mirror

The mirror does not need regular cleaning. The dust you see in the viewfinder is not on the mirror. There is absolutely nothing to gain by "dusting off" in the mirror chamber, but you stand a good chance of harming the works. If you must blow off the mirror or the screen, use low air pressure, perhaps a squeeze-bulb.

If you must clean the mirror, do it the same way you cleaned the lens. Use tweezers to hold a tightly-folded piece of tissue as your cleaning tool. Wipe once in one direction only. Do not rub. The mirror coating is usually aluminum (softer than lens coating, much softer than glass). Some of the newer mirrors may have a thin glass coating over the aluminum. These are less vulnerable to cleaning than bare aluminum, but unless you know for sure, assume it's uncoated, and treat the mirror with utmost care.

### Cleaning the Viewfinder of an SLR

If the dust particles you see in the viewfinder are in sharp focus, they are between the screen and the pentaprism and not on the mirror. If they show up as soft blurry spots, they are on the under surface of the focusing screen. Anything on the mirror, on the lens, on the eyepiece, or between the eyepiece and the prism, forms no discernable image in the viewfinder.

If the system has a removable prism unit or a removable screen, getting to the dust and cleaning the viewfinder is easy. Otherwise, the only way to get to the dust is by removing the top cover and the prism. Many modern cameras feature removable screens (photo 11.2) which makes cleaning the viewfinder easy. To do so, remove the screen, and blow off both sides of it. Use moderate air pressure to blow off the underside of the prism through the mirror chamber.

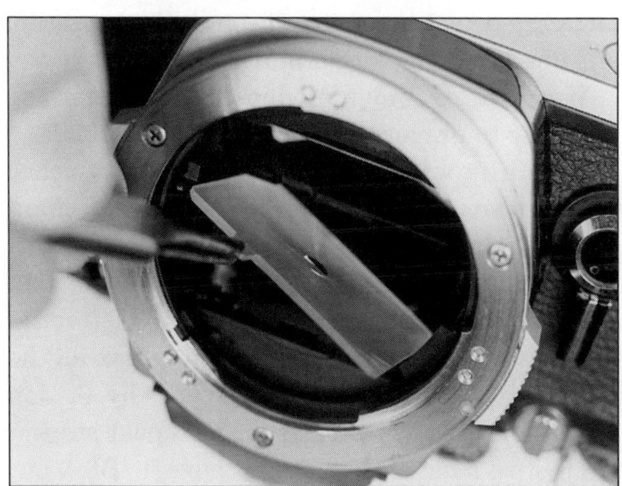

***11.2:** Removable focusing screen.*

If the screen has been contaminated, it must be removed for cleaning. Once out, spray a generous amount of Windex™ onto both sides of the screen, wipe it very gently with tissue soaked in Windex™ or with your finger tip. Then rinse it under running water, and blow it off. It must not be wiped dry. Be very careful with Fresnel™

screens. They are easy to damage, and many of them are expensive; others might be unavailable.

### Cleaning Optical Plastic

Optical plastic is soft! The more you clean it, the cloudier it gets. Dunk tightly-folded tissue in Windex. Squeeze it out between a folded paper towel. Wipe the optical plastic with the damp tissue carefully and only once. No rubbing! If the plastic is cloudy or grimy, use toothpaste to gently polish the plastic.

## Mechanical Cleaning (Book One)

### Flood-cleaning

This shortcut is effective for dissolving excessive oil or grime. 1. Squirt a generous amount of lighter fluid onto the parts to be cleaned. 2. Work the mechanism to dissolve the oil. 3. Blot up the mixture with tissue paper (not with cloth). 4. Repeat steps 2 and 3 several times. 5. Blow out the remaining liquid. (Hold the nozzle close to the parts.) Repeat 1 through 5 if some oil remains. 6. Dry the assembly with a hair dryer.

**Warning:** remove all loose parts from the assembly to prevent blowing them away.

**Flooding with graphite solution** is an easy way to clean and lubricate a complicated mechanical assembly. 1. Mix fine graphite powder with lighter fluid. 2. Stir with a folded tissue. 3. Dab the tissue to the assembly to be lubricated. 4. Repeat steps 2 and 3 until the fluid gets to all the parts. 5. Work the mechanism repeatedly. 6. Mop up the fluid with clean tissue. 7. Repeat steps 5 and 6 until most of the liquid is gone. 8. Blow out the remaining liquid and graphite powder. 9. Gently warm up the assembly with a hair dryer. Do all this fast. Make sure no liquid remains. Protect the optics from liquid or graphite.

## Resetting (Book One)

1. Attempt to reset a mechanical camera by disengaging the wind lock, then winding and releasing the camera. (The wind lock is often located at the bottom of the camera.) 2. Attempt to reset an electronic motorized P&S camera by inserting film and setting the rewind. 3. Attempt to reset an electronic SLR by exposing on its mechanical setting.

## Polaroid Mirror (Book One)

All reflex Polaroid cameras have a large front-surface mirror in them. Look for rigid bodies, such as the Pronto!™, the One Step™ or other inexpensive models. Break open the housing, and salvage the mirror.

## Recementing Compound Lenses (Book Two)

Compound lenses cemented with Canada Balsam often separate over the decades. Early signs of separation may be a rainbow discoloration or pale yellow stains around the edges of the element.

Canada Balsam melts at about 150° Celsius and is soluble in dimetilketon (Acetone™). If it's a relatively old lens, you can assume the cement used was Canada Balsam. You may then proceed with confidence. First, using a hair drier, heat up the lens to the resin's melting point. Build the lens around with plywood on five sides, and direct hot air from a hair drier into this enclosure. After an hour of heating the lens, take a linen or cotton towel or gloves (The lens is hot!), and attempt to slide the two elements apart. If it doesn't budge, don't force it. Up the heat and leave the lens for another hour in your make-shift oven. If it still doesn't budge, use it as is or write it off.

Canada Balsam comes apart easily once melted. It requires a minimum of force. Once apart, let it cool down naturally without being force cooled. Place a felt-pen mark on the outside surfaces just to be sure you don't mix up the sides. Soak a tissue in Acetone™ and wipe off the balsam with it.

When both sides are absolutely clean, place the concave element on a sheet of paper towel, and place a drop of optical cement on the center of it. Edmund Scientific (address in the appendix) carries a synthetic optical resin that cures in UV light, called Norland Optical Adhesive #60. The clear liquid can be applied directly from the bottle to the center of the lens. Apply one drop only and not a fat one at that. (Larger lenses require a larger drop.) Don't spread the resin. Just leave it there in a nice round bead. Now carefully place the center of the other element on top of the bead of resin and apply a gentle rocking pressure. Spread the drop slowly and evenly until it reaches the edges of the lens. You don't have to hurry. This resin remains liquid until UV light hits it. Once you're satisfied with the alignment, direct a UV lamp (sunlamp) onto the lens. Direct sunlight also does the trick. It takes only a few minutes for the resin to gel and not more than ten minutes to cure completely. Keep the elements aligned during the curing process. While the resin is still liquid, the elements may slip by their own weight. Clean the edges of any overflow of resin.

## Testing Shutter Speeds without Instruments (Book One)

It is possible to test shutter speeds to ballpark figures with your own senses. Set the camera onto 1/1000 second or the highest available shutter speed. With the lens removed, open the door, point the camera toward an evenly illuminated surface such as a white wall or a sheet of white paper. (It doesn't matter how far away the surface is.) Look through the frame as you trip the shutter. You should see the frame faintly light up (i.e. catch a glimpse of the wall through the shutter). If one side of the frame is darker than the other (usually the opposite side from the winding crank) it's called capping, and the shutter needs cleaning, lubrication and adjustment, or just adjustment if the capping is not excessive. If the frame remains completely dark on the highest shutter speed, try the next speed and the next. If they work or capping occurs, then the problem is the same as before only worse.

At shutter speeds slower than 1/60 second, the slow-speed escapement is engaged in its various modes. The length of the buzzing sound the escapement makes is an indication of the shutter speed. With a little practice, you will be able to tell the difference by ear between the slow speeds, and by eye between the high speeds. Practice on a good camera.

Suppose you want to test one of the bottom-feeder Leica models where you cannot see through the shutter for lack of a door to open. All is not lost. Slide a white sheet of paper under the pressure plate where the film normally goes, and look through the shutter from the front as you expose. Otherwise, everything is the same as before. Instead of looking at the wall from the back, now you're looking at the white paper from the front.

With a lens shutter the procedure is the same as with an SLR, only you won't see the whole frame illuminated. With the lens on, you can only see the circle of the aperture, and with a lens shutter, there is no capping.

## Mechanical SLR with Lens Shutter Configuration (Book One)

In this configuration the lens must be open for viewing. There is usually an extra cover flap behind the mirror to seal the film plane. The exposure sequence is as follows: the trigger releases a master ring which simultaneously closes the shutter and the diaphragm and flips up the mirror. Continuing its movement, it flips up the cover flap, then triggers the shutter. The shutter now opens and closes for exposure. After exposure, the master ring reverses itself and closes the cover flap first, then simultaneously opens the shutter and the diaphragm, and brings down the mirror.

At the end of its travel it kicks out the winding lock. Notice that the shutter timing is internal and independent from the master ring.

An interesting side effect of all this is that if the shutter isn't working properly, it sticks open rather than close as is usual with other lens shutters. Then the mirror and the cover flap take the place of the shutter. With the shutter stuck open, the cover flap is able to provide about 1/30 second exposure. Therefore, some of the pictures may even be well-exposed despite a non-functioning shutter.

A quick way to examine the shutter: set the camera on self-timer and to a one second shutter speed. Watch the blades. As you trigger the shutter, the blades must snap shut instantly with no hesitation.

When the timer triggers the shutter, the blades should snap open. After one second, you must see the blades momentarily closing before opening finally for viewing, at which time, the mirror comes down with a clank too.

Some of the earlier models, such as the Bessamatic, several models of the Contaflex, as well as the Nikkorex, have no instant-return mirror, as a result, the mirror will stay up with the shutter closed after each exposure. The mirror resets, and the shutter opens when you wind the camera on.

## Lubrication Recommendations

| Function | Parts | Lubricant | Source |
|---|---|---|---|
| Slow moving | rewind shaft, advance gears charging shafts cams, rack & pinions | light grease, silicon grease, light lithium grease | automotive, hardware |
| Fast moving small surface | focal-plane shutter, shafts in bushings, curtain shafts, curtain take-up drum (down side), timing gears, master shaft, ratchet claws (pivot) | light, oil 3in1™ light silicon oil, graphite powder in lighter fluid | household, electronic supply, camera distributor, automotive |
| Fast moving large surface | lens-shutter blades & control ring, automatic diaphragm blades & control ring | no lubricant graphite in lighter fluid or dry graphite rubbed on | automotive, camera distributor, locksmith |
| High friction, high load | shutter tensioning claw mirror catch lever, master ring catch | molybdenum or lithium paste, graphite paste | automotive camera distributor |
| Helical threads | focus ring in separate lens assemblies or built-in lenses | heavy, viscous grease, bearing grease | automotive |
| Plastic parts | for all plastic parts | synthetic-based grease, lithium paste | automotive electronic camera distributor |

***Note:*** *There are many lubricating agents that have been formulated for some specific purpose and may not be the best for cameras. If possible, obtain specifications or recommendations for usage. Do not use any product if you're not sure what it is or what it is intended for. You must never use any oil or grease intended for cooking or cosmetic purposes.*

# Appendix

## Glossary

**Bellows tool:** Modified pliers for removing bellows from folding cameras.

**Capping:** 1. One side of a frame is either black or darker than the other side. 2. The malfunction in a focal-plane shutter causing unevenly exposed frames, caused by unequal shutter curtain speeds.

**CdS (CadmiumSulfide):** Photoresistor. As a sensor for a light metering system, requires battery power to operate. Very slow responding—especially under low illumination.

**Cocking (charging, tensioning):** The readying of an assembly (shutter or mirror) for exposure. In some of the latest P&S models, no cocking of the mechanism occurs, but stepping motors operate all major moving parts without the intervention of springs. (The shutter mechanism in even the most sophisticated SLRs is still operated by springs, thus require cocking before exposure can occur.)

**Cyanoacrylate:** A fast setting cement. Sets by the action of humidity in the air. A well-known brand is Krazy Glue™, also called fast glue, instant glue, Instabond™, Super Glue™, and other names. Temperature, humidity, the material being glued, depth and freshness of the glue (fresh glue sets faster) influence setting time. Once the tube is opened, the unused liquid tends to thicken, and at room temperature, it gels and becomes useless in about one to two months. If kept in the fridge, it lasts longer.

**Escapement (governor):** A mechanical timing device works on the same principle as clock movements do. Usually found in self-timers, shutter timers, "M" sync timers, AF sequence timers.

**Glue Pen™:** Plastic paper glue in a tall, slander container. Dries to a flexible, transparent plastic film. May be used for repairing bellows.

**Graphite:** In powder form, a good lubricating agent for cameras. May also be used as a filler agent in composite materials to improve the physical properties of some plastics.

**Graining paper:** Stiff cardboard embossed on one side with a negative leather-grain pattern. Comes in a vinyl repair kit and intended to impress a grain pattern into newly applied vinyl paste.

**Group (front group, etc.):** A group of lens elements forming a discrete assembly. One front group and one rear group in a simple lens; usually front, rear, and two zoom groups in zoom lenses.

**Inertia timer:** A shutter timing device found in older or inexpensive mechanical cameras. After they are opened, the shutter blades are kept open for as long as it takes to accelerate a weight out of the way. This can be a swinging weight at the end of a pivoting lever or a spinning wheel accelerated through a rack and pinion arrangement.

**Intermittent malfunction:** Recurring and disappearing at random or at physical influence. Not steady or reliable.

**Pin-face screw:** It has a big flat head with two holes in it, such as found on top of many winding cranks or shutter-speed dials.

**Rewind button:** Usual placement on bottom right. Push to disengage the sprocket for rewinding the film. May be placed on the top as well, but always close to one end or the other of the film-advance sprocket.

**Rewind knob (rewind crank):** Usual placement on top left, for manual rewinding of the film.

**Selenium:** Photovoltaic cell. As a light meter sensor, it requires no battery but provides enough power to drive a galvanometer. Its color response deviates from that of the human eye.

**Shutter:** Device to let a controlled amount of light reach the film plate. Usual placement is either at the focal-plane or inside the lens between the front and rear groups. In simple designs, the shutter may be placed behind the lens, and on rare occasions, in front of the lens, such as in the case of the original Spy Minox.

**SOS™:** #00 steel wool impregnated with soap. Available where household cleaners are sold. Good to clean metal parts. Removes oxides, tarnish, etc. Good for cleaning and polishing fine metals.

**Sprocket:** A toothed wheel engaging with the film perforations. Uniformly advances the film the length of one frame. In the electronic P&S models, the sprocket as defined above is absent. The take-up spool advances (pulls) the film. There may be a single-disk sprocket which, rather than advancing the film, may fill a sensing and feedback task.

**Standard light:** A calibrated steady light source for testing and calibrating light meters.

**Stop:** 1. The difference of one in the EV value. 2. The amount of offset on any of the control dials that produces a difference of one in the EV value (often one physical click-stop).

**Variable Density Filter:** A circular or crescent shape filter in front of the light sensor. Usually attached to the ASA dial or aperture dial and has the property of passing more or less light through at different portions along its length. The variable density is often accomplished by a photographic emulsion on a film base or by partial mirrorization of film or glass. It can also be a slot or small holes in a metal plate.

# Suppliers

### Camera Bellows LTD

(stock and custom bellows)
Runcorn Works
2 Runcorn Rd.
Birmingham 12, England
tel: 0121-440-1695

### Edmund Scientific

(tools, optics, chemicals)
101 E. Gloucester Pike
Barrington, NJ 08007

### Efstonscience Inc.

(Edmund Scientific, Canada)
3350 Dufferin St.
Toronto, Ont. M6A 3A4 Canada
tel:(416)787-4581-5 fax:(416)787-5140

### Fargo Enterprise

(parts, tools, worldwide directory)
301 County Airport Rd. #105
Vacaville, CA 95688
tel:(707)446-1120 or (800)359-2878

### Noble Enterprises

(camera parts and manuals)
P.O. Box 46
Marion, IA 52302
email: gnoble@cedar-rapids.net

### Peachtree Marketing Inc.

(batteries, accessories, books)
85 Citizen Court, Unit 14
Markham, ON L6G 1A8 Canada
tel:(905)470-8822 fax:(800)363-9040

### Society of Photo-Technologists, Cam-Comp Inc.

(tools, parts, instruments)
325 Route 17M, Suite 5
Monroe, NY 10950
fax:(914)782-4248

**Timesavers**
(clock parts, tools, fasteners, oils)
Box 12700
Scottsdale, AZ 85267
tel:(602)483-3711 fax:(602)483-6116

**Western Bellows Company**
(custom bellows)
9340 7th St., Suite G
Rancho Cucamonga, CA 91730-5664
tel: (909)980-0606

# Recommended Readings

### Camera Shopper

A monthly periodical. At least half of the magazine is filled with classified ads of cameras and photo equipment, the balance is committed to articles on antique and collectable cameras. A calendar of camera shows and swap-meets is included at the end of the magazine.

### Kovels' Antiques & Collectibles Fix-it Source Book

By Ralph & Terry Kovel (1990) Contains mostly names and addresses of suppliers of hard-to-find items and substances for restoring any type of collectibles. Some methods and ideas for restorations are also included. (ART 707.3 K88kf)

### Lind's List Camera Price Guide and Master Data Catalog

Includes over 13,000 current prices. Lists cameras from 1939 to modern times.

### McBroom's Camera Bluebook

By Michael McBroom. This is a complete, up-to-date price and buyers guide for new and used cameras, lenses and accessories. (Amherst Media)

### McKeown's Price Guide to Antique and Classic Cameras

Includes over 10,000 current camera prices. This book is updated bi-annually.

### Restoring and Preserving Antiques

By Frederic Taubes (1969). Comprehensive restoration and finishing instructions for wood. Contains interesting finishing techniques, gilding, antiquing etc. Stone, metal and paintings restoration is also included. Lavishly illustrated. Artificial patina application on wood and metals. (707.3 T22r)

### Shutterbug

A monthly periodical. This magazine is crammed full with used and new photo equipment and services ads.

# Index

# Other Books from
# Amherst Media

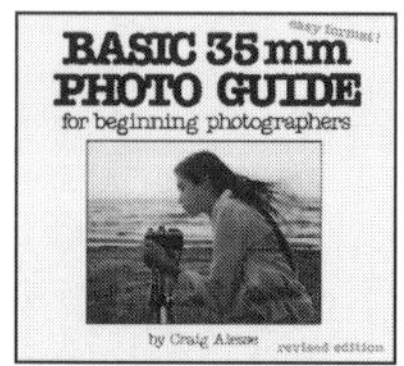


## Basic 35mm Photo Guide

*Craig Alesse*

Great for beginning photographers! Designed to teach 35mm basics step-by-step — completely illustrated. Features the latest cameras. Includes: 35mm automatic, semi-automatic cameras, camera handling, *f*-stops, shutter speeds, and more! $12.95 list, 9x8, 112p, 178 photos, order no. 1051.

## Build Your Own Home Darkroom

*Lista Duren & Will McDonald*

This classic book teaches you how to build a high quality, inexpensive darkroom in your basement, spare room, or almost anywhere. Includes valuable information on: darkroom design, woodworking, tools, and more! $17.95 list, 8½x11, 160p, order no. 1092.

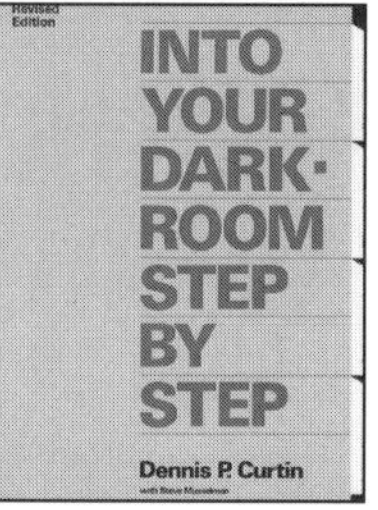


## Into Your Darkroom Step-by-Step

*Dennis P. Curtin*

This is the ideal beginning darkroom guide. Easy to follow and fully illustrated each step of the way. Includes information on: the equipment you'll need, set-up, making proof sheets and much more! $17.95 list, 8½x11, 90p, hundreds of photos, order no. 1093.

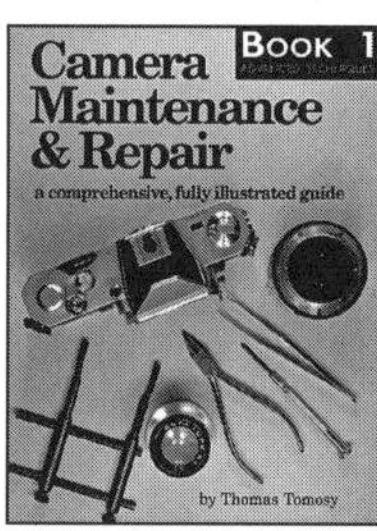


## Camera Maintenance & Repair Book 1

*Thomas Tomosy*

A step-by-step, illustrated guide by a master camera repair technician. Includes: testing camera functions, general maintenance, basic tools needed and where to get them, basic repairs for accessories, camera electronics, plus "quick tips" for maintenance and more! $29.95 list, 8½x11, 176p, order no. 1158.

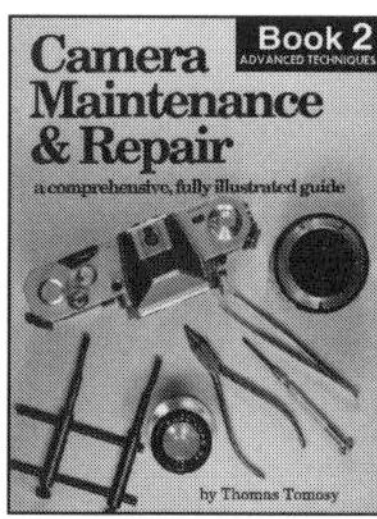


## Camera Maintenance & Repair Book 2

*Thomas Tomosy*

Build on the basics covered Book 1, with advanced techniques. Includes: mechanical and electronic SLRs, zoom lenses, medium format cameras, and more. Features models not included in the Book 1. $29.95 list, 8½x11, 176p, 150+ photos, charts, tables, appendices, index, glossary, order no. 1558.

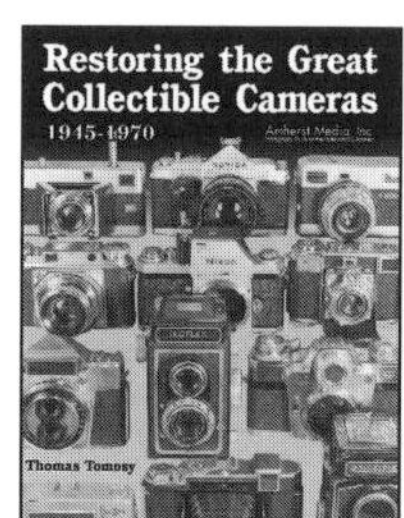


## Restoring the Great Collectible Cameras (1945-70)

*Thomas Tomosy*

More step-by-step instruction on how to repair collectible cameras. Covers postwar models (1945-70). Hundreds of illustrations show disassembly and repair. $29.95 list, 8½x11, 128p, 200+ photos, index, order no. 1560.

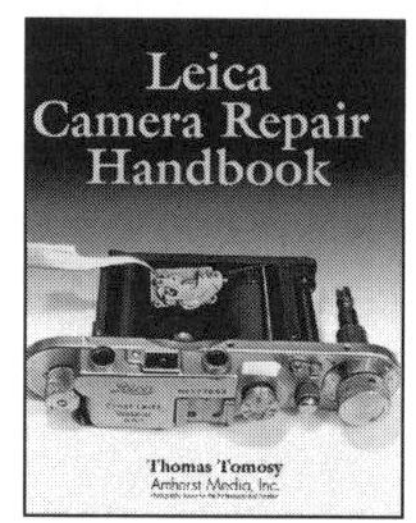


## Leica Camera Repair Handbook

*Thomas Tomosy*

A detailed technical manual for repairing Leica cameras. Each model is discussed individually with step-by-step instructions. Exhaustive photographic illustration ensures that every step of the process is easy to follow. $39.95 list, 8½x11, 128p, 130 b&w photos, appendix, order no. 1641.

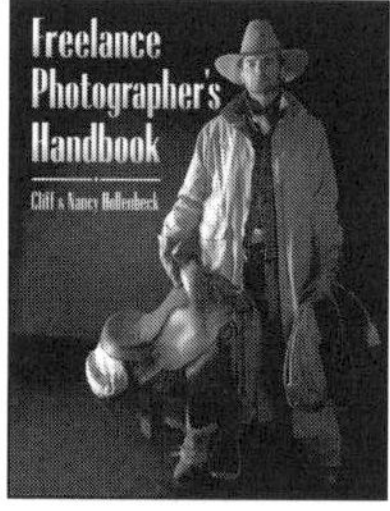


## Freelance Photographer's Handbook

*Cliff & Nancy Hollenbeck*

Whether you want to be a freelance photographer or are looking for tips to improve your current freelance business, this volume is packed with ideas for creating and maintaining a successful freelance business. $29.95 list, 8½x11, 107p, 100 b&w and color photos, index, glossary, order no. 1633.

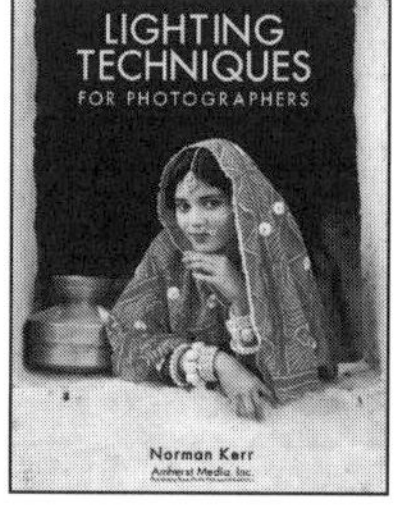


## Lighting Techniques for Photographers

*Norman Kerr*

This book teaches you to predict the effects of light in the final image. It covers the interplay of light qualities, as well as color compensation and manipulation of light and shadow. $29.95 list, 8½x11, 120p, 150+ color and b&w photos, index, order no. 1564.

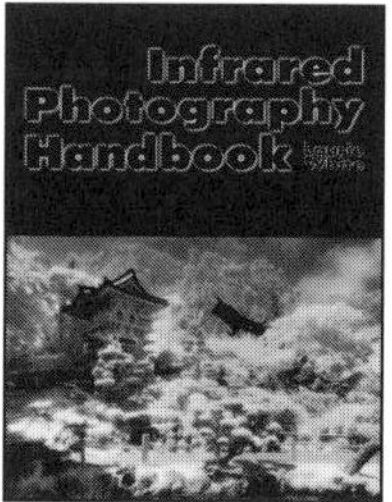


## Infrared Photography Handbook

*Laurie White*

Covers black and white infrared photography: focus, lenses, film loading, film speed rating, batch testing, paper stocks, and filters. Black & white photos illustrate how IR film reacts. $29.95 list, 8½x11, 104p, 50 b&w photos, charts & diagrams, order no. 1419.

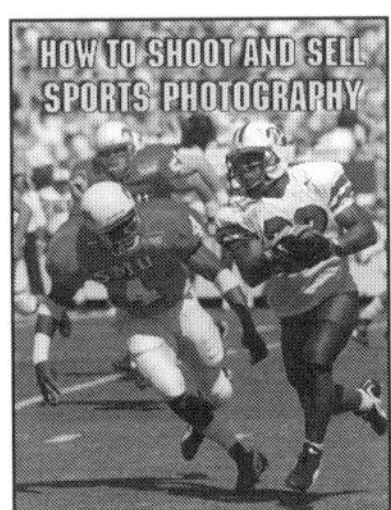


## How to Shoot and Sell Sports Photography

*David Arndt*

A step-by-step guide for amateur photographers, photojournalism students and journalists seeking to develop the skills and knowledge necessary for success in the demanding field of sports photography. $29.95 list, 8½x11, 120p, 111 photos, index, order no. 1631.

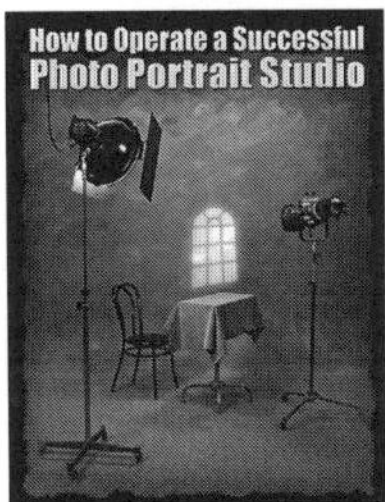


## How to Operate a Successful Photo Portrait Studio

*John Giolas*

Combines photographic techniques with practical business information to create a complete guide book for anyone interested in developing a portrait photography business (or improving an existing business). $29.95 list, 8½x11, 120p, 120 photos, index, order no. 1579.

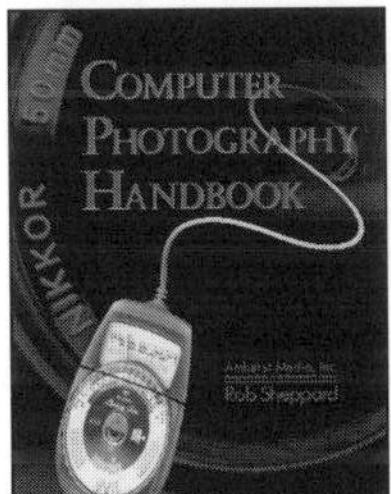


## Computer Photography Handbook

*Rob Sheppard*

Learn to make the most of your photographs using computer technology! From creating images with digital cameras, to scanning prints and negatives, to manipulating images, you'll learn all the basics of digital imaging. $29.95 list, 8½x11, 128p, 150+ photos, index, order no. 1560.

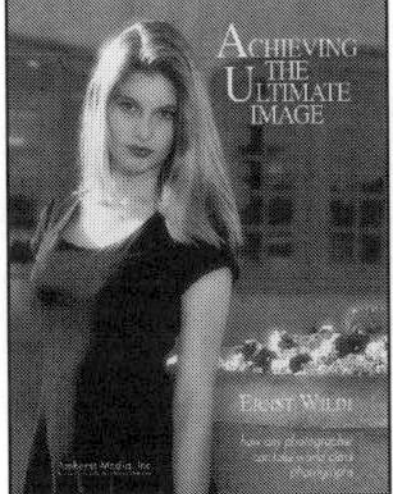


## Achieving the Ultimate Image

*Ernst Wildi*

Ernst Wildi teaches the techniques required to take world class, technically flawless photos. Features: exposure, metering, the Zone System, composition, evaluating an image, and more! $29.95 list, 8½x11, 128p, 120 b&w and color photos, index, order no. 1628.

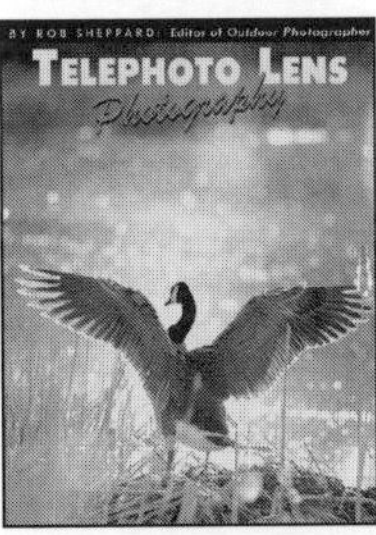


## Telephoto Lens Photography

*Rob Sheppard*

A complete guide for telephoto lenses. Shows you how to take great wildlife photos, portraits, sports and action shots, travel pics, and much more! Features over 100 photographic examples. $17.95 list, 8½x11, 112p, b&w and color photos, index, glossary, appendices, order no. 1606.

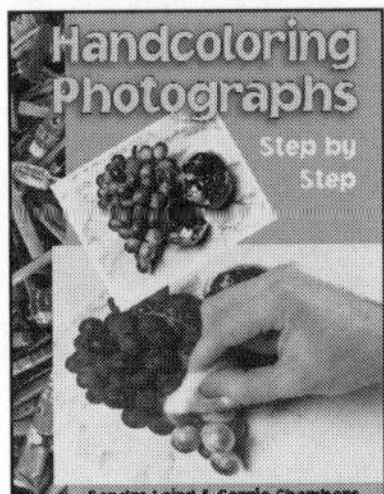


## Handcoloring Photographs Step-by-Step

*Sandra Laird & Carey Chambers*

Learn to handcolor photographs step-by-step with the new standard in handcoloring reference books. Covers a variety of coloring media and techniques with plenty of colorful photographic examples. $29.95 list, 8½x11, 112p, 100+ color and b&w photos, order no. 1543.

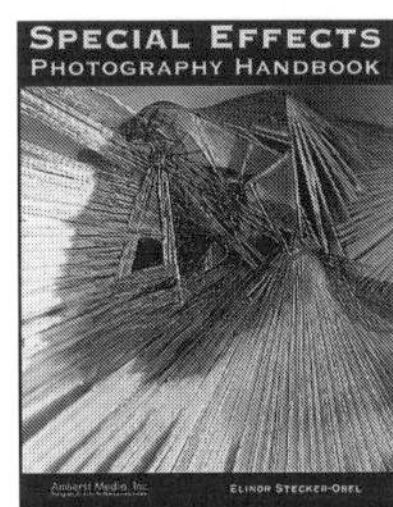


## Special Effects Photography Handbook

*Elinor Stecker-Orel*

Create magic on film with special effects! Little or no additional equipment required, use things you probably have around the house. Step-by-step instructions guide you through each effect. $29.95 list, 8½x11, 112p, 80+ color and b&w photos, index, glossary, order no. 1614.

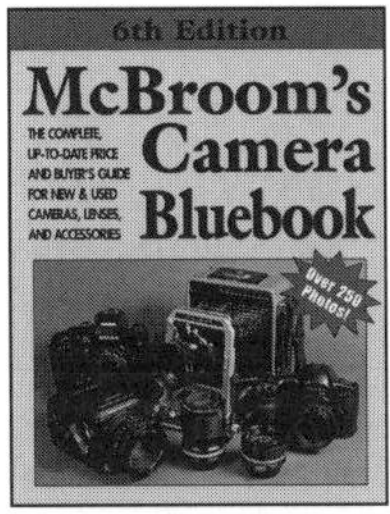


## McBroom's Camera Bluebook, *6th Edition*

*Mike McBroom*

Comprehensive and fully illustrated, with price information on: 35mm, digital, APS, underwater, medium & large format cameras, exposure meters, strobes and accessories. Pricing info based on equipment condition. A must for any camera buyer, dealer, or collector! $29.95 list, 8½x11, 336p, 275+ photos, order no. 1553.

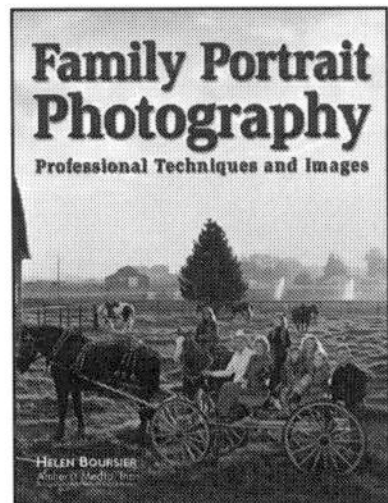


## Family Portrait Photography

*Helen Boursier*

Learn from professionals how to operate a successful portrait studio. Includes: marketing family portraits, advertising, working with clients, posing, lighting, and selection of equipment. Includes images from a variety of top portrait shooters. $29.95 list, 8½x11, 120p, 123 photos, index, order no. 1629.

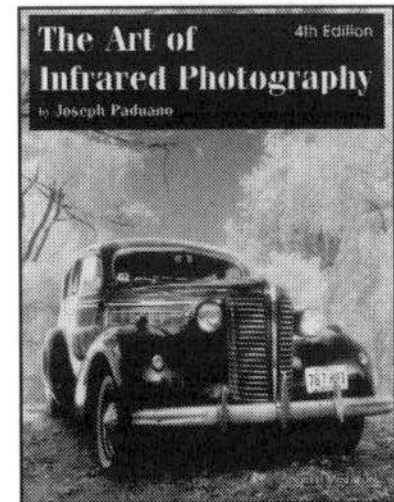


## The Art of Infrared Photography, *4th Edition*

*Joe Paduano*

A practical guide to the art of infrared photography. Tells what to expect and how to control results. Includes: anticipating effects, color infrared, digital infrared, using filters, focusing, developing, printing, handcoloring, toning, and more! $29.95 list, 8½x11, 112p, order no. 1052

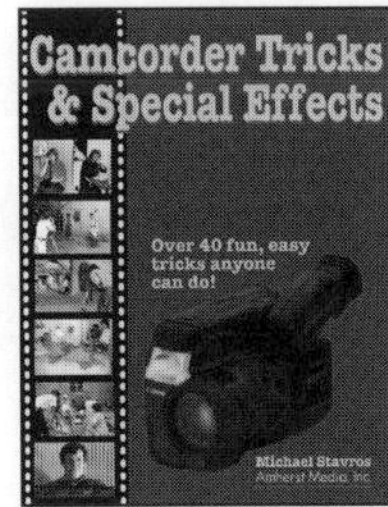


## Camcorder Tricks and Special Effects, *revised*

*Michael Stavros*

Kids and adults can create home videos and mini-masterpieces that audiences will love! Use materials from around the house to simulate an inferno, make subjects transform, create exotic locations, and more. Works with any camcorder. $17.95 list, 8½x11, 80p, order no. 1482.

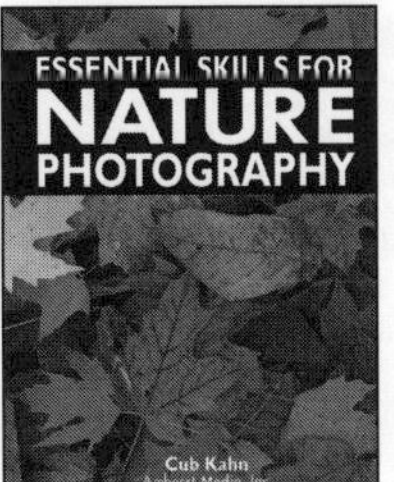


## Essential Skills for Nature Photography

*Cub Kahn*

Learn all the skills you need to capture landscapes, animals, flowers and the entire natural world on film. Includes: selecting equipment, choosing locations, evaluating compositions, filters, and much more! $29.95 list, 8½x11, 128p, order no. 1652.

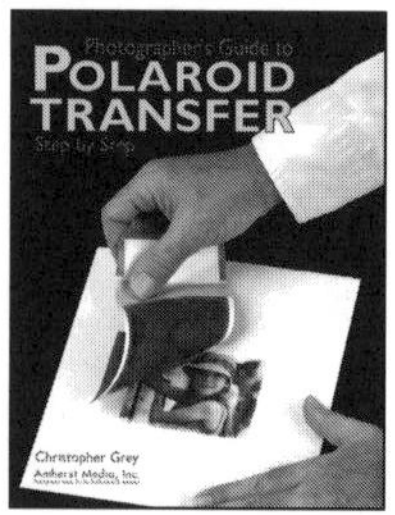


## Photographer's Guide to Polaroid Transfer

*Christopher Grey*

Step-by-step instructions make it easy to master Polaroid transfer and emulsion lift-off techniques and add new dimensions to your photographic imaging. Fully illustrated every step of the way to ensure good results the very first time! $29.95 list, 8½x11, 128p, order no. 1653.

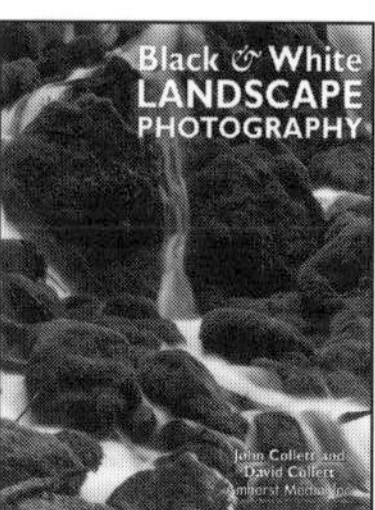


## Black & White Landscape Photography

*John Collett and David Collett*

Master the art of b&w landscape photography. Includes: selecting equipment (cameras, lenses, filters, etc.) for landscape photography, shooting in the field, using the Zone System, and printing your images for professional results. $29.95 list, 8½x11, 128p, order no. 1654.

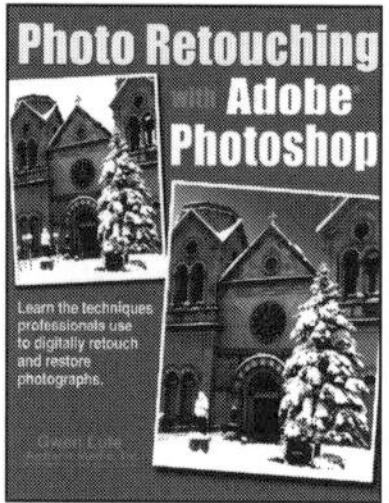


## Photo Retouching with Adobe® Photoshop®

*Gwen Lute*

Designed for photographers, this manual teaches every phase of the process, from scanning to final output. Learn to restore damaged photos, correct imperfections, create realistic composite images and correct for dazzling color. $29.95 list, 8½x11, 120p, order no. 1660.

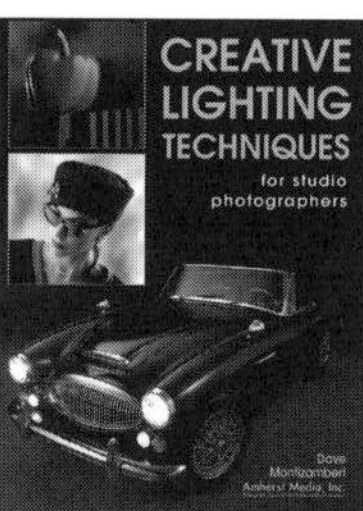


## Creative Lighting Techniques for Studio Photographers

*Dave Montizambert*

Master studio lighting and gain complete creative control over your images. Whether you are shooting portraits, cars, table-top or any other subject, Dave Montizambert teaches you the skills you need to confidently create with light. $29.95 list, 8½x11, 120p, order no. 1666.

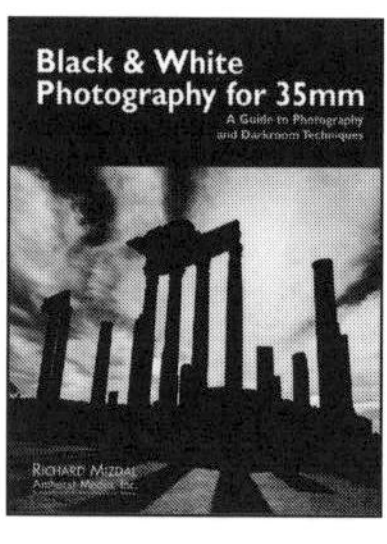


## Black & White Photography for 35mm

*Richard Mizdal*

A guide to shooting and darkroom techniques! Perfect for beginning or intermediate photographers who wants to improve their skills. Features helpful illustrations and exercises to make every concept clear and easy to follow. $29.95 list, 8½x11, 128p, order no. 1670.

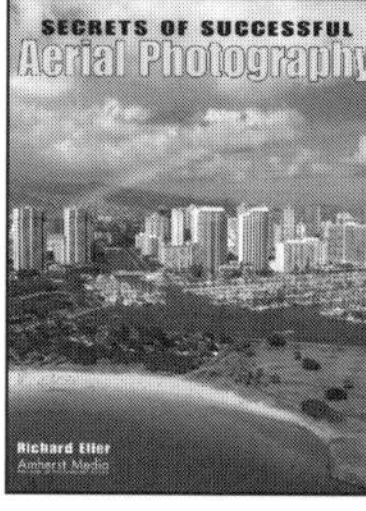


## Secrets of Successful Aerial Photography

*Richard Eller*

Learn how to plan for every aspect of a shoot and take the best possible images from the air. Discover how to control camera movement, compensate for environmental conditions and compose outstanding aerial images. $29.95 list, 8½x11, 120p, order no. 1679.

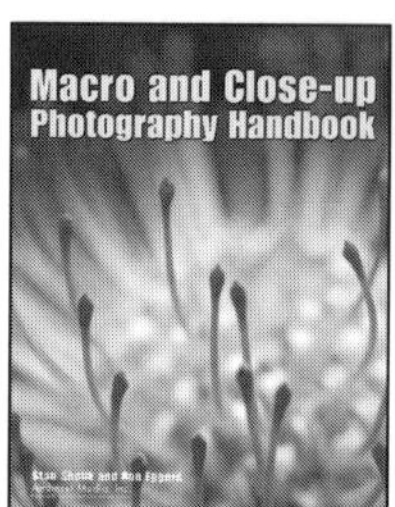


## Macro and Close-up Photography Handbook

*Stan Sholik*

Learn to get close and capture breathtaking images of small subjects – flowers, stamps, jewelry, insects, etc. Designed with the 35mm shooter in mind, this is a comprehensive manual full of step-by-step techniques. $29.95 list, 8½x11, 120p, order no. 1686.

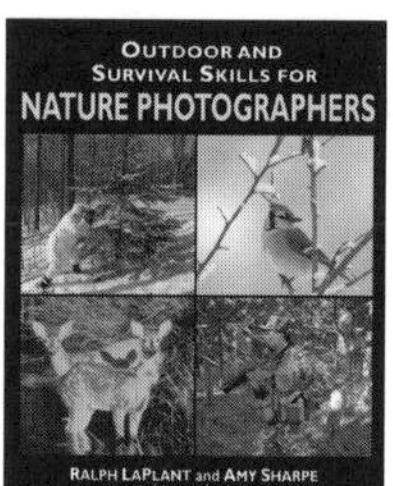


## Outdoor and Survival Skills for Nature Photographers

*Ralph LaPlant and Amy Sharpe*

An essential guide for photographing outdoors. Learn all the skills you need to have a safe and productive shoot – from selecting equipment, to finding subjects, to preventing (or dealing with) injury and accidents. $17.95 list, 8½x11, 80p, order no. 1678.

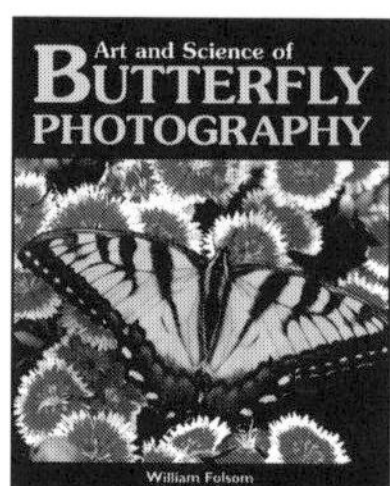


## Art and Science of Butterfly Photography

*William Folsom*

Learn to understand and predict butterfly behavior (including feeding, mating and migrational patterns), when to photograph them and even how to lure butterflies. Then discover the photographic techniques for capturing breathtaking images of these colorful creatures. $29.95 list, 8½x11, 120p, order no. 1680.

# More Photo Books Are Available!

## Write or fax for a *FREE* catalog:

AMHERST MEDIA
PO BOX 586
AMHERST, NY 14226 USA

Fax: 716-874-4508

www.AmherstMediaInc.com

**Ordering & Sales Information:**

*INDIVIDUALS:* If possible, purchase books from an Amherst Media retailer. Write to us for the dealer nearest you. To order direct, send a check or money order with a note listing the books you want and your shipping address. U.S. & overseas freight charges are $3.50 first book and $1.00 for each additional book. Visa and Master Card accepted. New York state residents add 8% sales tax.

*DEALERS, DISTRIBUTORS & COLLEGES:* Write, call or fax to place orders. For price information, contact Amherst Media or an Amherst Media sales representative. Net 30 days.

*All prices, publication dates, and specifications are subject to change without notice.*

*Prices are in U.S. dollars. Payment in U.S. funds only.*

CUT ALONG DOTTED LINE

# *Amherst Media's Customer Registration Form*

Please fill out this sheet and send or fax to receive free information about future publications from Amherst Media.

## CUSTOMER INFORMATION

DATE

NAME

STREET OR BOX #

CITY STATE

ZIP CODE

PHONE ( ) FAX ( )

## OPTIONAL INFORMATION

I BOUGHT *RESTORING CLASSIC AND COLLECTIBLE CAMERAS* BECAUSE

I FOUND THESE CHAPTERS TO BE MOST USEFUL

I PURCHASED THE BOOK FROM

CITY STATE

I WOULD LIKE TO SEE MORE BOOKS ABOUT

I PURCHASE BOOKS PER YEAR

ADDITIONAL COMMENTS

**FAX to: 1-800-622-3298**

IF MAILING, FOLD IN NUMBER ORDER ALONG DASHED LINES.

①

②

Name________________________________
Address______________________________
City_________________________State______
Zip___________________ — ___________

Place
Postage
Here

**Amherst Media, Inc.**
**PO Box 586**
**Buffalo, NY 14226**

③

IF MAILING, PASTE UNDERSIDE OF FLAP, OR TAPE HERE.